Capital Markets

Bernard J. Foley

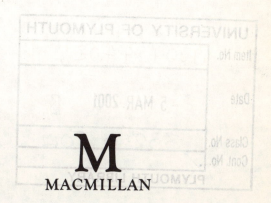

M

MACMILLAN

First published 1991

Published by
MACMILLAN EDUCATION LTD
Houndmills, Basingstoke, Hampshire RG21 2XS
and London
Companies and representatives
throughout the world

Edited and typeset by Povey/Edmondson
Okehampton and Rochdale, England

Printed in Hong Kong

British Library Cataloguing in Publication Data
Foley, Bernard J.
Capital Markets.
1. Great Britain. Capital markets
I. Title
332
ISBN 0–333–52332–6 (hardcover) ✓
ISBN 0–333–52333–4 (paperback)

To my mother Sarah and in memory of my father
James Joseph Foley

Contents

Preface

This book is primarily written for students but will also prove of interest to anyone who wishes to understand the operation of the world's key capital markets. The intention of the author is to inform and not to intimidate hence the book deliberately addresses a wider audience than those who will become academics or financial analysts. Nevertheless it will provide a useful introduction to undergraduates choosing finance and banking courses as well as those currently engaged on an MBA who do not wish to specialise in finance.

One of the major problems in this area is to find books which offer an adequate mix of theoretical discussion and institutional description. If I have erred toward the latter this reflects the fact that there are a large number of excellent, mainly American, textbooks which can take the reader through the arcane mysteries of Arbitrage Pricing Theory or the Black-Scholes Option Valuation Model. There is no point, except to display a certain academic machismo, in repeating the exercise. The book should therefore be seen as complementary to texts which are more formally concerned with financial analysis.

Acknowledgements

Writing a book is merely one stage in a process of production which involves many people, not all of whom are aware of their contribution. I would like to thank the International Stock Exchange, the Association of Investment Trust Companies, NASDAQ International, the Société de Bourses Françaises and the Federation of German Stock Exchanges for their kind responses to my periodic requests. In particular staff at the Liverpool office of the Stock Exchange proved very helpful at a crucial stage in the proceedings. My thanks are also due to the University of Liverpool and Professor Noel Boaden for the study leave which enabled me to make a substantial start, to my editor Steve Rutt, who has been courteous and encouraging throughout, and to Keith Povey, whose suggestions improved the typescript considerably. Finally my deepest gratitude is owed to my wife Polly and our two wonderful sons Tim and Stephen Patrick (S.P.) who had to put up with my absences and the continuous tapping of the word processor during the time that I took to finish this book.

Formby   BERNARD FOLEY

List of Tables

List of Figures

List of Abbreviations

ADR	American Depositary Receipt
AFDB	Association of Futures Dealers and Brokers
AIBD	Association of International Bond Dealers
AITC	Association of Investment Trust Companies
AMEX	American Stock Exchange
APT	Automated Pit Trading
BIS	Bank for International Settlements
CAPM	Capital asset Pricing Model
CATS	Computer Assisted Trading System
CBOE	Chicago Board Options Exchange
CBOT	Chicago Board of Trade
CD	Certificate of Deposit
CFTC	Commodity Futures Trading Commission
CLOB	Central Limit Order Book
CLOSE	Central Limit Order Service
CME	Chicago Mercantile Exchange
DDM	Dividend Discount Model
DOTS	Designated Order Turnaround System
DTI	Department of Trade and Industry
ECD	EuroCertificate of Deposit
ECP	EuroCommercial Paper
ECU	European Currency Unit
EMH	Efficient Markets Hypothesis
FCM	Futures Commission Merchant
FIMBRA	Financial Intermediaries, Managers and Brokers Regulatory Association
FOX	Futures and Options Exchange
FRN	Floating Rate Note
FSA	Financial Services Act
GEMM	Gilt Edged Market Maker
HGSCI	Hoare Govett Smaller Companies Index
ICCH	International Commodities Clearing House
IDB	Inter Dealer Broker
IET	Interest Equalisation Tax

ILGS	Index Linked Government Securities
IMM	International Money Market
IMRO	Investment Managers Regulatory Organisation
INS	Institutional Net Settlement
ISE	International Stock Exchange
JSDA	Japanese Securities Dealers Association
LAUTRO	Life Assurance and Unit Trust Regulatory Organisation
LBO	Leveraged Buy Out
LDE	London Derivatives Market
LIFFE	London International Financial Futures Exchange
LIBOR	London InterBank Offered Rate
LOCH	London Options Clearing House
LME	London Metal Exchange
LTOM	London Traded Options Market
MATIF	Marché à Terme International de France
MOF	Multi Option Facility
NASDAQ	National Association of Securities Dealers Automatic Quotation System
NASDIM	National Association of Securities Dealers and Investment Managers
NIF	Note Issuance Facility
NMS	Normal Market Size (UK usage)
NMS	National Market System (US usage)
NYSE	New York Stock Exchange
OARS	Opening Automated Report Service
OTC	Over the Counter
PSBR	Public Sector Borrowing Requirement
PSDR	Public Sector Debt Repayment
RPI	Retail Price Index
RIE	Recognised Investment Exchange
RUF	Revolving Underwriting Facility
SAEF	SEAQ Automatic Execution Facility
SDR	Special Drawing Rights
SEC	Securities and Exchange Commission
SEAQ	Stock Exchange Automatic Quotation system
SIAC	Securities Industry Automation Corporation
SICAV	Société d'Investissement à Capital Variable
SOES	Small Order Execution Service
SRO	Self Regulatory Organisation
TAURUS	Transfer and Automated Registration of Uncertified Stock
TOPIC	Teletext Output of Price Information by Computer
TSA	The Securities Association
TSE	Tokyo Stock Exchange

Introduction

The object of this book is to give the reader an insight into the operation of some of the world's major capital markets. It goes almost without saying that financial markets of every kind have been transformed out of all recognition in the past 25 years and furthermore the pace of change shows no signs of slackening. In the 1950s and 60s capital markets were highly protected, insular, almost ossified structures whereas what we now see is a landscape in which distinctions between financial institutions are rapidly disappearing. Previously cartelised equity and bond markets are opening up to competition, a range of markets based on derived instruments such as futures and options have emerged in many centres and a torrent of new financial instruments is being proffered to all manner of potential users. It is by no means clear therefore how capital markets will look even three or four years from now.

The changes which have occurred so far are the outcome of a number of factors some of which are related to developments in the nature of the global economy while others are specific to finance itself.

1 GLOBAL FACTORS

(i) One of the most remarkable of features of the past decade and a half has been the intellectual conversion by political elites to the power of markets as instruments of economic change. The 1970s saw the rise of liberal economic ideas which challenged the dominance of socialist and Keynesian perceptions as to the economic role of the state. In the 1980s this resulted in a headlong rush by parties of the right and the left to put more emphasis on the market as a means of achieving social and economic objectives. The culmination of this process saw the beginning of the dissolution of the communist dominated bloc in Eastern Europe and the attempted replacement of command planning by market oriented systems of allocation within the USSR itself.

(ii) New patterns of international payments caused by the rise in oil prices in the 1970s produced a number of mechanisms designed to cope with the resulting financial flows. In particular the syndicated loans market by

1

which groups of commercial banks facilitated lending to sovereign states in the Third World and the Communist bloc became extremely important. The so-called Eurocurrency markets had already produced a growing degree of internationalisation in the 1960s but it was accelerated by the results of the oil price increases.

(iii)   The gradual recovery of the world economy from the stagnation of the 1970s produced a period of sustained growth in the 1980s which increased real incomes substantially and perhaps more significantly restored profit rates in the capitalist world to levels that had last been experienced in the 1960s. This in turn produced greater flows of savings throughout the system. Japan and to a lesser extent West Germany were the primary sources of these savings flows while the United States became the biggest net beneficiary.

(iv)   The reduction in rates of inflation in the 1980s encouraged people to place more trust in financial securities particularly bonds and other fixed interest instruments. At the same time privatisation of public assets and the sustained recovery in equity markets from the lows of 1974 until the Crash of 1987 induced an unprecedented degree of interest in equity markets. While the Crash induced new caution, the fact that the underlying economies continued to grow much as before indicated a hitherto unsuspected resilience of the market economies to such major shocks.

(v)   The move to floating exchange rates and more volatile interest rates in the 1970s, which were an aspect of the slide into inflation, introduced additional elements of uncertainty into international trade and capital movements when compared with the relatively tranquil 1960s. Hence new ways of coping with those uncertainties were developed. This spawned a completely new series of markets and products specifically designed to allow investors and/or traders to hedge different species of risk.

(vi)   Finally in the field of technology, the availability of cheap computer power and increasingly sophisticated communications have made their impact felt in a variety of ways. At the simplest level for example the majority of financial transactions and payment systems have come to rely on electronic means of transmission and storage. In addition more and more activity in world markets either relies directly upon or is supported by electronic hardware in the form of screen based systems or computer assisted trading. The integration of computer power with international communications in turn allows securities houses to carry out their business in a number of different market places on a 24 hour basis.

Another impact of computer power has been to give dealers in complex securities, foreign exchange and financial products a rapid evaluation of their position. The whole area of derived markets – traded options, index options, options on futures, swaps, swaptions, warrants, and so on – is made comprehensible and therefore feasible by being able rapidly to assess the 'fair value' of the relevant product.

2 MARKET FACTORS

The specific changes which have been under way in capital markets have taken a number of forms.

(i) A major feature of the financial scene in the past decade has been the twin processes of disintermediation and securitisation. *Disintermediation* occurs where borrowers and lenders come into direct contact with each other rather than via financial intermediaries such as the banking system. Eliminating such intermediaries has become feasible because many issuers of debt have a better credit rating than the banks themselves. This is particularly true since the international debt crisis of the early 1980s caused a rerating of many of the larger banks. Thus investors may rate IBM or Volvo more highly than major banks and be prepared to accept their paper at lower rates. *Securitisation* is the process whereby banks package existing debts which they have on their balance sheets and sell them to a subsidiary. By removing them from the balance sheet in this way the bank frees itself to undertake further lending. The bank's subsidiary pays for the debts from the proceeds of bonds sold to end investors. The interest on the bonds is channelled to these investors from the revenue which accrues as the original debt is repaid. For example mortgage backed securities emerged in the United States in the 1980s and more recently they have made an appearance in the UK.

(ii) Rapid innovation in financial products and markets introduces constant change which causes problems for regulatory regimes and may introduce new forms of systemic risk. For example it has become common for banks to act as counterparties in swaps and options taking on the risk themselves. Because these are *contingent* liabilities they are defined as 'off balance sheet' products and they may fall outside the scope of conventional regulations as to required capital backing. The use of novel and relatively untried devices may mean that unknown combinations of risk can result in overexposure or commitments which the banks may have difficulty controlling. Another example of the effects of untested financial techniques may have occurred in the Crash of 1987, when institutions in the US seemed to believe that they could lock in gains made in bull markets by new trading techniques such as 'portfolio insurance' (Chapter 8).

(iii) Then there is the issue of institutional dominance: collective investment schemes in the form of occupational pension funds, savings-linked life assurance, and unit and investment trusts have become progressively more important and, despite the effects of privatisation on individual share ownership, they continue to grow. Their investment philosophy can have significant implications for market volatility, mergers and acquisitions, the level of share turnover and in some markets the use of highly technical hedging/trading strategies.

(iv)   The last two decades have also witnessed an enormous expansion of derived markets which offer methods of dealing with uncertainty. The general public has yet to make up its mind about these rather more esoteric devices as they look like a sophisticated form of gambling. Yet they can be justified in terms of protecting companies from movements in underlying factors such as exchange rates or interest rates.

Forward and futures markets have been around for many years particularly for international commodities while traditional options on individual shares have long been an established feature of equity markets. There has however been an explosion of novel forms of investment which two decades ago either did not exist or did so in a primitive form. The following is not meant to be an exhaustive list but simply indicative of the bewildering variety of new products: for example in bond markets there are floating rate bonds, zero-coupon bonds, puttable bonds, stripped bonds, dual currency bonds, index-linked bonds, mortgage backed bonds; in the money markets there exist negotiable Certificates of Deposit, a Euro Commercial Paper Market, money market funds, foreign currency accounts; in the derived markets there are traded options on equities, index options, index participations, futures, options on futures, currency warrants and money back warrants; in the swaps market there are currency swaps, interest rate swaps, options on swaps (swaptions) and so on!

Many of these 'products' owe their existence to the economic instability of the 1970s and 1980s. Most of them are exchange traded products but some international banks and securities houses offer their corporate clients 'financial engineering' services ie the facility of designing specially tailored solutions to cope with individual species of risk identified by the company in question.

(v)   Finally in the 1980s governments which at one time monitored and regulated capital markets very tightly embarked on processes of liberalisation and the relaxation of controls. At the same time stock exchanges themselves complemented these changes by simplifying their listing requirements. The effect of these measures has been to make access to public capital markets easier and cheaper. Accompanying liberalisation of domestic capital markets there has also been increased internationalisation. Bond markets have been moving inexorably down this path since the 1960s but in the 1980s there has been a substantial growth of international *equity* offerings.

In addition various exchanges have been pushed by their domestic authorities and competitive pressure into permitting foreign houses to establish a presence. London's Big Bang in 1986 came some eleven years after New York's in 1975 but was merely a prelude to deregulation in Japan, Germany and most spectacularly France.

As the process of internationalisation gathers pace it is also possible to discern various degrees of convergence. For example minimum capital requirements ('capital adequacy') for banks have been agreed via negotiations under the auspices of the Bank for International Settlements. The Group of Thirty is attempting to establish common clearance and settlement procedures in securities markets. And finally the approach of the Single Market in 1992 implies greater uniformity of market practice and standards within Europe. The Council of Ministers has already accepted a number of Directives relating to co-ordination of insurance, minimal requirements for admission and listing on exchanges, minimum disclosure provisions, harmonisation of prospectuses and minimum standards for collective investment undertakings.

It is clear therefore that given the forces which continue to impinge on capital markets we are a long way from settling down into a steady state condition and we are equally far from knowing the final outcome of the processes which were sparked off some two decades ago.

In concluding this introduction perhaps I may be permitted a personal note. The original outline of this book included a final chapter provisionally entitled 'Do we need stock markets?'. In the event the chapter was broadened in scope to summarise a number of major criticisms about the way markets currently work. Imagine my surprise to find that just as the book was nearing completion that august keeper of the free market faith *The Economist* published one of its excellent surveys ('A survey of capitalism', May 11 1990) that comes down heavily against what it racily calls 'Punter Capitalism'. The article is not an attack on Capitalism per se - far from it - instead it points to the merits of 'Proprietor Capitalism'. However the author does speculate about the wider consequences for economies where markets dominated by financial institutions, in particular the US and the UK, drive a wedge between ownership and control and ultimately induce 'a change in the meaning of ownership' (p. 8). Nor is this a simple re-run of the arguments put forward over fifty years ago by Berle and Means (1933) and Burnham (1939).

There are in any case other issues which need to be addressed before the question 'Do we need stock markets?' can be fully answered. I hope this book goes some way to helping the reader make up his or her own mind.

1 The Role and Function of Capital Markets

1 INTRODUCTION

Capital markets perform a number of important functions. First they are mechanisms which facilitate the transfer of investible funds from economic agents in financial surplus to those in financial deficit. This is achieved by selling securities – shares or bonds – to those with surplus funds. As a result companies, governments, local authorities, supranational organisations and so on have access to a larger pool of capital than would be available if they had to rely exclusively on generating their own resources.

This is the so-called *primary market* where new issues of equity or debt are arranged in the form of an entirely new flotation or in the form of an offer to existing investors. In either case the organisation concerned raises new cash in exchange for financial claims. For a company the financial claims may take the form of equity (shares) or perhaps debt (bonds) whereas public authorities invariably issue bonds. Having a public quotation on a stock exchange is a major advantage to listed firms when they need to raise more capital although as we shall see this is does not take place on as large a scale as is frequently supposed.

It is perhaps the second function of capital markets which is the focus of more attention – that of acting as a *secondary market* for securities which may have been issued at some time in the past. The market allows owners of shares or bonds to sell their holdings readily and hence it assures them a degree of liquidity that otherwise would not be feasible. *The existence of a secondary market therefore makes the primary market operate more effectively*. When making the decision to invest in these particular financial assets, the investor can feel confident that he or she is not locked in but can in fact turn the investment back into cash at any time. The secondary market in other words provides a facility for the continuous reallocation of financial assets among various investors allowing some to divest themselves of such assets while others can use their surplus funds to acquire them.

The main users of capital markets are companies, sovereign governments and supra-national bodies such as the World Bank or the European

Investment Bank. Chapter 3 examines the nature of bond markets in which governments, and supra-nationals borrow. This chapter examines corporate finance and identifies the various securities which companies issue.

2 COMPANY FINANCE

Companies need capital for a variety of purposes. Working capital is employed in the conduct of day to day operations while longer term finance is needed to undertake fixed capital formation, to finance expansion and to develop new processes or new products. This long term capital is generated internally, via the company's cash flow, or externally, via the banking system or the public capital markets depending upon the size and nature of the firm.

Despite the media attention devoted to stock exchange activities, the issue of securities to raise capital is not the most important way in which companies finance their activities.

Table 1.1 indicates the relative importance of various sources of company finance in the UK over the past decade.

TABLE 1.1   Sources of funds – UK industrial and commercial companies, 1980–9

	1980	1981	1982	1983	1984	1985	1986	1987	1988	1989
Total £m					35 506	45 309	48 941	69 764	85 737	95 810
Internal (%)	64.2	63.1	62.4	77.3	80.7	68.1	56.4	49.5	41.4	30.3
External (%)	35.8	36.9	37.6	22.7	19.3	31.9	43.6	50.5	58.6	69.7
of which										
Bank										
Borrowing	21.9	17.9	22.5	4.7	20.5	16.5	18.6	17.4	36.2	34.8
UK Capital										
Issues	4.9	7.4	4.4	7.3	3.9	11.0	16.1	23.4	9.2	9.8
Other*	9.0	11.6	10.7	10.7	−5.1	4.4	8.9	9.7	13.2	25.1

*Mortgages and other loans/Capital issues overseas/Overseas direct investment in securities.
Adapted from *Financial Statistics*, No 339, July 1990.

Table 1.1 illustrates the contributions of various sources of funds required to carry out all operations: thus working capital and longer term financing are not distinguished here. A number of features are immediately apparent:

o Except for the latter years of the decade the most important source of finance derives from internally generated funds;
o Bank borrowing is the second most significant source of funds: it tends to be used in the main to finance short term or working capital;

o Capital issues normally comprise less than 10% of the total except in the period 1985–87 when this source of finance increased considerably. This clearly reflected the fact that companies were taking advantage of the rising equity market which was about to crest in the third quarter of that year.

This pattern of financing is not a new phenomenon and has been a cause of comment for many years (*Bank of England Quarterly Bulletin*, Sept. 1980). Similar orders of magnitude can be found in the 1960s and while rather wider variations were a feature of the 1970s internal funding remains by far the most important source of company finance: access to the capital market seems to be marginal as a source of funds.

Table 1.1 however describes the financing of *all* industrial and commercial companies and in so far as this includes a large number of concerns without a public quotation it will understate the significance of the stock market. Furthermore it may be argued that stock markets are more important as a way of financing *long-term investment* so we should really focus on the significance of markets as a source of finance for this purpose. Does a different picture emerge in the case of quoted companies?

The short answer appears to be 'No'. Mayer (1987) for example suggests that over the period 1949–77 the net financing of physical investment (ie longer term capital formation) in *quoted* companies (see Table 1.2) has been even more dependent on internally generated funds!

TABLE 1.2   Net financing of physical investment (quoted companies), 1949–77

	Percentage share
Internal funds	91.37
Net trade credit	− 1.31
Net bank credit	2.24
Net issue of securities	7.69

Mayer (1987).

It is difficult to say how far this pattern of financing reflects the preferences of the companies concerned (ie the demand side) as opposed to the nature of UK banking practice (the supply side). Certainly there is the view that the small proportion of long-term funding attributable to bank finance reflects the tendency on the part of UK banks to confine themselves to lending at the short end of the spectrum as far as the corporate sector is concerned. This contrasts sharply with their German and Japanese counterparts which have traditionally lent to industry over much longer time periods (Harris *et al.*, 1988).

The explanation for this bias toward internally generated funds need not detain us at this point. It is a matter which has vexed economists for some time and there are a number of competing explanations. It is sufficient to note that the phenomenon is both marked and persistent. Nor is the UK alone in this respect: Table 1.3 below illustrates the situation in the United States.

TABLE 1.3   Sources of funds – US non-financial corporations, 1958–88

	1958–60	1961–9	1970–3	1974–9	1980–1	1982–8
Total ($billion)	44.8	75.6	128.1	208.4	296.7	402.8
Internal (%)	76.5	73.1	62.0	72.1	74.1	81.3
External (%)	23.5	26.9	38.0	27.9	25.9	18.7
of which						
Loans	5.8	11.2	11.8	10.8	16.4	13.7
Bonds & Notes	15.4	14.0	18.3	14.0	10.5	19.6
Stock (shares)	4.0	1.5	7.0	1.5	0.2	−14.7
Other	−1.8	0.2	0.9	1.6	−1.3	0.1
Gross Capital Spending ($billion)	29.5	48.6	68.6	157.1	232.3	301.1
Capital Spending (%) of Sources	65.8	64.3	53.6	75.4	78.3	74.8

Board of Governors of the Federal Reserve System, *Flow of Funds Accounts*, 1989.

Again the dominance of internally generated funds is obvious and, while the importance of the US bond markets comes out clearly as a source of funds, the equity market has been insignificant. Indeed over the period 1982–8 there was a substantial move by a large segment of corporate America to buy itself back with the use of debt hence the negative value for equity issues.

In fact it is ironic that two of the economies which are regarded as having the most developed public capital markets appear to rely on internal funding to a greater degree than other developed economies (Bank for International Settlements, 1981 and 1989).

If external sources of finance play a relatively minor role in the provision of investment funds why do firms decide to use the capital markets at all? Selling debt or equity via an organised and recognised stock exchange yields a number of advantages and disadvantages to the firm.

as opposed to the economy
eg as efficiency via disclosure

Advantages

(i)   Growth

Access to external sources allows the firm to grow more rapidly: the ability to raise additional capital is considerably easier and more successful where the firm has a stock exchange quotation. Growth can occur via internal organic processes or via acquisition of other firms.

(ii)   Status

A stock exchange quotation confers status on a company and frequently allows it to obtain bank credit on finer terms than would be the case for similar sized non-quoted organisation. It also helps publicise a company bringing it to the notice of a larger clientele. A sufficiently large quoted company may well find that it is able to exploit international sources of capital by borrowing or issuing equity in another country or perhaps via the Euromarkets.

(iii)   Flexibility

The availability of stock exchange finance gives a firm more flexible capital structure. It is possible to vary the financial structure of the organisation more easily – altering the debt/equity mix to obtain finance on the cheapest terms. Issues can be arranged not only in conventional securities but also in hybrids such as bonds with an option to convert into equity at a later date or with warrants attached.

(iv)   Realisation of wealth

Owners of the company can, by selling shares, use the stock exchange to realise part of their wealth. As a company grows the value of the share holding will reflect that growth and an original investment of a few thousand shares may come to represent an extremely valuable claim on the assets of the company. However for as long as there is no market in the shares the individual is to a large extent locked into his holding and is simply a 'paper millionaire'. Furthermore the value of the shareholding is clearly vulnerable to a change in the fortunes of the company. 'Going public' offers the individual the opportunity to sell all or part of the holdings and to turn these assets into cash which can be used to diversify the individual's wealth.

Disadvantages

(i)   Disclosure

The decision to obtain a stock exchange quotation carries with it the duty to disclose information about the firm. This disclosure goes beyond minimal statutory requirements laid down in company legislation. Greater information about the firm, its markets, its capital structure and so on is demanded particularly at the time of flotation when a very detailed prospectus must be produced. The quantity of information and the frequency of reporting is increased. This imposes extra costs in the form of information collection and auditing and extra inconvenience on the company.

(ii)   Investor pressure

The fear of publicity operates as a useful check on the performance of company management and investor pressure may represent a further constraint. Although not over common, there are significant examples of company policy being altered because of grass roots pressure. As a result, managers may find themselves with less room for manoeuvre in terms of investment policy than is the case in a private company.

(iii)   Acquisitions

This is the downside to the advantage of being able to grow by acquisition: the firm is also vulnerable to the threat of takeover. Some observers regard this as a mechanism whereby greater efficiency is achieved either to fight off a prospective predator or as a result of coming under the control of a more go–ahead management. Large scale institutional ownership of blocks of shares may be particularly significant in this respect as it may be sufficient for a corporate raider to persuade a handful of major shareholders to part with their holdings.

(iv)   Insider dealing

This is the practice of making use of privileged, price sensitive information to take advantage of a subsequent move in share prices. It is not known how much insider dealing takes place although certainly there have been a number of well publicised cases in the US and the UK. Public suspicion remains high that it is a widespread practice. However this is a controversial and unsettled area of dispute: there are some academics who take the view that it is a 'victimless' crime which fulfils a useful economic function in enhancing the informational efficiency of the market while others see it as stealing from shareholders who have been kept in ignorance and are themselves unable to profit from the information.

It is often assumed that the balance of advantage favours going public and in the past it was then seen as a 'one way street' ie having made the decision to seek a stock market listing a company would thenceforth remain in the public domain. There have however been a number of cases in the United States (Levi-Strauss for example) and also in the UK where quoted companies have become private again (Virgin Records).

3 TYPES OF CAPITAL

A company's capital structure can be categorised into three broad classes:

1. *Equity capital* which usually takes the form of ordinary shares in the UK (common stock in the USA). Holders of equity capital are owners or members of the company and hence receive a return commensurate with the performance of the company;
2. *Preference capital* which also forms part of the equity of the company but which confers certain priorities compared with ordinary shares;
3. *Loan capital* (bonds) which includes debentures and unsecured loan stock. Interest is payable on bonds whether or not the company makes a profit. Most loan capital is redeemable although it is possible to have irredeemable loan stock.

Ordinary Shares

In essence a share certificate is a set of rights in a company. It indicates a degree of ownership of the company and at the same time defines the relationship between shareholders. Ownership is evidenced by entry on the company's register of members rather than possession of the share certificate itself. (Except in the case of 'bearer' shares where no name appears on the company's register and physical possession of the certificate is evidence of title. These shares are more common in Europe than in the UK or the US).

The various rights of different classes of shareholder on matters such as voting, dividends and liquidation procedures are defined in the Articles of Association of the company. There are two major categories of equity capital – ordinary shares (termed in the US 'common stock') and preference shares. It is possible to have ordinary shares divided further into certain sub-classes eg 'A' ordinary, 'B' shares and so on to confer or limit rights in particular ways although on the whole there has been a move away from these sorts of share. In some markets, the UK and Japan for example (although not in the USA), shares must carry a nominal or par value despite the fact that this may have little bearing on the actual price at which shares trade.

In the normal course of events, and unless indicated to the contrary, ordinary shareholders are entitled to one vote per share held, any dividends, and any pro rata share in the assets of the company on winding up. This right to participate in the residual profits and assets of the company distinguishes ordinary share capital from other forms of capital: it involves the greatest risk and in turn holds out the greatest potential return.

Finally if it is thought appropriate ordinary shares can be issued as redeemable at the option of the issuer or the holder. It is also possible for firms in the UK and the USA to repurchase their ordinary share capital.

Preference Shares

Essentially preference shares are shares which have a priority over ordinary shares. This priority extends to dividends and repayment of capital in the event of liquidation: typically preference shares offer the owner the right to a fixed dividend, higher priority than ordinary shareholders on winding up but restricted voting rights. Variations on the basic theme are also feasible. Thus 'cumulative preference shares' ensure that in the event of a company not paying a dividend in any one year the holder has the right to receive arrears of dividends from profits in the future before payment is declared for ordinary shares.

Companies in the UK have tended less and less to issue preference shares because the fixed dividend cannot be set against corporate tax liability whereas the coupon payable on debt issues is allowable.

It is fairly common for preference shares to be designated as 'redeemable' and redemption can be undertaken out of profits or from the money raised by a fresh issue.

Debt – Debentures and Unsecured Loan Stock

(i)   Debentures[1]

Debentures are securities issued by a company using assets of the company as collateral. This can take the form of a fixed charge against specific assets (such as a property) or a floating charge or both. A floating charge simply relates to all present and prospective assets of a company without specifying particular assets. This allows the company to use the assets freely without having to refer back to the debenture holders or the mortgage deed to secure permission. However, in the event of a default on the interest payable or the company being wound up the debenture holder can exercise the right to intervene, in which case the floating charge becomes a fixed charge on the assets of the company at that date. Debentures carry the highest priority in terms of payment of interest and repayment of capital on liquidation.

(ii)   Unsecured loan stock

This type of debt implies no specific charge against the company's assets and therefore ranks below debentures in terms of priority. As a consequence of the lower degree of income and capital security the interest rate (the coupon) offered by such debt is normally higher than for debentures issued by the same organisation.

In a similar manner to debenture holders, those holding unsecured loan stock have a trustee whose duty it is to see that the issuer fulfills the conditions of the trust deed. In this case however the deed or covenant does not specify charges on the assets of the company but identifies the amounts and types of other debt that the company can issue. For example there will be concern to ensure that the rights of present holders of unsecured stock will not be infringed by the issue of new debt with a higher or equal priority. This may be done by the use of a 'negative pledge' which prevents the issue of more secure debt without giving present holders equal rights. Alternatively it is possible that the company could impose a maximum limit on the ratio of debt to net assets.

Despite the higher degree of security attaching to bonds compared with equity there is nonetheless always the possibility of a default on the interest and/or the repayment of capital. It has been customary in the United States for bonds to be rated according to the risk of such default. This rating is formally carried out by one of the major rating agencies such as Standard & Poor's, Moody's Investor Services or Fitch & Co. (See Chapter 3 for an example of the rating criteria.)

(iii)   Convertible bonds

Convertible bonds are issued in a number of forms: for example they can be issued as convertible unsecured loan stock or as convertible preference shares[2]. These are similar to conventional loan stock and preference shares in that the holder is entitled to a fixed coupon until such time as the conversion option is exercised but they also carry the right to convert into ordinary shares at some defined ratio. This right is usually exercisable on a given date over a number of years. In the UK the issue normally specifies a period before the conversion option can be exercised and this effectively protects the company against early conversion. In contrast in the United States conversion can normally be exercised immediately.

Convertibles therefore are a hybrid security combining characteristics of equity and debt and to that extent can be perceived as a form of deferred equity: on conversion the holder relinquishes the right to a fixed coupon and takes on the rights of the ordinary shareholder.

4 RAISING CAPITAL – CHOICE OF MARKET

The decision to sell shares to the public ('to go public') presents a company with two problems: what market to use and what method of sale to employ.

There has been a considerable restructuring of markets in the UK in recent years. The 1980s had seen the existence of four distinct types or levels of market. Three of these were the responsibility of the International Stock Exchange while the fourth – the Over the Counter market – consisted of a group of security dealers licensed by the Department of Trade and Industry. Hence firms could choose among the following possibilities

   (i)   A full listing on the International Stock Exchange (ISE);
  (ii)   The Unlisted Securities Market (USM);
 (iii)   The Third Market [3];
 (iv)   The Over the Counter Market (OTC).

These were differentiated in terms of the listing and reporting criteria which they imposed on firms and therefore the degree of public scrutiny to which companies were subjected. By 1991 however as a result of pressure from the European Community to harmonise listing requirements the Third Market was merged with the USM and a number of other changes were introduced the more important of which are discussed below.

The International Stock Exchange (ISE)

The London Stock Exchange formally changed its name to the above shortly after 'Big Bang' in October 1986. A merger with the International Securities Regulatory Organisation (ISRO) was negotiated in an attempt to encompass dealings in international securities so as to prevent fragmentation of markets in London. The ISE is a Recognised Investment Exchange under the terms of the Financial Services Act 1986 and currently constitutes the largest market for raising equity capital in the European time zone.

Like other exchanges – Paris with its 'Marché Officiel' and 'Second Marché'; Frankfurt with the 'Amtlicher Handel' and 'Geregelter Markt' – the ISE decided in the 1980s to offer companies a graduated series of markets which were progressively more demanding for firms seeking a quotation.

Table 1.4 overleaf summarises the differences between the three tiers of the ISE.

Companies seeking a full listing therefore have to meet minimum qualifications (relating to the size of the company, the breadth of the likely market in its share capital and the amount and timeliness of information to which shareholders are entitled) while these matters were relaxed in various ways in the other two markets.

TABLE 1.4 Differences between International Stock Exchange markets

	Full listing	USM	Third Market
Trading	At least 5 years	*out of date, see across* At least 3 years	1 year normally can be less
Yearly turnover	No lower limit Sponsors usually expect more than £10m	No lower limit	No lower limit
Yearly pre-tax profit	No lower limit Sponsors usually expect more than £1m	No lower limit but usually over £500 000	No lower limit
Market capitalisation	£700 000 equity Sponsors usually expect over £10m	No lower limit	No lower limit
Latest audit prior to flotation	Six months	Nine months	Nine months except where still in project stage
Percentage of shares in public hands	At least 25%	At least 10%	No lower limit
Information to shareholders on substantial capital changes – disposals and acquisitions	Where 15% or more of assets profits or equity involved	25% or more of assets or profits equity involved	No limit

Advertising/Publicity

Placings & Introductions	Formal notice in one national daily paper and listing details in Extel Statistical Services	Formal notice in one national daily paper plus circulation of prospectus via Extel	Formal notice in one national daily paper plus circulation of prospectus via Extel
Offers for sale	Listing details in two national daily papers and circulated in Extel	Formal notice in one national daily paper	Formal notice in one national daily paper

ISE, *Quality of Markets Quarterly Review*, Winter 1988/9.

In fact the two junior markets – the USM and the Third Market – were relatively recent innovations in the UK: the former came into operation in 1980 while the latter commenced with the trading of shares in eight companies in January 1987. They were introduced to compete more effectively with the burgeoning OTC market and to provide a sort of step ladder by which smaller companies could in time graduate to a full listing. By 1990 the USM comprised some 450 firms with an aggregate capitalisation in the region of £9b while the Third Market consisted of approximately 70 companies with a total capitalisation of £600m.

At this juncture however the implementation of two EC directives, first proposed in the 1980s, brought about a further series of changes in the ISE. One directive (The Prospectus Directive) implemented in April 1991, requires the publication of a prospectus *whenever* securities are offered to the public whether or not an exchange listing is sought. This implied a tightening of conditions for a quotation on the Third Market. The other directive (The Mutual Recognition of Listing Particulars) implemented in January 1990, meant that listing criteria which apply in one Member country would be accepted by other Member countries. As London generally imposed tougher standards for a full listing than European bourses, compliance with the directive would have meant that the ISE would have to accept various securities meeting different criteria. Hence the Exchange decided to alter its own criteria to conform to the less stringent conditions imposed in other countries of the Community.

The combined effect of these directives therefore implied a degree of convergence of existing ISE markets. Hence a decision was made to close the Third Market and to relax certain conditions in the others. For example in the main market a three year record is sufficient compared with five previously while on the USM a two year record is now required compared with three years before. In the latter case the period can be waived altogether for greenfield projects.

The emergence of simpler, less costly routes to obtaining a public quotation reflected the Stock Exchange's reaction to a gap which was said to exist in the provision of finance for smaller companies (The Stock Exchange, 1977). In fact a similar argument had been made nearly sixty years ago in the Report on the Committee on Finance and Industry (1931) – the so-called Macmillan Report. The 'Macmillan Gap' had been a constant source of reproach to the Stock Exchange in the intervening years.

The net effect of the various changes has gone some way to fulfilling the broad objectives of the Exchange: to encourage more listings and to facilitate access by smaller firms. Thus a USM quotation is clearly cheaper than obtaining a full listing: advertising expenses are lower and Exchange and professional fees are less onerous. It has been estimated by Clements (1988) that the USM is 40 to 50 per cent cheaper than the main market. It is however extraordinarily difficult to be precise as legal expenses, accountancy costs, and of course the size of the issue are variable.

An analysis conducted by the ISE itself (*Quality of Markets Quarterly Review*, Winter 1988/9) came to the following conclusions:

o In all markets, costs measured as a percentage of the money raised, tend to fall as the issue gets larger;

o A USM flotation is cheaper than the Official List except in the case of very small placings;

o Cost differentials between the two markets were understated in so far as the analysis did not take into account the so-called hidden costs of preparing a five year trading record compared with a three year record and so on;

o Finally costs of a flotation had fallen compared with a Bank of England study for the period 1983–6 ie prior to 'Big Bang'.

o While it was hoped that firms obtaining a USM quotation would in time 'graduate' to a full listing in the event less than 10% of firms had done so up until 1989. Nevertheless it seems reasonable to argue that the USM will continue to play a significant role in providing an organised regulated market for the shares of medium and small companies in growth sectors.

The Over the Counter Market

Any individual authorised to conduct investment business by a self-regulatory organisation recognised under the Financial Services Act of 1986 can make a market in company shares outside the Stock Exchange. Originally dealers and investment brokers who were not members of the Stock Exchange were licensed to deal in securities under the Prevention of Fraud (Investments) Act of 1958 but they also carry out other activities in the investment field eg discretionary investment management, financial advice and planning, and the retailing of shares already traded on the Stock Exchange.

Many OTC dealers were members of the National Association of Security Dealers and Investment Managers (NASDIM) which has been absorbed into the Financial Intermediaries, Managers and Brokers Regulatory Association (FIMBRA). The latter is a recognised association and is accepted as the relevant Self Regulatory Organisation under the Financial Services Act, 1986.

Some dealers are prepared to sell or buy the shares of companies which do not have a Stock Exchange quotation hence they will often be referred to as 'unquoted' or OTC shares. In 1986 this 'market' comprised some forty licensed dealers conducting business largely by telephone in the shares of around 160 companies (Goodhart, 1987). The inauguration of the Third Market in January 1987 increased severely the degree of competition facing

OTC dealers and some of them applied to become members of the Stock Exchange. Also a number of companies whose shares were trading on the OTC expressed interest in transferring to the new market. In effect the Stock Exchange captured a considerable part of the business previously done by the expanding OTC market. This was of course a prime motive for introducing the new set of arrangements.

Shares acquired in the OTC market are riskier than those quoted on the Stock Exchange for several reasons: frequently the companies concerned are small with a short trading history; the degree of disclosure by such companies is limited largely to statutory requirements; relatively few shares are held by the public so that the level of trading activity tends to be restricted. (This of course makes for considerably greater volatility.) Finally, investor protection while improving is still below the standards of the Stock Exchange.

Trading practices in the OTC market are in any case undergoing change imposed via the Securities and Investment Board. Buying was always easy but selling was problematical – thus some dealers quote a buying and selling price (a 'spread') at which they will deal immediately but others may not make a two-way market on a continuous basis: they may only offer to 'match bargains'. Indeed Granville's, perhaps the most important of the OTC dealers, indicates precisely this in its advertising

This simply means that they will maintain a register of would-be buyers and sellers and try to match them up. The dealer then charges a commission for this to buyer and seller. It is obvious that selling shares in such an inactive market could take a long time and at prices which are difficult to determine. In effect the holder of such shares has an asset which is very illiquid and very risky.

The number of companies dealt with on the OTC remains fairly small (aggregate capitalisation is very much smaller than the USM) but the growth of this market in the 1970s was indicative of the costs of obtaining a full Stock Exchange listing. Furthermore the introduction of the Business Expansion Scheme (BES) in 1983 gave a considerable stimulus to the Over the Counter market. The BES was introduced as a way of stimulating the growth of new business – hence it gave income tax relief of up to £40 000 per annum (at the highest applicable rate of tax) to individuals buying shares in qualifying companies whose securities were not listed on the USM or the Stock Exchange. This, in its turn, lent impetus to the development of the Unlisted Securities Market and the Third Market by the Stock Exchange.

It is clear nonetheless that compared to the United States where the National Association of Securities Dealers (see Chapter 2) provides a highly integrated and transparent market there is in fact no unified OTC market in the UK but instead a number of 'markets' offered by individual dealers of varying quality. As a consequence the market has been, with honourable exceptions, one of the shadier areas of the UK securities industry: regulation was supposed to be the responsibility of the DTI but there have been a number of lamentable cases which suggest that the degree of regulation left much to be desired (Bosworth-Davies, 1988).

A stronger regulatory framework has been developed by the body which now oversees securities markets in the UK – the Securities and Investment Board (SIB). For example firms wishing to act as market makers in a particular share must make the Board aware of this fact. They will also have to indicate the securities which they will buy and sell and the SIB will then require the organisation to publish firm two-way prices in reasonable bargain sizes. The practice of 'backing away' from a price once customer interest has been elicited will therefore become more difficult. A dealer may be able to withdraw a security from the market once the Board has been notified but he will only be allowed to re-introduce it after a specified lapse of time. In addition a list of daily closing prices must be notified to the SIB or a designated information network. If a dealer is the only market maker in a share then this must be made clear to the public and the dealer must not give the impression that the security is traded on a registered exchange by making use of expressions such as the 'market price'. This again is designed to indicate to the potential investor that there is limited marketability in the share and hence a possible restriction on its liquidity.

While these changes improve various practices in the UK's OTC market, there is a long way to go before it approaches the supervision and integrity of the American equivalent. The Over the Counter market in the US is of course much larger and has a considerable number of members with individual seats (membership) on major exchanges so that it is in many ways an entirely different creature. Nevertheless it is a model which the UK would do well to follow.

The structure of public capital markets in the UK suggested the eventual development of a hierarchical arrangement with companies 'graduating' to a full listing via a series of progressively more stringently regulated and larger (in terms of access to capital) markets. It is not yet clear however that this is the way matters will in fact turn out: the 1980s were generally favourable to company growth yet only 10% of USM-listed firms moved on to the main market. This suggests that a degree of fragmentation will remain and the fluid movement between markets that might have been hoped for will not occur. On the other hand the effect of EC directives may lead not just to the integration of capital markets horizontally (ie across frontiers) but also vertically with the convergence on to a single set of listing requirements.

5   RAISING CAPITAL – CHOICE OF METHOD

As indicated earlier, companies wishing to raise capital have a number of possible sources which vary according to the status of the organisation.

Small private companies will generally have to rely on a limited group of existing shareholders, bank loans and/or leasing arrangements. Medium sized public companies with a market listing are able to sell new shares or issue debt to existing shareholders or to new subscribers. Large well established publicly quoted companies are able to tap a much greater variety of sources including in some cases foreign and international capital markets.

New issues are arranged in several different ways

o Private placing
o Public placing
o Offer for sale – fixed price
           – by tender
o Introduction

Private Placing

Private companies in the UK are prevented by the Financial Services Act (1986) from advertising an offer of new securities to the general public[4]. This does not apply in the case of advertising shares to those with the expertise to evaluate the risks or where the advertisement has a private character in the sense that there is a relationship between the issuer and the investor.

Hence such a company is limited to raising new equity capital by selling shares to existing members or perhaps to employees or possibly to third parties with sufficient financial competence. Obviously the placement of shares to securities houses and other such institutions comes into the latter category.

It is possible therefore for *both* private and public companies to use a private placement by circulating an offer through a merchant bank or a broker who may have a list of potential subscribers.

Private placements are not necessarily welcomed by the end investor unless the company in question is looking for a market quotation in the reasonably near future.[5] This is because institutions and other clients are being sold shares which may be illiquid in the sense that ready buyers are not available and therefore there is no immediate market price. Private placements nevertheless carry a number of major advantages:

o The fact that a well known broker arranges the issue gives investors confidence that there has been 'due diligence' in investigating the company;
o The securities house managing the placement has its own established list of clients – generally comprising major financial institutions which have a huge cash flow and a considerable appetite for new investment outlets;

o It is of course also possible for the issue to be underwritten but while this guarantees a successful outcome its adds to the cost of the operation;
o An issue which has the support of institutional investors facilitates further borrowing of for example bank capital on finer terms;
o Issuing costs via a private placement are generally very much smaller than a public offering.

Private placements are not as widely used in the UK as in the US where it is estimated that volume of capital raised in this way amounted to upwards of $170 billion in 1989 (Brady, 1990). Furthermore recent changes in Securities and Exchange Commission rules which govern such issues are likely to make it easier and cheaper for overseas borrowers to undertake this form of issue. The introduction of Rule 144a by the SEC in April 1990 relaxed the prohibition on the resale in the United States of non USA-registered securities by allowing qualifying financial institutions (those owning or investing at least $100m) to purchase eligible unregistered paper. At the same time the SEC allowed the resale of unregistered securities outside the USA. Quite what the impact of these changes will mean for existing international capital markets is too early to say at this juncture but it will certainly increase the competitive pressures.

Public Placing

Despite its name this technique does not involve a general offer of shares to the public, instead they are offered to institutional or individual clients of the securities house which is the company's sponsor. This method of making an issue is frequently preferred by companies as it is less expensive than most of the other issue techniques discussed. It can of course be very profitable for those fortunate enough to be on such a placement list as the relatively restricted distribution of the shares will generally mean that they can be sold at a premium.

To establish an adequate market in the securities however London's International Stock Exchange normally requires at least 25% of the shares being placed to be offered to market makers. This allows a wider group to gain access even though this access is to a smaller proportion of the shares in question. The fact that part of the equity is put into the public domain in this way distinguishes this form of placing from the private placing. The essential reason for the ISE's requirement is to improve the liquidity of the issue.

Offer for Sale – Fixed Price

Two techniques can be employed here: a direct sale to the public via an offer by prospectus or an indirect route by first alloting the securities to a broker arranging the issue and thence to the public. In the UK the prospectus and application form is published in two national newspapers although copies can be obtained from the brokers or the bankers to the issue. The major problem with any fixed price offer is pitching the price so as to ensure that the company gets the best possible deal while making the shares attractive enough to provoke investor interest. This is not easy and gross mistakes can and have been made by way of underpricing. Thus some issues, including some early privatisation issues, have been oversubscribed by a multiple of twenty or thirty-fold. As a consequence considerable premiums have emerged in the after-market to the benefit of the buyers.

On the other hand there is a danger that the issue will not be fully taken up which would then leave the company short of its funding. Most issues therefore are normally underwritten by institutional investors for a fee and this has the effect of guaranteeing the sale of those shares not taken up by the public. Any serious underpricing therefore implies paying fees for very little risk particularly in rising markets. Although even 'underpriced' attractive issues can fail in particular circumstances – a spectacular example of this was the BP issue which occurred in 1987 and fell foul of the October Crash.

Selling the shares via a securities house and thence to the public represents another way of undertaking the fixed price offer: having purchased all the shares the securities house then offers the shares to the general public at a higher price and the difference comprises the commission. If existing shareholders want to sell part of their holdings these can be bought by the issuing house and they are offered to the public at the same time as the new shares. With this procedure the securities house is taking a risk with its own capital so the issue will again be underwritten or sub-underwritten by the institutions as a way of reducing the risk.

Offer for Sale – by Tender

The difference between this technique and the above lies in the mechanism by which the price is set. In the case of a fixed price sale if the brokers underestimate demand the offer will be oversubscribed and when dealings start in the secondary market the share price will rise. The company will consequently do less well than it should have done and the buyer of the shares obtains a capital gain. This also has the effect of encouraging investors to subscribe for more shares than they really want in order to resell immediately at an expected premium. These so-called 'stags' have been the subject of criticism from time to time but the real problem is not the stags but the initial underpricing by the arrangers of the issue.

The Tender Offer is designed to get around this problem and it can be described as a 'price discovery mechanism'. The broker sets a minimum price for the shares and invites offers from the public at this *or at higher prices*. As offers come in the shares are allocated to the highest bids and then the broker moves down the scale allocating shares to successively lower bids until the whole of the issue has been accounted for. The price at which sufficient bids are received to allocate all the shares on offer becomes *the striking price*. Applicants who have offered this or higher prices then normally receive their allocation. In addition it has been general practice to reimburse investors offering more than the striking price with the difference between the strike price and their offer.

The arguments in favour of this procedure are as follows:

o It establishes a better test of market demand and reduces the chances of gross underpricing;
o The existence of a single striking price makes dealing less problematical in the after-market when the issue is complete;
o The reimbursement of money to investors bidding more than the striking price means that there is no discrimination between shareholders.

On the other hand the shares can still go to a premium when secondary dealings start as clearly the existence of higher bidders shows that there are some investors who were prepared to pay more. While the sale by tender might achieve a better result than the fixed price offer it can still be argued that the issuer could have done even better by not reimbursing the investors. This is precisely what occurred in the privatisation of British Airways. The normal procedures of reimbursement were not followed: the UK government allocated shares on the basis of successively lower offers until the issue was exhausted but did not arrive at a striking price – instead investors simply paid what they offered. This was in response to a considerable degree of criticism of earlier privatisations which had been viewed as absurdly generous and therefore rewarding investors at the expense of the Exchequer.

Introduction

A final way for a company to obtain a listing is by way of an Introduction. In this case no new issue of equity is undertaken provided the securities are sufficiently widely held to ensure adequate marketability. For example when a company is already listed on another exchange an Introduction may be preferred to a full listing. The company concerned is not necessarily interested in raising more capital in the short run but rather it may simply want to increase its visibility in another capital market. In this way it would be in a position to tap that market and extend its range of financing alternatives. Sometimes such a listing has been termed a 'vanity' listing as it does not make a substantial difference to the company concerned. On the other hand given the growing internationalisation of capital markets it is a simple and cheap way of obtaining an international presence.

Rights Issues

A rights issue is a means of raising more capital from existing shareholders. It involves the allocation of more shares on a pro rata basis (eg one for three or one for two) at a fixed price usually set at a discount to the current market value of the shares. Such rights are usually exercisable over a fairly short period of time (two to three weeks) during which time shareholders must decide whether they wish to buy the new shares at the subscription price. Should the shareholder decide not to exercise the rights then it is possible to sell the 'allotment letter' for whatever price it will fetch – after all it gives the holder the right to buy shares at a price less than the going market price. Because the rights have been issued at a discount to the price of the underlying shares there will usually be a premium provided the market price of old shares stays higher than the issue price of new shares. It is a fairly simple matter to work out the value of the rights in these circumstances.[6]

Shareholders can decide to do nothing in which case the company may sell new shares not taken up and distribute the proceeds to those who failed to exercise their rights. On the other hand this is not compulsory and shareholders may therefore lose out in these circumstances.

In the UK there has been some discussion about abolishing the right of existing shareholders to have first refusal in this way (pre-emptive rights as they are called). This is because rights issues are relatively cumbersome and take time which leaves the issue exposed to extraneous events which might undermine its success. Issuers therefore may prefer other ways of raising the extra capital – for example a placing is quicker to arrange and hence more predictable.

Capitalisation issues [7]

This is also known as a bonus or scrip issue. This is where the company issues shares free of charge on a pro rata basis to existing shareholders. In essence it is a balance sheet operation which is undertaken when the company's accumulated reserves are out of line with its issued capital. Theoretically the operation should leave the investors' overall position intact because the market price of the share should adjust to take account of the number of new shares in issue. For example a one for one bonus issue leaves twice as many shares in the market as before and therefore should cause the share price to halve. In some cases however it is argued that a bonus issue can improve the marketability of a share and this might increase the 'ex capitalisation' price if, for example, a share has a particularly heavy price.

NOTES

1. In the US the term 'debenture' refers to the unsecured obligations of a company while in the UK it means that there is a specific charge – for example a mortgage.
2. There are minor differences between convertible loan stock and preference shares with regard to conversion. If convertible loan stock is not converted into ordinary shares the stock will be redeemed at its due date and the holder will receive the redemption value of the bond. Convertible preference shares will be automatically converted into shares at the end of a specific period unless they are *redeemable* convertible preference shares.
3. Firms on the Third Market were not *directly* regulated by the Exchange: companies coming to the market by this route did so under the aegis of a member firm. This member firm or 'sponsor' had the responsibility of overseeing the activity of the company.
4. A private company is defined as one not formed or re-registered under the Companies Act 1985.
5. In fact Stock Exchange rules prevent brokers from placing securities unless a listing is under consideration.
6. The procedure is to calculate the 'ex rights' price ie how much all the shares theoretically be worth once the rights issue is completed

$$\text{'Ex rights' share price} = \frac{N \times \text{Price of old shares} + \text{Subscription price}}{N + 1}$$

where N = the number of old shares for one new share.

Suppose existing shares are selling at £10.00 and the individual has a rights offer of one for three at £8.00 the ex rights price where the existing share price remains constant is

$$\frac{3 \times £10.00 + £8.00}{3 + 1} = \frac{£38.00}{4}$$

$$= £9.50$$

Thus this ex rights price stands at a premium of £1.50 to the subscription price and this would be the price at which the new shares are quoted in their 'nil paid' form before the £8.00 becomes payable to the company.
7. In the US and the UK capitalisation issues are calculated in slightly different ways. In the US they are referred to as *stock splits*. For example in the UK a 4:1 capitalisation issue would leave the investor with five times as many shares as before (four new shares + one old share) whereas in the US a 4:1 stock split means the shareholder will have only 4 shares (ie one old share exchanges for four new ones).

2 Equities and Equity Markets

1 INTRODUCTION

Investors are attracted to equity markets because ordinary shares have risk/ return characteristics which make them a desirable part of a financial portfolio. Clearly they do not offer the security inherent in bonds but they compensate for this by offering the opportunity to enjoy greater capital gains and growing dividends. However one problem for investors is that of understanding the factors which influence the value of shares. This remains a highly controversial issue on which there is no major consensus outside the academic world.

2 EQUITY VALUATION

In some respects it is easier to say what *should* affect share prices rather than what *does* affect them: there are a number of theories about what determines the price of shares.

In the final analysis any price is determined by market forces – by supply and demand. In the case of shares, the flow of new issues (the supply) is small in relation to the current stock. Demand factors will therefore tend to be more important especially in the short run. But this only presents us with the problem of what influences the demand for and therefore the price of shares.

Demand may be based on rational criteria such as an assessment of the company's earning potential and therefore the prospective yield of the investment. Clearly however in so far as some view of future prospects and earnings is undertaken there is considerable room for error, disagreement, excessive optimism and excessive pessimism. Occasionally too irrational forces may come to bear in the form of fear and panic.

In the view of some the value of a share should reflect the underlying 'economic worth' of the company. The share price might fluctuate around this value but ultimately will tend to gravitate toward it:

earnings do ultimately and solely determine the value to be derived from shareholding and if shareholders do learn at all well from their experience,

27

their purchasing patterns will, in the long run, force stock prices to conform rather closely to these prospective earnings opportunities of the firms whose shares they buy. We have strong reasons to suspect that in a rough and ready way, security prices do follow closely the developments in company prospects. (Baumol, 1965)

If one takes this view then it leads to a particular investment philosophy: identify shares which, when compared with their true or fundamental value, are currently underpriced or overpriced with a view to buying/holding the former and selling the latter.

There are however others who feel that this search for the 'true' value of a given share is something of a waste of time: in their view other approaches to buying shares or constructing a portfolio will generate better outcomes/ returns. These other approaches are based on different notions about how share prices are determined and they derive their investment philosophies accordingly.

There are basically three major schools of thought:

1. Technical analysis;
2. Fundamental analysis;
3. The Efficient Markets Hypothesis.

Technical Analysis

Technical analysis, also referred to as Chartism, takes the view that in attempting to predict the future course of share prices it is useful to focus on the past behaviour of such prices. Chartists argue that share prices move in trends and patterns which periodically repeat themselves so the key to making gains is to recognise these patterns before others. According to technical analysts it really does not matter in which industry or markets the company operates, the use of a chart is sufficient to detect the likely movement in the price of its shares. At any one time prices reflect the balance of supply and demand so that changes in price result from shifts in the balance of sentiment between buyers and sellers. Hence by tracking price behaviour it is possible to develop insights into their future movements.

Thus analysts make use of different types of charts which indicate price changes over time in the hope that recognisable patterns will emerge. A repetition of such patterns would then present opportunities which may be exploited by 'out-guessing' the other market participants as to the next move in the share price. The search for patterns has produced a whole set of jargon words and concepts such as 'double tops', 'double bottoms', 'head and shoulders', 'triangles' and the rest. These are relatively simple concepts and other chartists employ more sophisticated techniques such as moving averages over various time periods (200 day/40 day etc), momentum indicators, relative strength, advance/decline ratios and so on.

There are a number of chart services which sell their products to the public and several large securities houses retain technical analysts to monitor various sectors of the market.

Technical analysis is regarded in some quarters however as vested interest in quasi scientific clothing. The most damaging criticism of chartists comes from the idea that the market is informationally efficient. This view which has considerable academic support suggests that in a market where the participants are intelligent, self-motivated profit maximisers there will be a built-in incentive to exploit available information to form expectations about the likely behaviour of prices. Indeed if share prices do not reflect such information they will be misvalued and it will be worthwhile for some members of the investment community to take advantage of the fact and buy or sell the shares as appropriate. Thus before a change in trend is picked up in the charts the market will already have digested the relevant information and the technical analyst will be too late to make use of his observations.

In any case at a common sense level one might ask why if the chart techniques work at all the analyst does not keep the good news to exploit for himself? The essence of being a successful trader is to be one step ahead of the market by using information which gives an advantage over the rest. The answer to the question must be that it is more profitable to sell chart recommendations than to use them to exploit market inefficiency. Of course it may well be the case that some technical analyst somewhere has actually discovered a consistently successful set of indicators which allow him to outwit the market. However the very act of making it public will undermine its efficacy!

Finally at an empirical level, there are a large number of academic studies which show that observation of past movements of share prices are of little use in predicting future behaviour (Brealey and Myers, 1981). The only circumstances in which chart *predictions* appear to work is if enough market participants follow the advice of a particular analyst. Thus if one were to say that the chart indicates a significant upward move in the price of Macdonald's or British Telecom and enough people buy on the strength of this statement the price would indeed move in that direction. However this does not work to the advantage of the people who rush in to follow the buy recommendation but to the existing holders of the shares. In this respect the technical analyst may be compared with the newspaper tipster whose advice is followed by readers: they find it difficult to make gains because the market makers monitor the financial columns and adjust their prices accordingly.

Given these various criticisms of technical analysis why do securities houses retain the no doubt expensive services of chartists? One reason may lie in the fact that when some participants in the market use the technique their decisions or expectations will be influenced by charts, hence this has to be taken account of in other people's decisions. For example in an investigation of the use of charts in the London foreign exchange market the Bank of England (*Quarterly Bulletin*, Nov. 1989) found that 90% of respondents used charts as an input to their short-run expectations – intra-day to a week – and 60% judged charts as at least as important as fundamentals.

A further reason charts may be used is that from time to time a bit of technical jargon can give an authentic ring to a sales pitch.

Fundamental Analysis

Fundamental analysts examine the underlying economic factors which they argue ultimately determine the value of equities. Some of these factors are based on balance sheet information and some are derived from measures of income. For example some analysts utilise information relating to earnings per share, assets per share, profit margins, turnover and so on as indicators of corporate performance and hence underlying share value. Thus a whole battery of financial ratios may be deployed in an attempt to assess how far a share's market price is out of line with some notion of its intrinsic value.

This intrinsic worth is estimated as the discounted present value of all its *expected* future dividends. For this reason this approach to valuing shares can be termed the Dividend Discount Model (DDM). Obviously a share would command a zero price if the owner never expected to be paid a dividend. In addition for purposes of valuing the share expected capital gains can be ignored as they can be subsumed into the concept of long-run dividends. The relevant formula is as follows

$$P = \frac{D_1}{(1+r)} + \frac{D_2}{(1+r)^2} + \dots \frac{D_n}{(1+r)^n}$$

$$P = \sum_{t=1}^{n} \frac{D_t}{(1+r)^t}$$

A formula similar adapted from equation (2) can be employed here provided the growth rate of dividends is expected to be constant

$$P = \frac{D}{(r-g)}$$

It is then argued that the market price will tend to gravitate toward this underlying value. This proposition would be true provided the investment community employs share valuation techniques based on estimating this flow of dividends and also provided that there is a reasonable consensus in dividend forecasts. However this is rarely the case: the forecasting accuracy of analysts appears to be fairly poor. A number of studies (Cragg and Malkiel, 1982) show that forecasting errors are very substantial with the *average* error being in the region of a third of the central forecast! Yet the validity of the whole procedure hangs on the proximity of forecasts to the actual outturn.

The Efficient Market Hypothesis (EMH)

Academic criticism of Fundamental Analysis and Chartism commenced over thirty years ago with the idea that share prices follow a random walk and the related idea that financial markets behave in accordance with the Efficient Market Hypothesis.

(i) The random walk hypothesis

Empirical support for the view that share prices do not behave in a systematic manner but are more akin to a random walk was initially put forward by Professor M. G. Kendall in the early 1950s (Kendall, 1953) and has since been supported by many other studies of share price behaviour. Fama (1970) provides a comprehensive review of the early development of both the theory and empirical work. A random walk simply means that successive price changes are independent of each other, ie that they are uncorrelated, hence attempting to predict the next movement in a particular time series will not be helped by a study of previous movements.

There has, as a consequence, been a degree of antagonism between chartists and academic supporters of the random walk idea (Levy, 1967).

(ii) Efficient market hypothesis

The Efficient Market Hypothesis supplies a theoretical framework which lends support to the random walk character of share prices. But what exactly do we mean by an 'efficient' market? An efficient market is one where at any one time prices take into account all available information. Market participants are assumed to act in an intelligent, self-motivated manner and to assess and act upon available information about share prices when formulating their buy or sell decisions. If some available information about a specific share is *not* acted upon then an opportunity will arise for at least some market participants to use that information to their advantage by buying or selling the share. Thus as market individuals or organisations act upon this information the price of the share will adjust accordingly until there are no further profit opportunities. This has been referred to as 'information arbitrage' efficiency by Tobin (1984).

It is important to note that this is a very particular and highly restrictive definition of efficiency: it refers to the ability of the market to process information in such a way as to use it to best advantage. It does not imply that stock markets are efficient in the economist's more normal sense of the word – ie providing services at least cost in terms of resources employed. Indeed throughout the period when the question of 'market efficiency' first began to impinge on the consciousness of financial analysts there was relatively little attention paid to issues such as freedom of entry and the widespread use of fixed commissions – blatantly anticompetitive and inefficient practices. It was not until 1975 (New York) and 1986 (London) that such practices were abandoned in two of the world's acknowledged 'informationally efficient markets'. Indeed it is still the case that they linger on in other markets. At the same time the operational efficiency of many stock exchanges was appalling as evidenced by the settlement failures in the back office crises experienced in New York in the late 1960s and London in the 1980s.

With that proviso in mind let us examine the concept of informational efficiency more closely. Analysts classify market efficiency into three possible varieties:–

1. Weak form efficiency – prices are said to reflect all *past* information;
2. Semi-strong form efficiency in which prices fully reflect all publicly available information;
3. Strong form efficiency where prices are said to embody all information – whether or not publicly available.

The weak form of efficiency is a sufficient condition to undermine technical analysts' claims to be able to generate consistently higher profits by making use of charts of past price movements.

The semi-strong form of the EMH takes us one step further by arguing that not only is past information taken into account so too is all publicly available information. There is considerable evidence that most of the major stock markets are efficient in the weak form of the hypothesis and some are consistent with the semi-strong form.

In the case of a market characterised by strong form efficiency it would be impossible for an investor to take advantage of new information from whatever source. This is because a market operating at this level of efficiency already exploits *all* information relevant to the share. This in turn means that insider information will also have been included in determining the share price.

While the strong form of the hypothesis has little empirical support it may be influential in affecting perceptions of how markets *should* operate.

Thus 'insider dealing' (ie the use of undisclosed, price sensitive information to take a position in shares) is regarded by most authorities as pernicious and has been made a criminal offence in several countries. It is not however always easy to define[1] and it is possible to justify some activities which are said to be insider trading as they tend to take markets closer to the position of strong form efficiency. Thus there are some who take the view that certain types of insider trading should not be seen as criminal because they can improve market efficiency by moving market prices toward their 'true' or fundamental value (Grossman 1986). For example the activities of the insider may at times convey information to other market participants with beneficial effects:

Trading on insider information is valuable . . . When others see insiders trade, that often tells them nearly as much as outright disclosure, and tends to push the stock's price closer to its real worth, that is, where it would be if the insider's information had been disclosed outright. (Herzel and Katz, 1987)

This is undoubtedly an interesting point but it assumes that investors know who the insiders are and this may be problematical when shares are bought via a nominee account or a series of such accounts. In addition it seems to take the view that the 'insiders' repeat their activities sufficiently frequently for the market to learn who they are and trade accordingly. What of the insider who simply makes his killing and leaves for sunnier climes?

Whatever one's view about these rather arcane arguments the most important implication of market efficiency is that price misalignments will be rapidly eliminated until, taking the logic to its conclusion, no profitable opportunities are feasible because the market adjusts too rapidly. Therefore on the average it is not possible to trade profitably on publicly available information. Insider dealing of course can consistently make money precisely because the individual concerned is able to act on information which the market has not yet taken into account.

Portfolio Theory and the Capital Asset Pricing Model

Investors have been instinctively aware for many years that to reduce risk it makes sense to hold a number of different securities. One result of Portfolio Theory has been to give scientific support to the old saying about not putting all one's eggs in the same basket. Such notions about diversification provide a major selling point for mutual funds/unit trusts as far as the smaller investor is concerned. Portfolio Theory however provides a mathematical framework for selecting the shares which should make up this basket.

In this respect the most important result derived from Portfolio Theory is to demonstrate that by constructing a portfolio of shares according to particular criteria it is possible to reduce risk *yet still maintain the weighted average rate of return of the individual securities.* (The proof of this proposition is not strictly relevant to our purpose here and can be found in a variety of text books – see Levy and Sarnat, 1984.) Hence it is possible for the investor, institutional or private, to select a group of securities which result in a risk/return profile that best suits that investor's attitude to risk.

The key to reducing risk is to choose securities, the returns to which are *uncorrelated* because they are affected by different factors – indeed it is even better to select securities which are negatively correlated (Brealey, 1983). Increasing the number of uncorrelated shares therefore reduces the degree of risk of the whole portfolio and by the time 20 diversified shares are in a portfolio almost all the risk associated with individual shares has been eliminated (Modigliani and Pogue, 1974).

Taking the procedure to its logical conclusion produces an interesting result which is fundamental: by adding more and more shares the investor will eventually hold shares in the whole market. The specific risk associated with particular shares will become less and less significant and eventually the risk of the portfolio will simply converge toward the risk of the market! At this point it is not possible to lower total risk any further – investors are left with an irreducible element – the risk of the market as a whole.

Of course this result applies not merely to national markets but also at an international level. The risk inherent in any particular market can be lowered by diversifying the portfolio into other world markets. Once again the most effective way of reducing risk is to combine markets which themselves have low correlation coefficients.

It has become commonplace for some investment funds to offer global asset allocation and this is a logical extension of Portfolio Theory. However the decision is made more complicated by the extra dimension of exchange rate risk and the fact that liquidity in some smaller markets eg Norway, Sweden, Spain, Ireland and so on may be much less than in established locally deeper markets.

When Portfolio Theory emerged it provided the ability to construct optimal portfolios for investors with different risk/return preferences. Academics readily accepted the idea, but until cheap computing power became available the unwieldy procedure involved in establishing and using the statistical relationships was a barrier to its practical use.

The Capital Asset Pricing Model (CAPM)

A rather simpler procedure was developed in the form of the so-called Capital Asset Pricing Model (Sharpe, 1963). This builds on the key notion that diversification works by reducing unsystematic risk until finally once one holds a portfolio which reflects the market as a whole it is not possible to reduce risk further and there remains an irreducible market risk.

Return = Risk free rate (1-Beta) + Beta (Expected market return) *(Bank)*

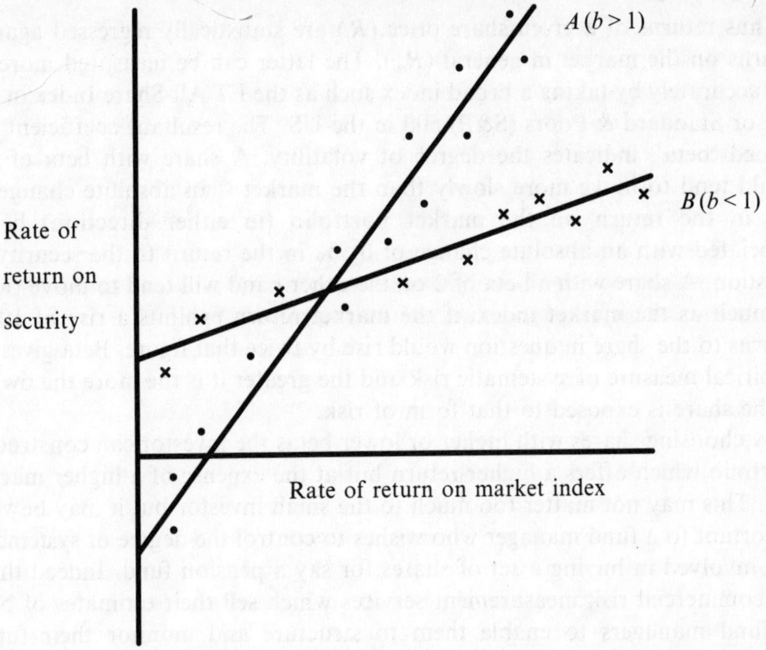

Figure 2.1 The relationship between security returns and the market index

Every security has two species of risk associated with it – unsystematic risk which is a feature of that particular security alone and systematic risk which is a measure of the relationship between the security and the market as a whole.

Some shares appear to be more volatile than others: they offer returns which vary by more than a given variation in the return on the market as a whole. Hence such shares are said to be aggressive. Other shares appear to be *less* volatile: when returns on the market index vary the returns on these shares change more sluggishly. These therefore are said to be defensive.

This can be illustrated graphically as shown in Fig. 2.1: Security *A* is more aggressive than security *B*.

It is possible therefore to assign a mathematical value to this volatility and that is indeed what the CAPM theorists have done over the years. Essentially the volatility of a share is estimated via the following equation

$$R_i = a_i + b_i R_m + e_i$$

where: R_i = the return on the ith security
R_m = the return on the market index
a_i = the vertical intercept of the security
b_i = the security's variation with respect to the market index
e_i = the unsystematic risk

Thus returns of a given share price (R_i) are statistically regressed against returns on the market in general (R_m). The latter can be measured more or less accurately by taking a broad index such as the FT All-Share Index in the UK or Standard & Poors (S&P) 500 in the US. The resultant coefficient 'b', termed 'beta', indicates the degree of volatility. A share with beta of 0.5 would tend to move more slowly than the market – an absolute change of 1% in the return on the market portfolio (in either direction) being associated with an absolute change of 0.5% in the return to the security in question. A share with a beta of 2 on the other hand will tend to move twice as much as the market index: if the market return exhibits a rise of 10%, returns to the share in question would rise by twice that figure. Beta gives an empirical measure of systematic risk and the greater it is the more the owner of the share is exposed to that form of risk.

By choosing shares with higher or lower betas the investor can construct a portfolio which offers a higher return but at the expense of a higher market risk. This may not matter too much to the small investor but it may be very important to a fund manager who wishes to control the degree of systematic risk involved in buying a set of shares for say a pension fund. Indeed there are commercial risk measurement services which sell their estimates of beta to fund managers to enable them to structure and monitor their funds appropriately.

After enjoying a period of sustained dominance over rival ideas the EMH and the CAPM have been the target of much recent critical analysis. This has tended to take two forms:

(i)   the first strand of criticism has focussed on the nature of beta as a measure of systematic risk, its stability and the methodology of its estimation;

(ii) the second strand derives from studies of market behaviour which appear to have thrown up observations contrary to the most fundamental implications of the EMH.

(i)   Estimating beta

Methods of estimating beta are not free of criticism for a variety of reasons. Calculations of beta almost invariably use *past* data and yet reliance on the past to predict the future has been a critical charge levied at both fundamentalists and technical analysts.

Betas can change: an obvious source of such change is the effect of divestment, mergers and acquisitions. Companies which grow through acquisition may have the same name and the same shares in issue but they may be in entirely different markets with very different features by the time the process is complete. Hence the share may develop different characteristics *vis-à-vis* the market.

Another, perhaps more fundamental, criticism concerns the question of 'the market' against which the share price is compared. By definition a market index is merely a representative measure which proxies the whole market or perhaps segments of the market. Clearly different indexes can be constructed which perform this role more or less adequately. If the beta of a share is calculated against different indexes then it is possible to obtain different results. That is to say in some cases the beta may be greater than 1 and the share would be classified as aggressive or volatile while in others it comes out as less than one implying that the share is defensive and not volatile!

If the beta of a share is sensitive to the index against which a comparison is made then it becomes extraordinarily difficult to assess the systematic risk to which the investor is exposed when adding a specific share to a portfolio. It would be like having a measuring rod that gives different results on different occasions.

(ii) Market anomalies

A key feature of the EMH is the conclusion that in an efficient market it is not possible to make consistently higher returns except by holding a portfolio with a higher level of risk. However, rather peculiar anomalies began to emerge in relation to what has become known as the 'small firms effect' or the 'smaller companies puzzle'. In both the United States and the United Kingdom (acknowledged to have the most informationally efficient stock markets in the world) evidence points to the existence of consistently higher returns from investing in the shares of smaller companies (Friend and Lang 1988, Dimson and Marsh 1989).

This would come as no surprise if it was also the case that such shares exhibited a higher beta because the higher returns would simply reflect the greater risk. The evidence however points to the opposite!

For example in the UK the Hoare Govett Smaller Companies (HGSC) index provides superior returns yet at the same time the beta of the HGSC is *lower* than the beta of the FT-Actuaries All Shares Index suggesting that in fact the smaller companies portfolio is less volatile and therefore on average less risky than the overall market index (Dimson and Marsh, 1989). In the United States where the size effect was first noted (Banz, 1981, Keim, 1983) similar results have been observed and investigations of other stock exchanges seem to have thrown up similar results (Guletkin and Guletkin, 1983). These results flatly contradict the CAPM.

There is no shortage of explanations for this apparent contradiction of the conventional theory of efficient markets. For example smaller firms may offer greater growth prospects; they may be less marketable; they may expose investors to other extra sources of risk etc. But none of these satisfactorily explains why it is that the profit maximising intelligent investors who are central to the theory did not recognise the disparities in returns and move in such a way as to eliminate them.

The small firms effect however is not the only anomaly which has been thrown up in recent years: a further problem for the EMH is presented by *seasonal variations* in returns. The so-called January effect came to light in 1984 (Keim and Stambaugh, 1984). This seems to show that in the US nearly all the differential size effect occurs at the turn of the year ie during the early part of January. Similar seasonal effects have been identified in other markets.

This constitutes a further puzzle: the very thing which random walk theory seemed to dismiss – the existence of persistent and replicable market behaviour seems to have risen from the dead! It is fair to argue that here we are discussing the seasonal patterns as they apply to segments of the market or to market indexes rather than individual share prices but it still leaves a fairly uncomfortable problem for proponents of the EMH. If the market is informationally efficient why do seasonal regularities occur and why do market participants fail to exploit and thereby eliminate these seasonal effects?

One possibility is that the anomalies are there but are simply below an exploitable threshold. Share transactions are subject to dealing costs and hence if the disparities in returns are insufficiently large then trading will not be able to take advantage of such effects. In this case we would observe the existence of a variety of so-called irrational seasonal effects but these would be quite compatible with a slightly modified form of the Efficient Market Hypothesis (Keane, 1989).

The 'size effect' and its close relative the seasonal effect are not the only observations which appear to be inconsistent with the EMH however. There is a growing literature which seems to point to a greater degree of volatility in share price behaviour than would be predicted on the basis of the Efficient Market Hypothesis (Shiller, 1981, Grossman and Shiller, 1981, Bulkley and Tonks, 1989).

There is also evidence which points to the fact that share prices overshoot in reaction to new information. This may be a consequence of myopic behaviour in the sense that shareholders give too much emphasis to recent events and hence overreact. This has been tested in the UK by Nickell and Wadhwani (1986). They simply questioned whether the significance given to present dividends relative to future dividends was 'too high' and indeed found that this did appear to be the case.

If we accept the evidence for the volatility of share prices why is this not mitigated by the activity of speculators? There are two possible answers here. The first is that the costs of dealing are too large to make speculation sufficiently profitable (Keane, 1989). Perhaps more telling however is the notion that markets may be characterised by *speculative bubbles* (Blanchard, 1979).

This argues as follows – 'Suppose an investor knew that today the market price of a share actually stands above its true or correct value, how might that investor behave?' If the Efficient Markets Hypothesis is operative then the market should react by adjusting the price downward in line with the correct value. However at the current market price there are really two probabilities: either the price will go down or it may continue to rise. If the probability of a continued rise is big enough to compensate for the risk that the price will fall then it is rational to hold or buy the share and hence there need be no pressure for the price to gravitate to its correct value. Hence prices may oscillate by a greater amount than the fundamental value would suggest.

The notion of speculative bubbles is particularly significant since the collapse of equity prices in October 1987. The EMH certainly struggles to explain what new information could have caused the shift in the valuation of stocks on one day compared with the previous day. Some authorities have instead argued that the events are better described as the result of a speculative bubble. Shiller (1987) for example points out that *before* the Crash occurred surveys estimated that over 80% of institutional investors and more than 70% of individual investors took the view that the market was over-valued! This hardly seems compatible with the EMH: why did not those believing the market to be over-valued act on their beliefs and sell earlier? This would have stopped the rise in stock prices in its tracks.

However if there is a speculative bubble individuals can be aware that prices are out of line with 'fundamentals' but continue to buy or remain invested if they assess the probability of the bubble being maintained is greater than the probability that it will burst. Investors may be prepared to ride the bubble upwards and hope to get out of the market before everybody else.

This sounds like an academic version of the 'greater fool theory' which argues that it is always worth buying a security provided that there is a greater fool to take it off your hands at a higher price. Hence individuals will continue to buy shares at continually rising prices provided that they believe that the next move will be upwards!

There remains the problem of explaining how speculative bubbles emerge in the first place. De Grauwe and Matthews (1988) for example take the view that inexperience in the development of financial innovations may produce conditions in which speculative bubbles may occur or be prolonged. In particular the use of Portfolio Insurance (see Chapter 8) in the US may have lulled certain institutions into a feeling that they had placed a floor under potential losses resulting from a market fall hence they would tend to stay in the market in spite of evidence that prices were getting out of line with fundamentals.

Where Portfolio Insurance accounts for a large segment of the market the attempt to sell simultaneously as investors revise their estimates of the probability of a bubble continuing would produce the kind of crash experienced in October 1987. While this sort of one-off event is not conclusive in the debate about the EMH, it is clear that coming on top of a number of accumulating anomalies, the Crash shook the faith of practitioners in the theory of rational markets.

In addition the Crash raised a number of question marks about the operational characteristics of the world's larger equity markets. This is an issue to which we now turn.

3   THE NATURE OF EQUITY MARKETS

Markets vary in terms of their jargon, trading practices and settlement techniques. One generic difference distinguishes Over the Counter and exchange floor markets: OTC markets are geographically dispersed, deals are done by telephone and buyers or sellers are forced to contact several dealers and if necessary negotiate prices. Such markets lack *transparency* and could be referred to as 'negotiated markets'.[2] Exchange floor markets on the other hand work by assembling buy and sell orders in a central location. In this latter case there can be other structural differences:

o   For example most European exchanges are 'matching markets' where brokers marry up buy and sell orders on behalf of their clients;
o   In London prior to Big Bang in 1986 there were firms which were exclusively market makers on the exchange floor – stock jobbers – who bought and sold shares for their own account and dealt with brokers acting for the public;
o   Finally there are floor exchanges which are a mix of the above – for example New York, Amex and Tokyo – which are in essence broker exchanges but have 'specialists' who can take on a market making function to provide a 'continuous auction' market.

Whichever is the case, current buy and sell orders are exposed to participants in a single location and in this way, it is argued the final customer can obtain 'best execution' – the best price.

The new technologies offering automated quotation screens and computer based order-matching systems have gone a long way to narrowing the gap between OTC and floor markets: electronic displays provide the necessary information on prices and bargain sizes to participants simultaneously.

There still remain some differences however in the degree to which systems are *price driven* or *order driven*. In the case of price driven systems competing market makers are interposed between buying and selling brokers. The market makers indicate prices and bargain sizes for the shares in which they deal: in essence the market makers act as wholesalers in the relevant equity. London and the National Association of Security Dealers' Automated Quotations Sytem (NASDAQ) are major exchanges which operate on this principle. In an order driven system however the buying and selling brokers come together directly or input their orders to a central computer and execution occurs via a process which *matches* buy and sell orders. European exchanges such as those of France and Germany operate this sort of system while Tokyo and the main American floor exchanges use a similar approach with the addition of 'specialists' to provide a continuous auction market.

4   THE UK – THE INTERNATIONAL STOCK EXCHANGE (ISE)

Stock exchanges can be measured in a number of ways: in terms of market capitalisation, turnover, number of listings and so on. In addition there can be substantial and rapid changes in these values. For example in the first half of 1990 Tokyo lost nearly 30% of its market value while turnover on all the main exchanges has fallen markedly compared with the period prior to October 1987. Hence any ranking of exchanges in terms of size can only be provisional and depends on the criterion employed.

In June 1990 there were some 2035 companies listed on the main London market – the International Stock Exchange. They comprised some 1484 domestic and 551 overseas registered companies In total there were 5050 company securities in issue while the aggregate value of *domestic* equity was £487 billion.

As can be seen in Table 2.1 London has a larger number of companies listed than any other exchange except the electronic Over the Counter Market in the US (popularly known as NASDAQ – the National Association of Securities Dealer Automatic Quotation System) which boasts 4264. However in keeping with its reputation as an international financial centre there are more foreign companies listed on the ISE than any other exchange and trading in foreign equities accounts for nearly 30% of total turnover.

The fear that large international companies and investors would gradually desert London in favour of bigger and cheaper markets, combined with the desire to see London as the pre-eminent stock market in the European time zone led directly to the decision in the mid 1980s to open up the London market to external capital and therefore competition from overseas securities houses. The effects of 'Big Bang' as this process of deregulation became known have been threefold:

TABLE 2.1 Major stock exchanges, March 1990

	Value of domestic equity		Total Equity Turnover 1st Quarter 1990		Listed companies	
	£b*	($b)**	£b*	($b)**	Domestic	Foreign
Tokyo	1899	(3229)	227	(386)	1610	120
NYSE	1764	(2998)	211	(359)	1650	91
London	487	(828)	86	(146)	1484	551
NASDAQ	229	(389)	68	(116)	3983	281
Frankfurt	232	(394)	104	(177)	378	351
Paris	204	(347)	19	(32)	456	226
Zurich	102	(173)	n/a	n/a	177	232

* Figures rounded up
** Exchange rate $1.70 = £1.00
ISE, *Quality of Markets Quarterly Review*, Summer 1990.

1. The dismantling of fixed commission charges which were characteristic of former dealing arrangements;
2. The opening up of the London Market to outside securities houses particularly American and Japanese;
3. A move to a screen-based electronic market place similar to that operated in the USA since 1971 by NASDAQ. The Stock Exchange Automatic Quotations (SEAQ) system operates via a central computer to which price quotes, market size and transactions are reported by market makers. This information is then distributed to subscribers by the Stock Exchange's TOPIC – a videotext information – service. The move to this decentralised screen-based system has led to the demise of the market floor and the emergence of off-floor dealing rooms.

The Dealing Mechanism

The old arrangements were replaced by a system in which as many as twenty five to thirty registered competing market makers undertook to make a two way market in particular shares. Each dealer indicates a bid (buy) and offer (sell) price in given size of bargain and brokers or other market makers can deal at or close to these prices.

From 1986 to 1990 the SEAQ system classified all securities into four categories – Alpha, Beta, Gamma and Delta. Depending upon the classification which a given security received there were implications for market makers in matters such as the minimum size of bargain, the firmness of the prices quoted, the amount of information provided on the screen and so on. In July 1990 the Council of the Stock Exchange accepted certain recommendations from a Special Committee on Market Development (the 'Elwes' Committee) which will involve changes in this system. These changes are discussed further below (p. 45). The following deals with the operation of the system prior to the implementation of the new structure.

(i) Alpha securities

These are the 138 most actively traded securities as measured by volume of turnover. In this case the SEAQ screen displays the various prices quoted by market makers and these are regarded as firm and good for the stated size of transaction. The Stock Exchange imposes a minimum size which market makers are required to offer in these Alpha shares (5000 each way) although it is common to see $L \times L$ on the screen which simply means 'Large' and implies that the price shown is good for deals of 100 000 shares or more. Average quote sizes vary but in 1989 were in excess of 85 000.

The best bid and offer prices (the so-called 'touch' price) is highlighted in a yellow strip across the SEAQ screen for easy inspection. Until 1989 *all* trades in alpha securities were supposed to be reported within five minutes. Despite the apparent rapidity of reporting this compares less than favourably with NASDAQ where deals are reported within 90 seconds.

In addition other information is displayed on the screen such as the closing price the previous day, cumulative trading volume for the current dealing day, the recent prices at which transactions have occurred as well as periodic indications that particular news about a company is imminent.

(ii) Beta securities

Beta shares comprise the next 500 or so most actively traded equities. Again price and quote sizes are firm. As the Beta shares are not quite so liquid the price spread tends to be rather larger and the size of the quote smaller. Not quite so much detail is displayed: for example bargains are reported but need not be displayed on the screen and there is no indication of cumulative volume.

(iii) Gamma securities

These are the least actively traded of the SEAQ securities. As a consequence the dealers will only display 'indicative' prices and sizes at which they will deal. Actual prices have to be ascertained by telephoning the relevant market maker. Again trades are reported but not displayed.

(iv) Delta securities

These comprise any domestic securities not quoted on SEAQ. Prices are distributed via the Stock Exchange's TOPIC service.

As one would expect the spread between bid and offer prices widens as one moves from the Alpha to the Delta securities as the lower the level of activity the less the pressure of competing market makers. Of course this also implies that Gamma and Delta shares are far less liquid than the Alpha and Beta counterparts.

The primary objective of the screen based quote system has been to give the market that transparency which keeps all market participants fully and rapidly informed. This accords with the generally held precept that markets need information to work efficiently and the more rapid and widespread is the dissemination of information the less likely that profit can be made via access to privileged sources. Transparency is a significant way of minimising abuse and therefore establishing confidence in the system as far as the investing institutions and clients are concerned.

Effectiveness of the New System

The screen trading system has only been in operation for a comparatively short period of time and has come in for a number of criticisms: it is still to some degree in the process of evolution as from time to time new rule changes are suggested. Apart from periodic technical failures of the type that seem to afflict many computer based systems, there have been other more important factors at work which have led users to query the present set up compared with the former trading floor or the NASDAQ system which served as something of a model for SEAQ.

(a) During the collapse in equity prices in October 1987 it was said that many market makers simply refused to answer their telephones. Indeed this accusation had been made earlier during the less marked fall in equity prices in August 1987. Although this was vigorously denied at the time and has been since, nevertheless the suspicion remains that in a severe bear turndown it is easier for market makers to avoid their prime function than was the case in the old system where bargains were struck on a face to face basis.

(b) The fact that market makers are required to deal with each other and also to publish their prices and *the deals they transact* left some of the larger market makers in a vulnerable position in the sluggish post-1987 market. There may have been an element of special pleading here but nonetheless the ISE treated the complaint seriously enough to amend its rules in two major respects:

○ Market makers were not required to deal with each other;
○ Details of trades of more than £100 000 in value did not need to be published on the screen until the following day.

These rule changes protected the position of those larger market makers who could feel more confident about accepting larger orders because they had the distributional capacity to sell it on to their client base. At the same time they were able to avoid acting as 'jobber of last resort' to the smaller market makers.

The problem is that in delaying the publication of large deals the market is no longer transparent and some dealers are unaware of the true state of market demand. Thus the integrity of the market is effectively compromised to cope with a possibly temporary difficulty in the market – that of overcapacity. In particular the new arrangements had the effect of protecting market makers with a substantial UK client base and therefore the changes were seen as biassing the system in favour of the home side. This is not consistent with London's claim to be treated as a prime international market and is a retrogressive step in relation to the ideas which lay behind 'Big Bang'.

An additional problem is that the ability to keep back information about large trades inserts a wedge between the spot market for shares and the futures and options market. As the latter are derived markets they are driven by the price movements of the underlying equity to which they relate. But if substantial transactions are kept out of the market, dealers in the derived sectors form their price decisions on inadequate information.

In July 1990 the ISE accepted a further series of reforms by the Special Committee on Market Development (the Elwes Committee). The fourfold classification of shares will be abolished and replaced by a system where market makers quote a price in a Normal Market Size (NMS) for each share. The normal size relates to a shares liquidity in relation to trading volume and should be approximate 2.5% of the average daily turnover for that particular share but there will be 12 standard sizes.

Furthermore the reporting system for larger market deals – those exceeding three times the value of NMS – will be tightened up again to 90 minutes. The obligation of market makers to quote prices to each other will also be reimposed within limits – ie to the extent of the SEAQ minimum quote size. This backtracking over the reporting and dealing rules reflects the sensitivity of the Exchange to the accusations that the market had become less transparent and while they go some way to meeting the criticism there is still a considerable delay which is well in excess of the Wall Street or NASDAQ reporting rules.

In addition market makers will be assessed periodically in terms of the amount of time their quotes are observed on the 'yellow strip' and there will be further study of the notion of a Central Limit Order Service (CLOSE).

See p47

On the positive side the new structure has produced a much more competitive environment with many of the larger deals being done on a net basis (free of commission). Table 2.2 indicates the behaviour of commissions for institutional and individual investors between 1986 and 1989.

TABLE 2.2   Commission rates in London since 'Big Bang'

		Commission rate (%)	
		Commissions included	All bargains (including deals net of commission)
1986	Individuals	0.86	0.86
	Institutions	0.39	0.39
	All investors	0.43	0.43
1987	Individuals	0.93	0.78
	Institutions	0.30	0.21
	All investors	0.45	0.30
1988	Individuals	0.84	0.64
	Institutions	0.24	0.19
	All investors	0.37	0.28
1989	Individuals	0.87	0.74
	Institutions	0.24	0.16
	All investors	0.36	0.26

The Economist (16–22 Dec. 1989), Survey of Europe's capital markets.

As well as these lower commissions for the most heavily traded Alpha stocks there has also been a narrowing of the spread between bid and offer prices. By late 1989 the average touch price (the difference between the best offer and bid price in the market) had fallen to 0.80% compared with 0.83% in September 1987 just prior to the October crash which brought about a temporary widening of the spread to 2.0% (*Financial Times*, 7 Dec. 1988, p. 29).

Undoubtedly then institutional customers have gained from the new regime thus far but the same cannot be said of the smaller private client. Table 2.2 indicates that private individuals face commissions of 0.74% of the bargain compared with 0.16% for institutions. A survey conducted by *The Observer* (5 Feb. 1989) confirmed that London based brokers had raised minimum charges considerably on small deals and private client business appeared to be growing rapidly for provincial brokers. With a few exceptions however provincial brokers appeared to be maintaining the commission scales applied to bargains prior to Big Bang.[3] The smaller investor has not gained markedly from the new regime.

This would be consistent with the experience on Wall Street after the abolition of minimum commision charges in 1975. In effect the cross subsidy which the private investor enjoyed at the expense of the institutional investor has disappeared. From the point of view of economic rationality this has much to commend it but it is not necessarily consistent with the position of the Thatcher government which expressed a desire to see growing private ownership of shares.

The Elwes Committee Report officially acknowledged that the smaller investor has 'had a raw deal out of the market since Big Bang' and addressed the problem in a number of ways. For example in a recommendation which has since been turned down by the Council of the Stock Exchange, it suggested that the dealing screen should have an additional *green* strip which would indicate the best prices offered by a market maker for small sized deals to be handled by the SEAQ Automated Execution Facility (SAEF) – the facility for small bargains. This would be the price at which brokers acting for smaller investors would have to deal. As mentioned earlier the report also recommended the setting up of an experimental Central Limit Order Service (CLOSE)[4] which will allow investors to place orders which are executed only when prices reaching prescribed levels. If this were allied to a proposed paperless settlement system it might be possible to achieve lower costs for smaller clients. Some of these changes would clearly enhance the current service and the use of a limit order system would increase the similarities between SEAQ and NASDAQ.

It is clear that the effects of increasing competition among the world stock markets and the overall fall in business since the Crash of 1987 has made the ISE think hard about the position of the small investor both to improve the service and to reduce the costs. In this respect the decision by the UK government to abolish duty payable on share transactions as from 1991 will go some way to helping achieve that aim.

Settlement and the Account System

One aspect of the London Market which differentiates it from the Japanese and American markets is the account system. Buying and selling shares in London is not undertaken for immediate cash settlement, instead settlement is carried out across a series of 'accounts'. These normally last for two weeks – opening on a Monday and closing two weeks later. Buy and sell orders can be placed at any time during the account but settlement in terms of cash or the delivery of the relevant share certificates does not take place *until some ten days after the account closes*. Thus an order to buy can be placed and almost three weeks can elapse before payment is required.

This system has advantages and disadvantages: from the point of view of a seller it means that a fairly lengthy period may elapse before the proceeds of a sale are actually realised and the loss of three or four weeks interest should be figured into the calculation. On the other hand as a buyer the payment for an order can be delayed for a period of almost three weeks so there may be interest gained on that side of the transaction.

One of the criticisms levelled at the account system in London is the opportunity it gives for speculation. Thus it is perfectly feasible to buy and sell the same stock within the account: opportunities thereby arise for taking a 'bull' or a 'bear' position in a stock in the hope that its price will move sufficiently to yield a substantial profit.

Example

An investor purchases 10 000 shares in a pharmaceutical company on the second day of the account at a price of £2.00 per share. If later that week an announcement is made that a new drug has been discovered by this company then the share price will rise to reflect the market's revaluation of the company's future profits. If the price rose to £3.50 then it would be possible for the investor to sell his 10 000 shares for £35 000 immediately and make £15 000 before expenses from the transaction. The bargain would be carried out and the investor need never have parted with any of his own money. A 'bull' therefore would place an order for a share in the hope that a price increase will allow him to sell again without taking delivery of the relevant share.

A 'bear' on the other hand will be able to make use of the account in the hope of a price fall. Here the investor *sells a share that he does not have* (this is the equivalent of a 'short sale' in the US) in the hope that its price will fall during the account. This will give him the opportunity to buy it at a lower price for delivery at the original higher price. Assume the investor had reason to believe that a report on the pharmaceutical company was going to be very unfavourable with respect to its top selling product. This will almost certainly damage its share price in the market so the strategy is as follows: sell 10 000 shares at £2.00. If the outcome is as expected and the price falls to £1.00 the investor buys the shares for delivery at this lower price and makes £10 000 less expenses.

The risks in the two positions are not of the same magnitude: in the case of the 'bull' position if the expected rise in the price does not materialise the investor can go ahead and take delivery of the shares for £20 000 or can sell them at a price close to the original purchase price and make containable losses. Indeed should the share price fall instead of rising the position will be a losing one but even if the share price fell to zero (a most unlikely event) losses will be confined to £20 000 plus expenses! The bull therefore can foresee his maximum exposure.

The bear who does not own the underlying shares would however be in a much more risky situation: if the outcome is not as expected and the price does *not* fall then to close the position, the individual has to go into the market and acquire the shares for delivery at a price which is unfavourable. For example if the adverse report on the company did not materialise or good news emerged unexpectedly then the price of the share could rise *theoretically with no upside limit*. Thus if the share price rose to £5.00 the investor would be facing a loss of £30 000 plus expenses.

The account system has been criticised as both an expensive anachronism and conducive to speculative abuse. In the past a rolling settlement system of five days as is the case in the US has been suggested as an alternative. A change of this magnitude however would, in current conditions, be virtually impossible given the back office difficulties experienced in some London houses after Big Bang and throughout 1987, when it appeared that settlement procedures were being overwhelmed by the sheer volume of business. The rise in the level of turnover was exacerbated by successive privatisation issues which brought millions of small investors into the market for the first time. As a consequence, with the existing account system, delays in settlement had reached the point where the Stock Exchange threatened to fine offending member firms. The fall in the level of business after the crash of October 1987 gave these firms a breathing space within which to clear the backlog of orders.

The experience however served to highlight certain aspects of the way in which some securities houses were managed: internal management control had been overlooked in the scramble to acquire jobbing and broking expertise and inadequate attention and training was given to the less prestigious but vital back office personnel.[5] Indeed it is not certain that the lesson has been entirely absorbed: some leading market makers having reduced their staff in the wake of the 1987 crash were taken by surprise by the upsurge of business in early 1989 and apparently again experienced settlement difficulties (*The Observer*, 5 Feb. 1989).

Part of the problem lies in the fact that the settlement system in London remains very largely paper driven – centred around the transfer of physical share certificates: the ISE has introduced a number of electronic services to facilitate more efficient trading which it is hoped will minimise the movement of paper but these have not yet penetrated the market on any great scale. Thus Institutional Net Settlement (INS) was introduced in Summer 1988 which allowed institutional investors to settle all of their day's transactions on a net basis by the transfer of a single amount.

In 1989 the so-called SAEF system (SEAQ Automated Execution Facility), an all electronic settlement procedure, went live but this system largely serves small orders in relatively active lines of shares. In this case when the dealer or the broker sees an acceptable buy or sell price on his screen he enters the order via a SAEF terminal and execution will take place at the best available price then displayed. The other aspects of the system then go into operation automatically – both parties are informed and the transaction confirmed, the records section is also informed and settlement takes place as a matched bargain.

While this SAEF mechanism only deals with smaller bargains it is quite feasible to see it or some such variant replacing the present paper driven system. This would speed up and reduce the costs of transactions considerably. If the system were sufficiently enlarged it would become simpler to eliminate the account system.

We should not be too optimistic about the fortunes of such systems however. The Stock Exchange has been discussing a fully computerised settlement procedure since 1982 – this is the so-called TAURUS (Transfer and Automated Registration of Uncertified Stock) system which has been discussed and postponed on several occasions. Two sets of objections inhibited the introduction of this arrangement. One was the issue of cost: it was estimated in 1989 that some £60m would be required to install the hardware alone and at a time when market makers were losing money this hardly seemed a welcome development. The other issue was perhaps more significant: there was a degree of vested interest involved in the paper driven system. Banks acting on behalf of some of the major institutional investors such as pension funds and insurance companies make profits in the process of handling settlement and these profitable activities would be compromised if the system were to move into an all electronic mode.

By 1990 however the ISE felt sufficiently confident to announce a specific timetable for the TAURUS system (*The Financial Times*, 10 Mar.). Thus the intention is to eliminate share certificates and achieve 100% 'dematerialisation' by 1993. There is also a decision to replace the current two week account system with a five day rolling settlement system as from October 1992. The resulting smoother flow of work should iron out the tendency for bunching of orders and the accumulation of backlogs which occurs in periods when turnover tends to peak. The development costs of the system up till 1993 are estimated to be approximately £50m and the annual operating costs to be in the region of £30/£35m. The net present value of the cost saving is put at somewhere between £225–255m over a period of ten years.

Whether the project eventually provides the level of savings looked for and the timetable proves realistic in view of previous experience, the long delayed move to a paperless system became more urgent in the late 1980s.

Competitive Pressures

London's position as the dominant stock market in the European time zone is not unassailable despite its having led the way in deregulation. A number of developments suggest that there will be sustained pressure from a variety of sources.

(i) Competition from other exchanges

Since 1988 NASDAQ has enjoyed Recognised Investment Exchange status in the UK. While on the whole NASDAQ has confined itself to trading UK equities in the form of American Depository Receipts it may in due course start trading UK equities and international equities currently traded on the ISE's SEAQ International.

Some continental exchanges also pose distinct threats to London. For example Paris has been deregulating faster than any other major exchange and, thanks to a combination of tax incentives and privatisations, the equity market has grown rapidly to be almost as large as the traditionally dominant bond market. Turnover has also been rising quickly and there has been a relaxation of listing requirements to improve access to the market by small and medium sized companies. In addition the French authorities opened the ownership of brokers (*agents de change*) to banks and foreign houses. Hours of trading were extended from 10.00 am to 5.00 pm and finally in July 1989 fixed commissions were abolished. As Paris had no tradition of independent market makers like London and New York the Bourse opted for a technology which involves the use of automated matching orders in a central market. Shares in Paris can be bought for cash ('*au comptant*') in the case of less actively traded issues or for monthly settlement ('*règlement mensual*' – RM) for the most active. Finally Paris offers a financial futures exchange – MATIF (the Marché à Terme International de France) which began trading in 1986 but by 1990 was trading a larger volume of contracts than the longer established London International Financial Futures Exchange (LIFFE).

The Federation of German Stock Exchanges (which comprises eight seperate exchanges dominated by Frankfurt) has been following the almost universal trend to simpler listing procedures, the setting up of a futures markets (the DTB) and the more extensive use of new technology. In the latter context the price information system (KISS) and the order matching system (BOSS) give markets both greater transparency and more rapid execution. In addition settlement in Germany is highly efficient taking place within two days. Turnover in both domestic equities and foreign issues has been rising much more rapidly than in London and was indeed greater in the first half of 1990. The obvious strength of the German economy endows Frankfurt with a more powerful domestic base and recently, as the shadow of the European Single Market in 1992 looms large, the authorities appear to have become more amenable to altering tax and regulatory regimes which have held back the growth of Germany's stock markets.

(ii) Fragmentation of the central market

A second source of competition which has to be considered is the effect of direct trading between institutional investors which by-passes the main market (Gordon, 1987). Instinet (Institutional Networks Corporation) has offered a service in the USA for some years which allows large investors to make bids and offers directly with each other and matches them accordingly. While not particularly significant at this stage there is no doubt that improved technology may enhance these facilities to the point where they might result in some loss of turnover.

Despite the ISE's dominant position *vis-à-vis* other stock exchanges in Europe the cumbersome and costly nature of transactions in London is clearly disadvantageous compared with other European bourses which have already begun the move toward nonpaper settlement arrangements. With the approach of 1992 the growth of potential competition has proved the spur which finally may have moved London toward a more efficient system.

5   THE USA

The United States has the widest range of financial services and markets available to savers and borrowers of any of the developed economies. This reflects the size of its domestic economy, its significance in the World Economy and its political commitment to Capitalism. New York remains the financial capital of the US with both the New York Stock Exchange (NYSE) and the smaller American Stock Exchange (AMEX). There are other exchanges: the Midwest Stock Exchange in Chicago; the Pacific Stock Exchange in Los Angeles; and smaller exchanges in Boston, Philadelphia and Cincinnati. In addition there is the nationwide all electronic Over the Counter market provided by NASDAQ.

The regional exchanges are overshadowed in terms of the volume of business and total capitalisation by the NYSE and NASDAQ. Indeed at one time it seemed as though companies sought a listing on the smaller exchanges simply as a staging post on their way to Wall Street. While the latter still carries enormous prestige there have been attempts in recent years to win business away from New York and NASDAQ in particular has been relatively successful in this respect. Despite minor differences in their regulations and operating practices the other exchanges are essentially similar to the so-called 'Big Board' in New York, hence practices in the NYSE can serve as a model to understand the operation of other floor exchanges in the United States.

The New York Stock Exchange

The NYSE is probably the most well known and for a long time was the largest exchange in the world measured in terms of market capitalisation. There are over 1600 listings with more than 2300 common and preferred stocks.[6] In dollar terms nearly 80% of US securities business is conducted there.

To obtain a listing on the NYSE requires the company concerned to meet a number of conditions which relate to matters such as minimum net assets, earnings, capitalisation and the number of shares publicly held.

Overseas companies are able to obtain a listing and more are in fact seeking one. For example large European firms such as British Telecom, Unilever and ICI as well as Japanese companies such as Sony and Matsushita Electric (Panasonic) are listed. In all there were 77 such listings in 1988 but this figure is fairly small compared with other markets. In part this reflects the more stringent and costly requirements which the NYSE imposes in terms of size, frequency of reporting and the quality of accounting information (Tondkar *et al.*, 1989). The basic requirement for foreign organisations is that a member firm on the Exchange should attest that there is a liquid market in the relevant shares but there are in addition a number of significant quantitative criteria. Having met the conditions and paid the initial fee as well as sundry other charges to obtain a listing, the company takes on obligations such as the production of certified quarterly financial reports, an agreement not to issue further shares without the permission of the exchange, the maintenance of a transfer agent to deal with shareholder records etc. The firm must also continue to meet other minimum market criteria to retain the listing: some of these criteria are more generous than the above but failure to meet them can result in a *delisting*.

The Dealing Mechanism

The NYSE operates an auction system in which brokers trade with each other on an open outcry basis hence it is essentially an order driven system. In addition however there are certain specialists who act to smooth the market in various ways principally by dealing for their own account. This competitive auction approach explains why dealing remains a central market floor-based process in New York and other US exchanges compared to London.

Deals are normally done in round lots of 100 shares (except for very inactive shares when lot size may be ten shares). Given that the price of shares in the USA is typically 'heavy' by British standards eg in 1989, on the NYSE, the average share price was $32, the price of a round lot was $3200. Institutional sized transactions usually take place in blocks of 10 000 shares. Trades can also take place in *odd-lots* – anything from 1 to 99 shares but such deals usually attract higher charges.

The market procedure works as follows: a broker executing a client's buy order approaches a particular location – a post – on the floor of the exchange where the relevant stock is traded. Some fifteen such posts exist and each is allocated about 100 stocks. An indicator board shows the shares traded in each section of the post and a price display indicates the last price at which a transaction occurred. It also shows whether or not this current price was greater or less than the previous price ie whether there was an 'up tick' or a 'down tick'. If the broker observes that the last trade took place at $21 per share it may nevertheless be possible that another broker is willing to sell at a lower price. The broker can ascertain the current bid/ask spread from the specialist who has a permanent location at the post or if there are other brokers present he can enquire of them without indicating whether he is acting as buyer or seller. This enquiry may elicit a response such as '$20\,^1/_2 - 21$' from another broker which means that $\$20\,^1/_2$ is the best bid, the most anyone will be prepared to pay for the stock, and $21 the best offer price, the lowest anyone will sell for.

   The buying broker can wait for other possible offers and if this fails to elicit better responses he may then bid eg '$20\,^3/_4$ for three hundred'. In other words he will buy 300 shares for $20.75 per share. In the event that this finds no takers he may raise the bid by a further $^1/_8$ of a point.[7] The new bid is now 'Seven eighths for three hundred' and this may be sufficient to persuade one of the other brokers to accept the bid by declaring 'Sold'. If on the other hand a broker decides at the outset to accept an offered price he will simply say 'Take it'. Each party to the transaction makes a note of the deal and settlement takes place later.

   In these days of screen based trading technology this procedure seems highly anachronistic but the open outcry system is defended by the NYSE as a way of preventing secret deals from taking place on the floor of the Exchange. (On the other hand sceptics have seen it as a way of preserving vested interests.) In addition brokers are forbidden from directly matching orders between their own customers: buy and sell orders for the same line of stock cannot be simply 'crossed' (or 'put through' to use British termino-logy). Both orders must be sent to the floor to face appropriate bids and offers and in this way each customer should get best execution. This sort of off-market cross is allowed in the case of block trades, where a considerable parcel of shares (10 000 or more) is to be bought and sold through a single broker. Even then however both buyer and seller must be apprised of the cross and permission must be sought from the Exchange.

   Thus far what has been described is the procedure involved in handling a 'market order' one which is to be executed as soon as possible when it reaches the market floor at the best price available. However the individual may want to buy or sell shares but *only if it can be done at a certain price or better*: it is possible that the broker may have been given a 'limit order' by his client, an order which will be good for a day, a week or simply good till cancelled. Thus the client's instructions may be to buy at $\$20\,^3/_4$ *or cheaper*. In this case the broker would not be able to raise the bid as described above but instead would leave his limit order with the market specialist until such time that it can be filled at that price. Limit orders work when selling shares too –

for example the broker may be asked to sell at $25 or better and again if he is unable to obtain this price the order is left with the floor specialist who for a commission known as floor brokerage would process the order later.

Indeed the specialist system emerged precisely because in a continuous auction market where brokers trade with each other there is no guarantee of a simultaneous coincidence of buyer and seller. The broker of course could always wait at the post until such time as a buyer or seller arrived. However it would save time which could be gainfully employed elsewhere, to leave the order on a limit basis with another broker. Over a fairly lengthy period brokers emerged who specialised in handling these limit orders and remained permanently at a specific post. If a specialist executes an order for another broker he is himself operating as a broker and will be paid a negotiated floor commission. In effect the specialist is paid for saving the time of the other brokers who can thereby move on to other posts. However there is nothing to prevent the function being carried out by a centralised limit order system held on a computer. This is indeed the way other markets eg Tokyo and Paris appear to be going.

The role of the specialist has evolved considerably and gradually so that some specialists started to act as principals buying and selling for their own account. They would buy or sell close to the previous price which had the effect of giving other brokers good and speedy execution and at the same time attracted future brokerage income. The role of the specialist became more and more significant and in 1934 the US Congress passed The Securities and Exchange Act which explicitly laid a duty on specialists to 'maintain a fair and orderly market' in the shares in which they specialise (Seligman, 1982). This role has been emphasised in subsequent legislation and in the adoption of a specific rule by the New York Stock Exchange (Rule 103) which threatens to suspend or cancel the registration of any specialist should the Exchange find

> any substantial or continued failure by a specialist to engage in a course of dealings for his own account to assist in the maintenance, so far as practicable, of a fair and orderly market.

In effect specialists have to act so as to maintain continuity of prices and stable markets which means avoiding any violent fluctuations in the price of any stock they handle. This is done usually by keeping the bid/ask spread in the region of half a point and it has been estimated that some nine-tenths of deals take place within a quarter of a point of the previous sale although higher spreads may occur for highly priced or thinly traded shares. Stable markets are usually attained by the specialist agreeing to lean against the wind by absorbing selling pressure onto his book or meeting buying orders from his book – even to the extent of 'going short' ie selling stock he does not have in the hope of buying it in later from another broker. The role of the specialist enhances liquidity in the exchange because he functions as a market maker for a broker in the absence of any other brokers. However the position is a difficult one given the obligations imposed by the Securities and Exchange Commission and the Exchange itself. In very active stocks there is no real problem as there are always many market participants but in thinly traded securities there is the obvious risk that capital will stagnate for considerable periods of time before a new buyer appears.

While operating as a market maker the specialist is acting in a similar manner to the old London jobber, however the role is somewhat broader and therefore more problematical. When the New York specialist deals for his own account he can only do so consistent with maintaining a stable market and price continuity. Thus if the specialist has a client's order to buy a particular share at $30 he is required to execute that first – NYSE rules impose an obligation on the specialist not take the stock onto his own book until *all* customer orders at that price are completed. On the other hand execution of another broker's limit order generates fee income.

It was estimated in 1988–9 that about 10% of exchange turnover was handled by specialists compared with nearly 13% in 1975 just prior to the abolition of fixed commissions. While at one time dealing for their own account made up about 50% of the broker's income (the rest coming from brokerage fees), it is argued that the larger proportion now comes from trading profits as opposed to acting as agents for other brokers. Clearly however the former is a riskier source of income than the latter and is likely to result in wider spreads.

By contrast, the duty to maintain orderly and continuous markets has never applied in the London Stock Exchange as the single capacity system meant that jobbers simply were acting on their own behalf and never as an agent for another party. Hence income derived either from the spread between bid and offer prices or by assuming a position in a particular share. As a result larger price discontinuities were commonplace in London.

The role of the specialist remains crucial to the operation of the NYSE: because he is frequently left to execute the various limit orders of brokers who have moved on to other posts he has an insight into the balance between supply and demand that the others lack. In other words he knows more than any other broker about the current market conditions for the stocks in which he deals. This knowledge allied to his duty to trade so as to maintain orderly markets puts him in a powerful position to influence the trend of prices. This is a factor which has exercised the Securities and Exchange Commission (SEC) greatly in the past and to prevent the abuse of this privileged position close surveillance of specialists' activities is maintained by the NYSE. Monitoring takes place on about eight occasions each year when details of all dealings over various one week periods are examined. This allows the Exchange to scrutinize the orderliness of the market, the degree of price continuity and the bid/ask spread in order to assess how successfully the specialist's function is being performed. In addition there is a weekly report made to the Exchange on trades specialists make for their own account. Finally there is computer surveillance of price behaviour. The computer is programmed to flag unusual price changes and allows the exchange to retrieve data and analyze it for suspicious movements.

Clearly however the obligation to maintain fair and orderly markets cannot always be fulfilled in the face of overwhelming market pressures such as hit the market in October 1987 as there is a limit to the capital which specialists can deploy.[8] Trading halts may well have to be resorted to in order to allow the market to stabilize and this of course undermines the continuity of prices – one of the key functions supposedly carried out by the specialist. Indeed it is the limit to the amount of committed capital which presents a major problem for the Exchange's specialists. As one might expect, given the larger overall size of the market and the price-heavy nature of shares on the NYSE the average capitalisation of New York's specialists was considerably greater than the equivalent London jobber prior to liberalization of the London market – a ratio of approximately eight to one (Thomas, 1986) – nevertheless in very uncertain and volatile markets turnover can be so large in the NYSE so to threaten the solvency of even the best capitalised specialists. This was amply demonstrated in October 1987 when trading halts were imposed: indeed the Brady Report (1988) commissioned in the wake of the crash was highly critical of some market makers whose performance was described as 'poor by any standard'.

There have been a number of longer term changes in market practice and technology which have been threatening the position of the specialist. The increase in block trading – transactions of 10 000 or more shares – which has been associated with the growth of institutional investors has taken business away from the specialist. The SEC's Institutional Investor Study (1971) showed that generally with an increase in the size of block trades specialists were used less and less, instead the institutions completed their block trading by making use of NYSE members who executed such orders off the Exchange floor in their 'upstairs' offices. Once all the details of the trade were in place they would then merely 'cross' such deals on the floor of the Exchange in order to conform to the letter of the rules. Block trades accounted for just over 2% of total NYSE volume in 1964, had grown to nearly 15% by 1970, and to 29.2% in 1980 (Seligman, 1982): by the late 1980s they comprised more than 40%.

In addition a great deal of block trading takes place off the Exchange altogether: the Instinet system for example has taken business away from the specialist.[9] Similarly the effect of computer trading for smaller lots removes turnover and therefore squeezes the specialist from the other direction. Furthermore the continuing growth of NASDAQ with its high tech, competing market maker approach also represents a threat to the traditional structures maintained by floor exchanges such as the NYSE and AMEX.

In the late 1980s there were about 500 firms which were members of the NYSE but the number of these acting in a specialist capacity has been in steady decline: from 67 in the mid 1970s the numbers have fallen to 49 by 1989.

Recent trends in the revenues and profitability of specialists point to the continued decline in their role (see Table 2.3).

TABLE 2.3   **Comparative income statements – NYSE specialists, 1st quarter 1987–9 ($m)**

	1987	1988	1989
Revenue	193	167	109
Expenses	70	75	73
Pre-tax Income	123	93	36
Tax provision	59	38	15
Net Profit	64	55	21

The Banker, Feb. 1990.

It is too early to write off the specialists as key players in the American system if only because they remain an important vested interest in the organisation of most exchanges. However it does seem to be the case that changes in technology, increasing competition and the more recent decline in the general level of trading represent threats which might have terminal consequences.

The American Stock Exchange (AMEX)

The American Stock Exchange is the second largest floor exchange in the United States, yet despite this it is very much smaller than its neighbour the NYSE. With something in the order of 950 ordinary and preferred issues traded, AMEX generates about 7 to 8% of the dollar volume compared with the Big Board or about 4% of the *total* volume of US securities markets (compared to a little over 8% some ten years ago).

Included in the 661 full members of the Exchange are all the major US brokerage businesses such as Merrill Lynch, Prudential Baache etc. There is also a category of associate member who is allowed to place orders via regular members. These associate memberships are often taken up by small or medium sized NYSE firms who need access to AMEX but do not have sufficient turnover to merit a full member's status.

Listing requirements in terms of net worth, income, market capitalisation and so on are less stringent than the NYSE but tougher than is the case for NASDAQ. As a consequence AMEX tends to be perceived as the junior exchange from which firms will graduate to the 'Big Board'. The fact that General Motors and Standard Oil were first listed there and some very considerable companies remain has done little to change this perception. Until the early 1950s it had been called the New York Curb Exchange as it had started as an outside market before it moved indoors in the early 1920s (Sobel, 1972).

The two exchanges work in a similar fashion with open outcry and specialist dealers playing a key role. Orders are handled in a similar manner as on the NYSE but the average size of transaction tends to be considerably smaller because prices on AMEX are generally lower eg the average share price in 1989 was $20. In some respects it can be argued that AMEX has been more innovative than the NYSE by installing computers at an earlier stage to handle and monitor trading and dealing activity. The more cynical observer however might question how far these moves reflected concern for modernisation and how far they reflected pressures brought on AMEX as a result of a number of major share scandals which occurred in the 1970s.

Given the similarities between the exchanges it is no surprise that from time to time there have been discussions about merging into one single market. The Exchanges do indeed cooperate in a number of ways – for example along with NASD – they united their individual clearing houses to set up the National Securities Clearing Corporation. This credits and debits the accounts of members for buy and sell transactions in a single consolidated bookkeeping process. AMEX and the NYSE also jointly operate their own subsidiary the Security Industries Automation Corporation (SIAC) originally formed to develop joint automation programmes and consolidate their technical facilities. This is also the vehicle through which they provide market data to the various commercial information suppliers. The idea of a full scale merger however was decisively rejected by AMEX in the 1970s but of course it is always possible that the matter will be re-introduced at some future date. This will obviously become more likely if AMEX continues to decline in the face of competition from NASDAQ and the NYSE: in addition to the contraction in market share mentioned above the number of company listings had been falling but by the late 1980s there had been something of a recovery (see Table 2.4).

TABLE 2.4 Number of companies listed on AMEX, 1980–8

1980	892
1982	834
1984	792
1986	796
1988	896

NASDAQ *Fact Book*, 1989.

Clearly the Exchange has suffered from the rapid advance in the visibility of the Over the Counter market and the relatively easier listing requirements demanded by NASDAQ. Thus far AMEX has refrained from diluting its own listing criteria but instead has attempted to cope with the situation by introducing new products such as traded options which have proved highly successful – particularly the index option based on the Major Market Index. Indeed in 1988–9 AMEX's various option contracts placed the exchange in second place behind the Chicago Board Options Exchange in terms of total US options trading. Success in this and a number of other areas however only serves to underline the relatively weak position in conventional equities trading and a prolonged period of stagnating volumes will increase the possibility of merger.

The Securities and Exchange Commission has long taken an even more radical view having several times discussed the notion of a *single* integrated national securities market for the US comprising not merely the major floor exchanges but NASDAQ as well (Seligman, 1982). While the technology is sufficiently sophisticated the remaining obstacles may prove to be rather more problematical as the various floor exchanges are clearly reluctant to face further increases in competition and there are clear vested interests in retaining the status quo.

National Association of Securities Dealers' Automated Quotations System (NASDAQ)

NASDAQ is a system run by the National Association of Securities Dealers which was largely responsible for the development of the Over the Counter Market in the US. With 4179 domestic and 272 foreign companies listed on NASDAQ at the beginning of 1989, the OTC market in America is a much bigger more sophisticated and better regulated operation than in the UK. Its very size and diversity makes it difficult to summarize easily as both the participants that figure in the market and the securities that are available are so heterogeneous.

The OTC market emerged originally as a way of buying and selling the shares of companies that were unlisted and therefore did not have a quotation on one of the main exchanges. However the dealers do not only handle this sort of transaction: as well as unlisted shares it is possible to buy the shares of many companies with a conventional exchange listing, Treasury bonds and some foreign securities in the form of American Depositary Receipts.[10] The trading of exchange listed shares was something of a bone of contention with the NYSE for many years. For members of the New York Exchange, the emergence and growth of this so-called 'Third Market' represented a threat and various unsuccessful attempts were made to get Congress and the SEC to prevent trading in NYSE listed issues.

NASD is a very extensive organisation comprising 6432 member operating over 22 000 branches. These member firms are extraordinarily varied: some may be one or two person operations located in the mid-West dealing in specific financial products such as mutual funds or specially tailored investment packages, others are well known securities houses with a presence on Wall Street and London (for example Shearson Lehman Brothers and Merrill Lynch). The latter use the facilities of the OTC market to trade large blocks of shares. Some firms charge a negotiated commission for their services and others levy a flat fee. Most member firms are brokers but there are over 500 active market makers in the system and the average number of market makers per security is 9.4 (NASD Annual Report, 1988).

NASDAQ has grown to become the second largest of US stock markets and in terms of the value of domestic equity is nearly five times larger than AMEX. It has never had a trading floor and prior to the development of the electronic network which links dealers the OTC market was extremely fragmented. Customers in different parts of the US could not be sure that they were getting the best price when selling or buying since dealers were physically separated and not in immediate contact with each other. As a result the same securities could well be trading at very different prices in different places. In addition trading was less transparent because transactions could be accomplished via negotiated prices rather than the auction procedure followed on the floor exchanges. In the latter case the specialist maintains a continuous market so that there was and is always a bid and ask price available.

While it was possible for a dealer to be in touch with some of the larger operators by telephone, clearly there was no way of being informed of what may have been happening in perhaps dozens of other locations. A partial way around this problem existed via a privately operated price information service – the National Quotations Bureau. This publishes via its *pink sheets* the wholesale prices of something in the order of 10 000 shares with almost half as many bonds. These sheets are printed overnight and distributed across the USA before the opening of AMEX and the New York Exchange.

The use of these pink sheets was of great concern to the SEC in the early 1960s as there was some feeling that dealers could publish prices and then later back away from them when enquiries came in. For example a bid price may be reported in a particular line of stock but when the seller offered the shares the dealer could refuse to buy or change price downward arguing that the market situation had changed since the day before. To overcome this problem a rule was imposed whereby if the dealer reports the same prices two days running then they become firm prices and he has to deal at them or risk official complaint and censure from the SEC.

Despite these measures the highly fragmented OTC market remained of some concern to the regulatory authorities for some time and improvements in computer technology and telecommunications were seen as the key to overcoming this fragmentation. Eventually in 1971 the NASDAQ structure was implemented. Dealers are now linked nationwide by an electronic screen-based system and price information is relayed instantaneously to offices throughout the United States. At any time during the trading day dealers can feed into the system bid and ask prices and they can also alter them according to what their competitors are doing.

The system provides different three levels of service to brokers and other market professionals:

> *Level 1* gives the inside quotations (the best bid and offer prices) for all NASDAQ securities, last sale information on those securities which qualify for NASDAQ's National Market System (NMS) as well as a variety of market summary data.
> Level 2 provides a service to trading rooms and in addition to Level 1 gives all the quotations by all market makers for every NASDAQ security.
> *Level 3* is the service used by market makers enabling them to enter prices and last sale information into the system.

Thus, should the prices quoted at Level 1 prove interesting for the customer the salesman, having ascertained the best quotes, simply contacts the market maker by phone and the deal is completed in the normal way. In the case of small lots it is even simpler as the Small Order Execution Service can handle the deal electronically. Clearing is handled by the National Clearing Corporation which is a subsidiary of the NASD. Of course these are wholesale price quotes and will not be the same for the customer but the NASD has on the whole taken the view that a markup (or a markdown when the customer is selling) of no more than 5% should be charged unless a security involves unusual effort and risk. The size of the markup has been an issue of some contention with the SEC and consequently in many cases dealers will disclose the size of the markup they have charged.

The NASD monitors the bid and ask prices on shares quoted on NASDAQ and the system checks newly entered price data against the *representative spread* ie the average spread for market makers in that share. A market maker is not allowed to put quotations in the system which exceed certain maximum allowable spreads approved by NASD Board of Governors (see Table 2.5).

If a dealer enters prices where the bid/ask spread is considerably larger than the average this will be pointed out to the dealer and unless it is corrected he may be subject to disciplinary action.

In addition NASD monitors member firms via regular inspections and maintains a watch over advertising practices. Finally the SEC itself also polices the OTC market by scrutinising price behaviour in order to pick up

TABLE 2.5   Size of bid/ask spreads, NASDAQ Quotes

Average Spread $	Maximum Allowable Spread $
$^1/_8$ or less	$^1/_4$
$^1/_4$	$^1/_2$
$^3/_8$	$^3/_4$
$^1/_2$	1
$^5/_8$	1
$^3/_4$	$1^1/_2$
$^7/_8$	$1^1/_2$
	etc.

NASD, *Reference Guide for NASDAQ Companies*, 1988.

suspicious movements. The degree of monitoring of the market plus the fact that dealers are wired into a nationwide network where price information is clear and instantaneous has transformed the OTC market and led to much greater confidence in it by American investors.

Originally NASDAQ started by indicating price quotes for about 2500 OTC shares and that number has increased gradually. Not only is the OTC market in the US larger and more sophisticated than its UK counterpart it is also better regulated (via the SEC), more transparent and, significantly, it is much more liquid. This is helped by several factors: there must always be two dealers who make a market in any given share; market makers are committed to buying and selling continuously and they must display firm bid and ask prices via NASDAQ. Companies quoted on NASDAQ also have to meet the usual sorts of quantitative criteria although they are less imposing than those of AMEX and the NYSE.

For a long time it has been possible to trade on NASDAQ the shares of companies listed in foreign markets in the form of American Depositary Receipts. These certificates, rather than the underlying securities, were traded actively on the OTC market and they were at one time rarely listed on the main exchanges. Over the last decade however they have become more common on the NYSE and are sometimes used by foreign companies as a substitute for obtaining a full listing on the exchange.

The OTC market is also very important in relation to US government securities, municipal bonds and corporate bonds. Over 90% of T-bonds, all municipal bonds and the great proportion of corporate bonds are bought and sold in this market rather than the exchanges.

In April 1982 the National Association of Securities Dealers introduced an improvement on the NASDAQ system termed the National Market System

(NMS).[11] Initially this covered only 40 issues but since then NASDAQ/NMS has grown to over 2500 companies. The system has been continuously upgraded since its inception and provides a number of important features. Thus the NMS imposes more rapid reporting requirements – price and volume data must be reported within 90 seconds of each transaction; in addition there must be at least four market makers as opposed to two for ordinary NASDAQ shares. There is also a Small Order Execution Service (SOES in operation since 1984) which enables brokers to trade NMS issues in sizes up to 1000 shares via computer as opposed to telephone as is the case with other types of NASDAQ deals. These SOES orders are therefore routed automatically to the market maker offering the best price.

At the same time tighter listing criteria were imposed for NMS shares. Consequently approximately a third of these companies are now able to meet the listing requirements of the New York Stock Exchange but have chosen not to transfer. Certainly there is a prevalent belief (which would be disputed by the NYSE) that NASDAQ's system of competing market makers provides deeper liquidity than is true of the floor exchanges particularly for smaller companies. NASDAQ also argues that the system offers a more continuous market because the specialist system may be subject to periodic trading halts as the specialist attempts to balance his books. On the other hand the experience in London during the Crash of October 1987 seemed to suggest that market makers could impose their own trading halts by simply ensuring that the phone is continuously 'busy'.

In many ways the NASD has been at the frontier of implementing new trading technologies and its success will continue to be influential in shaping markets in the future. It was NASDAQ's competitive market maker approach which London opted for in the post Big Bang era as London's jobbing system had been closer in spirit to the notion of competing market makers than to the NYSE's specialist system.

The degree of compatibility of the systems makes it feasible that at some future date a complete link between NASDAQ and London's SEAQ may be achieved (already links between NASDAQ and SEAQ have been set up and quotations and transactions on some 700 securities are in place). However recent pressures on the profitability of London market makers has moved SEAQ trading rules away from those of NASDAQ and this will clearly hinder any continued move toward integration of the systems.

Settlement

In the US there is no account system of the type employed in London instead settlement takes place on a rolling five day basis. Whereas in London buying and selling can occur within the account this is not possible in the US and therefore different procedures apply where customers wish to sell shares they do not currently own – 'short sales'. These are usually undertaken by borrowing the necessary shares for delivery (in the US all investors who maintain a 'margin' account with a broker sign an agreement giving authority to lend their stocks to others).

American markets allow shares to be bought on 'margin' ie only a proportion of the value of the purchase needs to be deposited with the broker. This proportion may be varied by the authorities, the Federal Reserve Board, depending upon the level of activity in the markets being raised or lowered accordingly. Since the 1930s it has varied from a low of 40% to as much as 100%.

6 JAPAN

There are eight stock exchanges in Japan. Only three of these exchanges are of any size – Tokyo, Osaka and Nagoya – which are responsible for 99% of all stock exchange activity. The Tokyo Exchange is the largest. In 1990 some 1730 companies (1610 domestic and 120 foreign) were listed and market capitalisation was some $3229 billion making Tokyo on this measure the largest of the world's exchanges.

An Over the Counter market is also operated by the Japanese Security Dealers Association (JSDA) and a number of commercial banks which are licensed to deal in government bonds. Over 90% of bond dealings take place via this OTC market but the volume of equity transactions is less than 7% of the equity business done on the exchanges. The JSDA has indicated an intention to follow the NASDAQ example and to move to a screen based system for the OTC market.

Japanese stock exchanges are organised on a membership basis and access to membership is achieved via the purchase of a seat. While Osaka appears to have been fairly liberal in creating new seats (in the late 1980s the number was increased from 58 to 82) the same could not be said of the Tokyo Stock Exchange (TSE) where only two seats were added beween 1949 and 1987. The alternative route is to buy into an existing member firm.

Nevertheless the Japanese stock exchanges are following the patterns observed in other countries in allowing access to *overseas* organisations. In 1987 there were just over 90 members of the Tokyo exchange and of these only six were foreign but by 1988 the numbers of seats had increased to 114 and a further sixteen foreign firms had been invited to become members bringing the total representation up to 22. There is clearly a degree of reciprocity involved here as since the mid 1980s Japanese houses have been establishing a major presence in London and New York. It remains to be seen how effectively these incomers will be able to compete as it has been estimated that the big four securities houses – Nomura, Daiwa, Nikko and

Yaimichi – together handle nearly 50% of all Japanese securities business. Another measure of the degree to which the Japanese markets are becoming more open is in the number of foreign listings which increased gradually throughout the 1980s. Nor is it only in the stock exchanges where a foreign presence is beginning to be felt: more than 30 foreign fund management firms have applied and been granted a licence to compete for management of pension funds, insurance and trust fund business.

The practice of the three major exchanges is to allocate *domestic* securities to one of two categories using criteria related to the volume of activity, the number of shareholders and the pattern of past dividends. Generally speaking the securities of major companies are found in the First Section. As of 1989 there were more than 1100 in this category accounting for almost 95% of the market's capitalisation. There are therefore over 400 securities in the Second Section mostly smaller companies and new listings. Foreign securities are placed in a third separate classification.

Membership of the Japanese Stock Exchanges is classified into three types: regular members, 'saitori' members and special members. Regular members trade securities on the exchanges either for their own clients or for their own account. Saitori members on the other hand are similar to New York's $2 brokers in the sense that they act as intermediaries between regular members and are not allowed to trade for their own account. The special members handle transactions on the Tokyo or Osaka Exchanges that cannot be dealt with on the other regional exchanges.

The Dealing Mechanism

Japanese exchanges are essentially auction markets: trading and the structure of the markets appear to be closer to the Wall Street model than that of London. Dealing on the three major exchanges takes place at trading posts to which securities are allocated depending upon the industry group of the listed company – electronics, chemicals and so on. Smaller Second Section shares are also assigned a specific floor location.

The process of trading is by auction carried out by specialist – 'saitori' or 'nakadachi' members who attempt to match offers and bids (Tagaki, 1989). Unlike NYSE specialists however the 'saitori' do not maintain their own position in any share. Instead they execute orders according to specific auction rules: bids and offers are dealt with according to priority of price and timing. The rules are marginally different however depending upon whether orders arrive during the trading day (9am to 11.00am and 1.00pm to 3.00pm) or prior to the opening of the market.

(i) In order to establish opening prices, orders which arrive before the opening of the exchange are treated as though they have arrived simultaneously. Each buy and sell order is compared until quantity and price are matched. This is the so-called 'itayose' method and in effect is a 'call auction' which attempts to set the price which will clear the market.

(ii) If orders arrive during the trading day they are dealt with by a *continuous* auction termed the 'zaraba' method whereby:

o The sell order with the lowest price and the buy order with the highest price take precedence – this is termed price priority;
o If two or more orders arrive at the same price then the earlier order is dealt with first – this is time priority.

The 'saitori' members are crucial to the transparency of the pricing process as all member firms are required to deal through them so that all orders are exposed to the market. Only the 250 most heavily traded issues are dealt with directly on the exchange floor of the Tokyo Stock Exchange, the others are traded electronically. Like Paris, Tokyo has chosen the Computer Assisted Trading System (CATS) developed by the Toronto Stock Exchange. Details are entered on the computer and buy and sell orders are matched on the screen. Completion of trades is then relayed via the screen to the member placing the order. Hence this approach does not affect the central market auction but instead copes primarily with the clerical/administrative support functions. Trading in all second category shares is conducted electronically and does not directly involve the saitori system.

Shares in the UK and the US have various par values but in Japan nearly all shares have a par value of 50 Yen. Orders are in round lots of 1000 shares for domestic issues while the lot size for foreign shares may vary depending upon their market price – sizes here may be 10, 50, 100 or 1000. Exceptions are also made for very price-heavy domestic shares, thus the lot size for Nippon Telephone and Telegraph is *one* share as when NTT was listed a single share was priced at 1.19m Yen and very quickly reached 3.18m Yen!

Market data are published in a various of ways. For example last trade prices are immediately relayed to securities firms and in addition the Japanese Securities Dealers Association publishes bid and offer prices of selected heavily traded shares on a daily basis. In addition Tokyo's Market Information Service monitors and provides information on price and volume of every security to the floor of the exchange and to security firms' offices.

Finally and interestingly in the light of discussions about market stability in the wake of the 1987 Crash there remain a series of price stabilisation rules which have attracted the attention of other exchanges. These rules impose a maximum daily price change of 2000 Yen for shares with a closing price on the previous day of 10 000 Yen or more. For shares which close below this figure there are lower allowable maximum price movements. How far these rules contributed to the relative stability of Tokyo is difficult to say as there are two other material factors which should be taken into account:

o The Japanese authorities seem more willing to intervene with 'advice' to
   the larger shareholders than is the case in other exchanges. The larger
   securities houses seem in addition more willing to accept that advice.
o In Japan there are very considerable *intercorporate* shareholdings so that
   on average less than 30% of equity is available to the public (Sakakibara
   et al., 1988). Hence it is possible that the same selling pressures were
   unlikely to develop.

Unlike other major world exchanges Tokyo still retains fixed brokerage
commission rates. While not as expensive as the old rates imposed in London
before Big Bang in 1986 it would come as no surprise to see Tokyo follow the
practice of London and Wall Street and abolish fixed commissions. On
ordinary shares the rates vary from 1.2% on deals up to 1 million Yen to
0.15% on deals over one billion Yen (Matsumoto, 1989). Commission rates
are lower for bonds ranging from 0.8% to 0.05% on straight bonds and 1%
to 0.15% on convertibles. In addition the government imposes a schedule of
taxes based on the value of the sale: equities carry a tax of 0.5%, straight
bonds 0.03% and convertibles 0.18%.

As in the US, investors in the Tokyo market are able to conduct
transactions for First Section shares via margin trading and indeed a
considerable volume of trading is carried out this way

> Individual investors are the major buyers of stocks on margin accounts and
> despite having to pay considerably higher interest on borrowing for margin
> investing, the volume of margin buying accounts on the Tokyo, Osaka and
> Nagoya represents about Y7 trillion, a figure that is still growing. (Matsumoto,
> 1989)

A legal minimum margin of 30% is required but as in the United States
this minimum requirement can be varied by the authorities (the Ministry of
Finance) depending upon developments in the market.

In addition the minimum requirement varies depending upon the nature of
collateral used. In 1988 the margin requirement was 70% for equities and 80-
90% for bonds.

Settlement

Settlement in Japan takes place on the third business day after execution for
almost all transactions. In this respect it is similar to American practice.
However there are three other possible settlement techniques:

(i)   Cash transactions which are either settled on the same day or the day
      immediately following;
(ii) Trades in new issues when the settlement date is fixed by the exchange;

(iii) Certain special transactions can be agreed for settlement within two weeks of the order. This is not in widespread use having been instituted to facilitate trading by overseas clients.

7 THE INTERNATIONALISATION OF EQUITY MARKETS

One of the most significant developments in equity markets in the 1980s was the growing trend toward the trading of equity across frontiers. While the international issuing of equities was damaged by the Crash of 1987 the primary market saw new issues of some $9 billion in 1988 and $14.9 billion in 1989. These figures make no allowance for equity related bonds which have been utilised by Japanese issuers in the Eurobond market. Indeed the growth of international bonds was a major pointer to what could be done, but bonds tend to be more homogeneous than equity and the fact that much of the bond market was accounted for by sovereign issuers gave potential investors a greater degree of security. Nonetheless some of the rather exotic bond offerings which have typified the Euromarkets in the last few years are testimony to the growing sophistication (some might say gullibility) of these markets.

The simultaneous trading of equities in a variety of foreign locations has not yet become a common phenomenon but in the 1980s there has been noticeable trend in that direction. In the United States foreign equities are traded in the form of American Depositary Receipts (ADRs) and NASDAQ has been a particularly active proponent of such trading compared with other exchanges – Table 2.6 compares the growth of ADRs in major US markets and illustrates the dominant position of NASDAQ.

TABLE 2.6 ADR Issues traded in the USA, 1982–8

	1982	1984	1986	1987	1988
NASDAQ	66	81	88	97	96
NYSE	14	17	23	34	46
AMEX	7	6	5	5	4

Note: The same ADR may be traded on several exchanges.
NASDAQ International.

In the case of London's International Stock Exchange trading in foreign equities accounted for nearly 23% of total turnover in 1988 and by 1989 this figure exceeded 25%. This is by some way the largest of any major exchange although some smaller exchanges such as Brussels (22%) and Luxembourg (14%) have a substantial proportion of turnover in overseas shares. Indeed the growth of this kind of foreign trading was undoubtedly a contributory

factor to the process of stock market deregulation which occurred in the
1980s as various European exchanges saw business leaking away to foreign
competitors. For example London's ability to transact block trades (£1m
plus) provided greater liquidity in several large European stocks than was the
case in their domestic markets.

The ISE's position as the leading international centre was strengthened in
1985 when the screen based trading system SEAQ International was
inaugurated. In 1987 there were 43 market makers providing firm quotations for over 190 foreign equities and indicative quotes in a further 600. By
1988 the £46.4 billion ($84 billion) worth of foreign turnover traded in
London represented more than 50% of global transactions in foreign shares.

Table 2.7 indicates the extent of the ISE dominance of international
trading in equities in 1989.

TABLE 2.7   Total equity turnover in 1989, selected markets

	Value of Turnover 1989	of which Foreign Equities	
	£b*	£b*	%
ISE	282.3	84.6	30.0
NASDAQ	262.8	14.2	5.4
W. Germany**	228.3	11.1	4.8
Paris	71.7	2.9	4.0
Tokyo	1448.9	12.1	0.008
NYSE	956.8	n/a	
AMEX#	17.2	1.4	8.1

*Rounded up.   **Federation of Exchanges
The NYSE does not provide a breakdown of domestic and foreign equity turnover.
ISE, *Quality of Markets Quarterly Review*, Spring 1990.

In 1989 the number of market makers had increased to 50 and of 707
shares being quoted some 302 carried firm prices (the other 405 having
'indicative' price quotes). London had also started to compete in 23 out of
the 120 American Depositary Receipts that are traded in US markets.

Table 2.8 compares the costs of trading (commissions, turnover tax, stamp
duty etc.) in different sized bargains on various exchanges. It shows that
London is highly competitive and offers particular economies on the larger
blocks: indeed for overseas investors the ISE is the most competitive in the
larger sized blocks. The decision in 1990 to abolish the remaining 0.5%
stamp tax will further increase that competitiveness.

As mentioned above NASDAQ has moved rapidly to extend its influence
in a variety of ways: in 1986 links with the ISE allowed the exchange of real-
time price quotations and by 1989 700 securities were quoted in this way on
the two systems. A similar sort of relationship has been developed with the
Singapore Stock Exchange.

TABLE 2.8 Costs of trading in various markets – buying and selling as a percentage of initial investment

	Investment of:			
	£10 000		£100 000	
Stock exchange	Domestic Investor	Foreign Investor	Domestic Investor	Foreign Investor
ISE (London)	2.47	1.90	1.12	1.04
New York	3.07	3.07	1.18	1.18
Frankfurt	1.70	1.45	1.70	1.45
Zurich	1.57	1.57	1.57	1.57
Paris	2.14	1.90	1.88	1.66
Tokyo	2.90	2.90	2.58	2.58
Amsterdam	3.19	3.19	2.65	2.65

ISE, *Quality of Markets Quarterly Review*, Spring 1989.

Internationalisation of markets is not confined to a growth in the cross-border *trading* of foreign securities; there is also the question of growing numbers of foreign *listings* of corporates in overseas markets. These are not necessarily connected: thus a listing on the ISE is not a prerequisite to being quoted on SEAQ International. Nevertheless London has a higher number of foreign listings than any other exchange – followed once again by NASDAQ. In mid 1989 some 505 foreign equities were admitted to the ISE's official list while some 21 were listed on the USM. This compares with NASDAQ's 196.

Despite stringent initial listing criteria as well as high fees and a variety of administrative and legal costs more companies appear to be seeking a foreign listing. The techniques of handling international equity issues are still in the process of development but the market has grown very rapidly from some $200m in 1982 to upwards of $11billion just prior to the Crash of 1987 which was something of a setback. This seems to suggest that the advantages are thought to outweigh the costs.

Advantages and Disadvantages of Foreign Listing

It is clear that one of the reasons why companies seek a foreign listing relates to lowering the cost of capital. Corporates which are confined to a single capital market may find that they are constrained in various ways. There can be regulatory problems: for example there may be queueing procedures imposed by the authorities or there may be restrictions on the issue of particular paper. Then the company might face a rising cost of capital in their domestic market. Hence it would clearly be advantageous to be able to issue debt or equity in other perhaps deeper capital markets.

The problem of rising cost of capital can be particularly acute in the case of very large organisations. Companies which have global operations may have such substantial demands for capital that they are obliged to tap several markets simultaneously. A presence in a number of markets can increase the size of any given issue and enhance the flexibility of capital raising techniques. Different markets have different preferences for such things as convertible issues, warrants and so on. The mix of instruments can be altered more readily to suit the company's financing needs.

In commercial terms issuing equity in other markets can help to raise the visibility of a company with potentially beneficial effects on sales. Finally having a presence in various markets may serve strategic interests. By broadening the shareholder base, the company may be better placed to resist takeover pressure and in turn may be able to undertake foreign mergers and acquisitions more easily.

There are of course some disdavantages to overseas listings not the least of which are disclosure requirements, investor relations and 'flowback'. The latter phenomenon is the tendency for shares issued into a foreign market to be sold back into their domestic market. This has the effect of depressing the price of the shares in the domestic market and could conceivably trigger a takeover bid while the shares are depressed. It was particularly marked shortly after the October 1987 Crash as investors looked to the relative safety of their domestic market.

Investor relations can obviously be a delicate issue and therefore may demand particular attention when a company decides to seek a foreign listing: cultural differences, perceptions and tolerance of risk, time preference, the significance attached to key data and so on can differ radically between different societies. Hence there is a need to maintain a considerable flow of information in several languages if investor loyalty is to be maintained and this in itself adds to the cost of documentation and communication.

Compliance with the listing and reporting requirements imposed by different stock markets is also a problem. Differences in the quantity of information, the frequency of disclosure and accounting procedures all pose burdens in both financial and managerial terms.

A variety of other barriers such as foreign exchange controls, limitations on domestic ownership of foreign securities, restrictions on issuing activity and different tax regimes have made international equity financing difficult in the past but these barriers are gradually being eliminated. Some of the major world exchanges have been modifying their criteria in order to attract new listings (Tondkar et al., 1989) and the use of new dealing technologies has facilitated trading between different markets.

One should remember of course that deregulation and the unfixing of commissions have had benefits for governments too – lowering their borrowing costs in domestic markets and facilitating reciprocal access to overseas markets. Hence governments in the larger economies have taken a more relaxed view about the use of their domestic capital markets, particularly where bond issues are concerned, hence bond markets are much further into the process of internationalisation than equity markets.

NOTES

1. A discussion of the various kinds of insider trading as well as a valuable summary of US case law is provided in Herzel and Katz (1987).
2. Transparency is achieved on many floor exchanges (eg NYSE and AMEX) by means of an open outcry system. Market participants hear all the bid and offer prices being called and have the chance to strike a deal accordingly.
3. Indeed a survey based on the Stock Exchange's Private Investor's Directory in 1989 showed that of 110 brokers some 95 had retained standard commissions of some 1.65%.
4. There are various types of order which buyers or sellers can ask a broker to carry out. A 'market' order means that the broker is to buy or sell at the best available market price. A 'limit' order for a buyer imposes a maximum price which he is prepared to buy. Thus if the current price is £4.00 per share the order might be 'Buy at £3.90 or better' (less). For the seller the limit order will establish a minimum price at which he is prepared to sell 'Sell at £4.10 or better' (more). This type of order will only be acceptable for reasonably large bargain sizes and will be reviewed periodically. A Central Limit Order facility would consolidate all these orders and execute them as the relevant limit prices are reached.
5. There is real irony here in so far as many securities houses employ investment analysts to comment upon and criticise the performance of quoted companies in the UK. "Physician heal thyself" would not seem out of place in the circumstances.
6. As usual American and British terminology differs rather confusingly: in the US ordinary shares are termed 'stocks' or 'common stock' whereas in the UK the expression 'stocks' normally refers to bonds.
7. $^1/_8$ of a point is the minimum allowable tick for the majority of shares. There is often a degree of puzzlement as to why pricing takes place in fractions of a point as opposed to decimals. The reason is that in an open outcry system there is less likelihood of an error if the quote is called in fractions. One of the advantages of going over to a screen based quotation system is that prices can be displayed in finer gradations eg $23.33 – $23.43.
8. This having been said it is difficult to conceive of many market systems which could have withstood those particular trading conditions with equanimity.
9. This is a privately owned computerized system to which subscribers pay a flat annual fee. It allows users to display their interest in buying and/or selling large blocks of shares. This private 'notice board' is said to have saved the users over 60% in commission compared with what they would have paid under the old scales.
10. An American Depositary Receipt is a device to facilitate the trading of shares of non-US companies in the United States. It is a negotiable certificate issued by a US bank which evidences title to a specific number of shares in a foreign company. The custodian bank takes care of administrative details such as dividend payments, proxies and any other rights that attach to the underlying

equity. ADRs are priced in US dollars and hence are readily traded without the physical transfer of the shares that they represent. Examples of some of the most actively traded ADRs in the US are those of Hanson, Reuters Holdings, BP and British Telecom. In the case of some ADRs it means that it is possible for a foreign company to have visibility in the United States without going through the formal registration process required by the SEC.

pb4

11.   This title was astutely poached from an expression which the SEC and Congress had used to describe what they regarded as a desirable *ultimate* objective for the securities industry in the US – the linking of all markets to form a unified system so as to afford best execution – see Seligman (1982) for a detailed discussion of these proposals.

3   Bonds and Bond Markets

1 INTRODUCTION

Bonds are a species of loan. As evidence of the loan the borrower issues a certificate which in the majority of cases promises the investor a predetermined rate of interest, called the coupon, plus the guarantee of repayment in nominal or cash terms at some future date. They are issued in various capital markets by public bodies such as supranational organisations, national and local governments and by corporate issuers.

What distinguishes bonds from other loans is that they are transferable or *negotiable*. A bank normally keeps a conventional loan on its book until it is repaid hence there is a continuing relationship between the lender (the bank) and the borrower. A bond on the other hand need not be held by the original lender (the investor) until it matures – instead it can be sold to another person or institution provided there is an adequate secondary market. This allows trading to take place in bonds which have been issued at some time before. The original buyer of the security is able to liquidate the investment and is not 'locked in' for the life of the bond.

In this way bonds offer the advantage of borrowing 'long' for the issuer while maintaining a reasonable degree of liquidity for any given lender – always with the proviso that a secondary market does exist and performs its function. This needs to be emphasised as there have been instances when a secondary market has become inactive and investors have found difficulty selling or face extremely wide spreads when they do sell. Recent experience in some segments of the Eurobond markets and the American corporate bond market (specifically 'junk' bonds) has borne this out.

The Coupon

The rate of interest which is the income accruing from ownership of a bond is called the coupon because at one time the majority of bonds were issued in *bearer* form and each certificate carried a series of coupons which the investor would clip off as each payment date fell due. The coupon would then be sent to the issuer's paying agent – normally a bank. Now many

75

bonds are registered so that ownership is known and the 'coupon' is simply a monetary transfer sent directly to the investor.

To take one example, the UK government has (among over 100 bonds currently in issue) £1050m of the following

Exchequer 10.5% 2005

In the UK bonds are normally quoted in units of £100 (in the USA or the Eurobond markets $1000) nominal or face value and the coupon is also quoted in relation to this value. In the case above therefore the holder will receive a coupon of £10.50 per £100 nominal each year until the redemption date. The bond will eventually be redeemed in 2005 by the UK government for £100 no matter what price the individual may have originally paid to acquire it. At any given time the market price of the bond may stand at a premium or a discount to the face value.

The fixed interest component – the coupon – is payable on an annual basis either as a single payment (most Eurobonds) or twice a year (the vast majority of UK and US government bonds). In some exceptional cases it may be paid quarterly eg 2.5% Consols.

Conventional fixed interest bonds are attractive to many investors because of the security of both income and capital compared with ordinary shares. For example the bonds of sovereign issuers, particularly mature democracies, are regarded as having first class security and corporate bonds rank higher than ordinary shares in the sense that payment of interest must be met before any dividends are declared. In addition should the firm go into liquidation bondholders have a prior claim to repayment of their capital.

2   CLASSIFYING BONDS

Bonds can be classified according to their financial structure and the market into which they are issued.

Financial Structure

The financial structure of a bond depends upon the nature of its coupon, maturity and redemption value. There are many variants within each of these characteristics.

The simplest example is called a *straight* bond or sometimes a *vanilla* bond as it has no complicating features: it carries a fixed coupon, a fixed maturity date and a known value (in nominal terms at least). Not all bonds are quite so simple – a few examples will suffice:

(a) *Perpetual* bonds or *irredeemables* have no specific maturity date. Some may be redeemed according to the wishes of the issuer for example the UK government's War Loan 3.5% is dated 1961 and after. Only if interest rates were to fall below the value of the coupon will the issue be redeemed.

(b) *Zero coupon* bonds pay no income in the form of a coupon but instead are sold at a deep discount to their face value. Hence all the return accrues in the form of a capital gain when the bond matures.

(c) *Convertible* bonds allow the investor to exchange the original bond for another security (eg another bond or the equity of an issuing company) on specified terms.

(d) *Warrant* bearing bonds carry a certificate which may be detachable and therefore negotiable giving the holder the right to buy another security at a fixed price at some future time.

(e) *Index linked* bonds are designed so that their value at maturity varies with some specified index. Since 1981 for example the UK government has issued Index Linked Government Securities (ILGS): both the coupon and the redemption value of these bonds are adjusted for movements in the Retail Price Index. Some corporate borrowers have issued bonds whose maturity value varies according to an index of equity prices. For example in January 1990 the Christiania Bank issued a Yen denominated bond for some Y2.9b, carrying a coupon of 8.75%. The redemption value of the bond was linked to the Nikkei-Dow stock index.

A sub species of this type of bond is one which links the final redemption value not to an index but to the price of a specific commodity such as oil, gold or silver.

(f) *Dual currency* bonds offer their coupon and redemption values in different currencies: for example the coupon may be payable in Swiss francs while the redemption value is in US dollars.

Markets

Most issuers whether sovereign governments, corporates or local authorities issue their 'paper' in their own domestic markets. It is also possible however to issue international bonds. By definition supranational borrowers, such as the World Bank, have no home market and therefore invariably issue international bonds.

These come in two main forms:

(a) *Foreign Bonds.* Borrowers may use a capital market which is different from their own domestic market because it is cheaper or more convenient. Obviously issuers have to meet the listing requirements of the relevant exchange and abide by the legal framework for the issuing of securities in the country in question. The most well known of this type of bond are called

'Yankee' bonds: here the borrower issues a bond denominated in dollars in the United States and hence must meet the various legal and regulatory requirements imposed by the US authorities. Similarly there are bonds denominated in Sterling and issued in the London market by foreign borrowers – these are termed 'Bulldog' bonds.

Foreign bonds pay interest gross of tax and are nearly always in bearer form. Their equivalents are found in other markets and go under rather exotic names for example in Japan 'Samurai' bonds and in the Netherlands 'Rembrandts'.

(b) *Eurobonds*. These are bonds issued and traded in many separate financial centres simultaneously. Although the major location of Eurobond issuers and dealers is in London it is really an international Over the Counter market where trading is carried out via the telephone and telex.

3 THE MARKET PRICE OF BONDS

Ultimately the market price of any security depends on the forces of supply and demand so when addressing the issue of what determines bond prices we are simply asking what factors lie behind supply and demand.

The *supply* of bonds is a function of the net financing requirements of the borrower – thus the UK government having been a very active issuer of bonds in the 1960s and 1970s as its borrowing needs expanded has recently been redeeming or retiring bonds earlier in their life as a result of its budgetary surpluses in the late 1980s. This contrasts with the position of the US government which has issued huge quantities of Treasury bonds in financing its enormous budget deficits.

As for the demand for bonds there are a number of factors of significance:

(i)   Changes in the credit status or quality of the borrower.
(ii)   Proximity of the bond to repayment or maturity date.
(iii) Investor expectations about the rate of inflation.
(iv)   The movement of interest rates.

In addition in the case of bonds denominated in a different currency from the domestic currency of the holder there is

(v)   The movement of exchange rates.

These factors give rise to various sorts of risk which bond-holders must consider – credit risk, inflation risk, interest rate risk and exchange rate risk.

Changes in the Status of the Borrower

This can have a marked effect on the market price of particular bonds. Thus doubts about an issuer's ability to meet interest due and/or the final redemption payment will result in investors shying away from such paper causing a considerable fall in its price.[1] For example in the corporate sector, the growth of takeovers financed by the issue of large amounts of debt, so-called Leveraged Buy Outs (LBOs), may result in unexpected changes in the capital structure of the target company with detrimental effects on the value of existing bonds. Although one might argue that it is a species of credit risk this has been termed 'event' risk.

Proximity to Redemption Date

This will affect the price of an issue because the market price will be drawn to the redemption price. Given that a bond is to be redeemed at full face value within a short space of time any hint of a fall in the market price will bring in buyers. Some authorities envisage this process as the redemption price acting like a magnet – pulling the market price toward it. Indeed it is sometimes termed the 'pull to maturity'

Expectations about Inflation

If inflation is expected to accelerate then fixed interest securities which pay their coupon and are redeemed in *nominal* terms will become less attractive than other assets better able to cope with inflation. In consequence the market price of fixed interest securities will fall and this will raise the yield on such securities. The rising yields go some way to compensate prospective buyers for the higher rate of inflation. At the same time the way in which the prices of bonds with different maturities behave gives a snapshot of what the market's views are about the likely course of inflation.

Movements in Interest Rates

Interest rates are an extremely important factor in determining the price of fixed interest securities. Everything else being equal their effect on the price of bonds occurs in the following manner: assume that interest rates have been stable at 9% for some period of time then one would expect the yields on various securities to have settled at a level which relates to this 9%. There will actually be a differential structure of yields which reflects things such as the maturity spectrum and the degree of credit risk associated with different issuers.

If interest rates start to rise then the yields on existing bonds will be out of line. Funds will flow toward those segments of the market offering the higher returns. Hence the price of bonds will tend to fall and, given the fixed coupon, yields will rise. This is not a smooth uncomplicated process and there may be circumstances where the relationship does not work. For example if bond prices have been depressed because of high inflation expectations then the rise in interest rates (which of itself would cause bond prices to fall) may be regarded as a sign of determination by government to squeeze inflation out of the system. Hence the market might in these circumstances react to the rise in interest rates with a *rise* in bond prices. In effect the negative impact of the higher interest rate has been offset by the positive impact of an improved inflation outlook.

Exchange Rate Changes

These apply where the bond is denominated in a different currency than the country of domicile of the bond holder. Clearly for example if the US dollar were to strengthen *vis-à-vis* the pound this would enhance the sterling value of dollar bonds. The effect of this is in turn to raise demand for such bonds tending to drive up their dollar price.

4   BOND ANALYSIS

Yields

Yields are important because they are primarily what the investor is looking to for his or her return. There are a variety of yields which can be calculated as a way of evaluating and comparing bonds (Phillips, 1987) but analysts identify two principal yields: the interest yield (also called the flat, running, or current yield) and the yield to redemption.

(i)   The Interest Yield

The interest yield identifies a return to a given outlay without reference to the time pattern of returns.

$$\text{Gross Interest Yield} = \frac{\text{Coupon}}{\text{Stock Price at Purchase}} \times 100\%$$

For example in September 1989, for the UK government bond Treasury 8% 2009 bought for £89.00 the interest yield would give

$$\text{Gross Interest Yield} = \frac{8}{89.00} \times 100\%$$

$$= 8.99\%$$

This represents the return gross of tax. The net yield to the investor is affected by his or her tax status and should be adjusted accordingly to get the net of tax yield.

$$\text{Net Interest Yield} = \text{Gross Yield} \times (1 - t)$$

where t is the rate of tax.

Hence in the case of a tax payer facing a rate of tax of 25% the net yield on the above bond becomes

$$\text{Net Interest yield} = 8.99\% \times (1.00 - 0.25)$$

$$= 6.74\%$$

As suggested earlier the interest yield is easily calculable as it is a simple ratio with no time dimension.

(ii)   The Yield to Redemption

The yield to redemption is more complex: it combines *both* the income accruing from successive interest payments plus any capital gain or loss as the security matures.

Calculating this yield is more difficult as it is the sum of two components

1.   the present value of a stream of future interest payments payable to maturity;
2.   the discounted value of any future capital gain or loss.

This requires the solution to the following formidable equation:

$$P = \frac{C_1}{(1+i)} + \frac{C_2}{(1+i)^2} + \frac{C_3}{(1+i)^3} \ldots \ldots + \frac{R}{(1+i)^n}$$

where P is the present market price paid for the bond;
C is the coupon payable until maturity;
R is the redemption value;
n is the number of years left to maturity;
i is the yield to be determined.

In the case of most conventional bonds four of these values are known: the present price (P), the coupon (C), the final redemption value (R), and the number of years to maturity (n) therefore it is possible to solve for the unknown (i).

The redemption yield therefore is that value of 'i' which just equates the flow of future coupons plus the final capital gain (or loss) to the *present* market price of the security. There is no direct or analytical solution to this equation; instead it is solved by inserting successive trial values for 'i' (iteration) and is commonly carried out now via the use of computers or investment analyst calculators. The easiest way of all of course is to look both yields up in the *Financial Times* or the *Wall Street Journal*!

In the case of the Treasury 8% 2009 the yield to redemption is 9.18% because in addition to the flow of future coupons there will also be an additional £11.00 capital gain if the bond is held to maturity. Of course given that a highly active secondary market exists for UK government bonds the holder may decide to sell the security before the maturity date.

The redemption yield gives a guide to the expected performance of an investment in circumstances where it is assumed that the rate of interest *does not vary* between the date at which the bond is acquired and the final maturity date. However this is a very strong assumption. If a bond pays half the coupon every six months then the investor may not be able to invest the interim receipts at the same rate of return. Thus if interest rates fall after the bond has been acquired then the cash flow from the investment can only be invested at lower rates and the original yield to redemption will overstate the true profitability. On the other hand if the rate of interest rises then it is possible to re-invest the coupon proceeds as they come in and achieve a higher rate of return. If this so-called 'roll up' rate is greater than the original yield to redemption then clearly the eventual realised return to the investment will exceed the redemption yield.

but.. but.. but..

(iii)   Performance yield

In calculating the redemption yield it is assumed that the investor holds the bond until redemption but this is rarely the case. In organised markets it is much more likely that the investor will sell the bond some time before its redemption date. In this case the investor will be interested in its expected performance between acquisition and disposal.

The performance yield is calculated in a similar fashion to the redemption yield except that the terminal value for the bond is simply the sale price and not the redemption value. In addition of course the time period over which the discounting procedure is carried out will be shorter. Thus in the case of the Treasury 8% 2009, if it were sold in September 1994 for £98 (ie after the receipt of five years worth of coupons) the yield would be 10.6%.

In this example we are able to calculate the performance yield precisely as we have imposed the terminal value and this can only really be done with certainty after the event. Of greater significance to the investor is the *prospective* outcome which implies estimating the future price at which stock may be sold. This in turn will depend on whether one takes an optimistic or pessimistic view of market performance.

These yields are obviously of major interest when comparing different bonds but, as is clear from the example of calculating performance yields, the behaviour of the market price during the period over which the investor intends to hold the bond is also a crucial consideration.

The Yield Curve

The concept of the yield curve was developed as a device to be used by market analysts in a variety of ways – to visualise the structure of market yields, to summarize market sentiment and possibly to identify anomolous behaviour on the part of certain bonds.

Bonds offer different yields according to their maturity and it is possible to plot these different yields on a graph. From a series of market observations taken at a particular time the analyst can estimate via statistical techniques a 'line of best fit'. This estimated line then becomes the resulting yield curve (see for an early example *Bank of England Quarterly Bulletin*, Dec. 1972– Sept. 1973).

Generally it is argued that one might expect two things to be true about the nature of yield curves:

(a) Longer dated bonds will tend to offer higher yields than shorter maturities to compensate for the longer period of illiquidity inherent to such bonds. This is the so-called 'liquidity preference hypothesis' which suggests that investors will require a 'premium' for giving up liquidity. The longer the period of illiquidity the greater the premium. In addition bonds with longer maturities tend to be regarded as being more exposed to possible adverse movements in interest rates. Such an approach would suggest that a graphic portrayal of the time structure of yields for securities of a given risk category would result in a monotonically rising yield curve.

(b) The yield curve of bonds with the greatest security or most credit worthy issuer should be uniformly lower than those of a lesser rated credit.

In other words we would normally expect the time structure of bond yields to produce a shape such as that illustrated in Fig. 3.1 below. This yield curve would also tend to change position as a result of changes in 'surrounding' factors such as interest rates, inflation, an adjustment in credit rating etc.

This simple liquidity approach is not of itself sufficient to explain the time pattern of yields actually observed in the real world however: for example in the London gilts market the yield curve tends to be distorted somewhat by taxation effects.

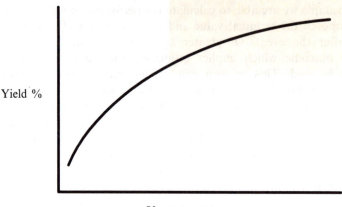

Figure 3.1   Yield curve

As indicated earlier interest on gilt-edged stocks is treated as income and hence attracts income tax at the standard rate deductible at source. Because gilts are free from capital gains tax however there is an advantage to higher rate tax payers to purchase those gilts where most of the yield comes in the form of a tax-free capital gain and less of it as taxable interest. Low coupon gilts standing at a considerable discount to their redemption value therefore tend to attract the attention of such taxpayers. This tax advantage means that low coupon gilts will experience greater demand relative to other gilts thus raising their price and lowering the yield by more than would otherwise be the case. Because of these distorting effects some authorities confine their observations for the yield curve in the medium to high coupon range.

Example 3.1

On 26 September 1989 the following low coupon gilts were quoted in the *Financial Times*

	Price £	Yield	
		Int.	Red.
Treasury 3% 1991	$90^3/_{16}$	3.33	9.65
Treasury 3% 1992	$84^3/_4$	3.54	9.51
Exch. 3% Gas 90–95	$75^1/_2$ xd	3.97	8.59
Funding $3^1/_2$%	$57^7/_{32}$	6.11	8.68

note: a long bond may be a substitute for a short, but not the other way round because of the pressure of imminent maturity.

...ption yield is considerably greater ...lects the contribution coming from

...be attractive for specific purposes has in fact led to the development of another possible explanation for the expected upward slope in the yield curve – this is known as the 'segmentation hypothesis'.

If short dated gilts and longer dated gilts are not regarded as good substitutes, because for example of different volatility *vis-à-vis* interest rate changes, then certain institutions may prefer to confine themselves to the short end of the spectrum while others see themselves as long run investors ie *segmentation* of the market may occur.

> The effect of the segmentation is that the assumptions and expectations of one set of investors may be inconsistent with the other. Put simply, the long term investors may be expecting the short term rate to rise while the short term investors may expect it to fall.
>
> If there are restrictions on the dealing between different segments of the market there is no particular reason why the assumptions should ever be consistent between long-term investors and short-term ones. Thus the persistent upward slope of the yield curve may simply represent the competition amongst buyers of bonds to hold short term instruments. This competitive pressure unless satisfied by borrowers, would make itself evident through a consequent rise in the price of short bonds and the associated fall in yield. (Peasnell and Ward, 1985, p. 121)

While a rising yield curve would be expected from *a priori* reasoning whether it be via segmentation, liquidity preference or whatever, actual observations of yield curves in the past 70 years have thrown up a number of different patterns. These have been:

(i)   Inverted – where yields on long bonds are below those on short bonds;
(ii)   The 'humped' version – where the yield curve rises between short and medium term bonds and then declines for long term maturities;
(iii)   Flat – where the yields on short and long maturities is broadly the same.

These various shapes appear from time to time and may be the result for example of operations by the authorities or of differential short term and long term expectations. These other variants of the curve are illustrated in Fig. 3.2.

The yield curve illustrates the relationship of the yields of a given category of bonds on a particular day and therefore it embodies a given state of expectations about the behaviour of economic factors such as inflation,

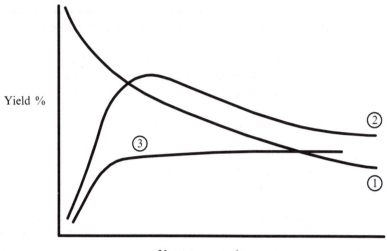

Yield %

Years to maturity

Figure 3.2   Hypothetical yield curves

interest rates or government policy. Obviously therefore from time to time the curve will shift as a result of changes in these expectations.

There are also the actions of the authorities to consider. Thus if a government is actively buying long dated gilts (as has the UK government in the past few years) then it will tend to push up prices in the long end of the spectrum (relative to shorter dates) and this will lower the yield on long dated stock.

Yield curves are used in a number of ways: for example monitoring the behaviour of curves and comparing international patterns is a way of summarizing aggregate market expectations as to potential inflation, interest rate movements and so on. Thus an upward shift in the Treasury bond yield curve in the United States may be indicative of growing market expectation of an interest rate increase. A downward shift may result from better than expected news about the rate of inflation or from a redirection of new funds into the bond markets as nervousness about equities develops.

When yield curves first emerged there was some scepticism and resistance to their use as a tool of analysis because of the problems involved in the lengthy calculations required to obtain the 'line of best fit' on the observations. The advent of cheap computer power however overcame this obstacle as it became feasible to calculate yield curves very rapidly for any number of different issuers and different economies.

This meant that analysts could calculate market yield levels at all or particular maturities so that it became possible to compare the yield on individual bonds against the 'central market yield' (Phillips, 1984). Differences between the *actual* yield of a given bond and the statistically estimated yield curve for that maturity then might provide a measure of how 'cheap' or 'expensive' a given bond may be. This it was hoped would allow the analyst to identify anomalies and to recommend switches between maturities. At first sight this seems to offer an excellent method of identifying buy and sell opportunities for the 'active' investor. Unfortunately however identification of securities as 'cheap' or 'dear' in relation to a given yield curve is sensitive to the precise position of the curve and this limits the usefulness of the approach.

The position of a fitted yield curve can vary because it depends upon:

(i)   The technique employed to fit the curve. There are a number of statistical methods which can be employed to determine a line of best fit hence variations in the precise position of the curve can occur depending upon which is the preferred method.

(ii) The set of observations against which the curve is fitted.

As a result there is no uniquely determined yield curve and analysts can and do calculate different yield curves with the result that contradictory recommendations about a particular bond could occur.

Yield Gaps

Yield gaps are a simple technique for examining the return from different classes of investment. The measured return achieved from one type of investment is subtracted from the return obtained over the same period from another type of investment.[2]

The most frequent comparison is between the interest yield on bonds and dividend yield on equities: the actual measures chosen may vary but the usual way is to compare the returns accruing from holding a basket of equities such as the *Financial Times*-Actuaries All Share Index and the return on undated gilts. In the US the comparison might be between the dividend yield on the S&P 500 and that on the longest Treasury bond.

Example 3.2

	9.5.89	25.9.89
Average Gross Yield on		
Irredeemable Gilts	9.07%	9.05%
Gross Dividend Yield on the		
FT-Actuaries All Share Index	4.21%	4.05%
Yield Gap	4.86	5.00

This gives a crude measure of the *income* foregone by deciding to hold a basket of shares compared with holding 'risk free' bonds. The behaviour of the gap over time can also be used to assess the relationships between equity prices in general and bond prices. Recall that yields move inversely with the price of the security then a widening of the gap may be used as an indicator of whether or not equities are overbought compared with their historical relation to prices in the bond market.

Thus for example in London in the period immediately prior to the 1987 Crash the yield on the FT's All Share Index was around 3% while on gilts it was in excess of 9%. In the US the yield on the S&P 500 was just over 2% while that on Treasury bonds and high quality corporate issues was more than 10% and many analysts felt that this was so far out of line with the normal relationship that some form of adjustment was needed.

The yield gap indicates that the income yield on equities is below that on less risky securities such as gilt-edged or high quality corporate stock. This apparent contradiction is easily explained however: in general ordinary shares offer a higher overall rate of return or yield than bonds *once one adds prospective capital gains to the dividend yield.* Equities also offer a better hedge against persistent inflation which appears to be endemic condition in both the US and the UK.

Volatility

Volatility is the percentage movement in market price for a 1% change in yield and therefore clearly a valuable factor in assessing switches as between different securities. Given the different features of bonds (level of coupon, years to redemption and so on) there are marked differences in the price action as a result of a given change in yields.

This is obviously more important to the active trader as it is a crucial factor for those who wish to increase or reduce their exposure to potential capital gains or losses. Everything else being equal three factors affect volatility – the bond's coupon, its maturity and the current absolute level of yields.

(i)   *Coupon*: the lower the coupon the greater the change in price for a given change in yield.

Example 3.3 Price movement per 100 basis points change in yield (eg 9% to 8%)

Different coupons (15 year maturity)		
Coupon	Absolute price change	% change in price
3%	51.6 – 57.2	10.9
5%	67.8 – 74.3	9.6
7%	83.9 – 91.4	8.9
9%	100.0 – 108.6	8.0

(ii) *Maturity*: the longer the maturity the greater the price change from any given change in yield.

Example 3.4 Price movement per 100 basis points change in yield

Different maturity (7.5% coupon)		
Years	Absolute price change	% change in price
5	94.2 – 98.0	4.0
7	92.5 – 97.4	5.3
10	90.4 – 96.6	6.9
15	87.9 – 95.7	8.9

(iii) *Level of yields*: other things being equal volatility tends to be greater the lower the absolute level of yields. Thus for example if yields are currently standing at 5% and they fall to 4% this will have a greater impact than if yields move from 10% to 9%.

In other words more volatility or *leverage* is obtained from a low coupon bond or a long maturity ('a fortiori' for bonds which exhibit *both* features) and therefore during periods when interest rates are expected to fall the investor can maximise potential profit by moving into this type of bond.

The above assumes that interest rates move the same way for all maturities ie that the whole of the yield curve shifts. This need not be true of course as the short-term rates may be more changeable depending upon expectations. For example there may be considerably more volatility in the prices and yields of short dated bonds if say inflation is expected to accelerate and then later decelerate.

Duration

A way of combining the effects of maturity and coupon can be encompassed in the concept of a bond's duration. This idea was developed by Macaulay (1938) as a way of describing the 'true length' of a bond. In effect he likened the future payments due on a bond to a series of individual loans which are to be paid back to the investor. Hence duration is the weighted average length of time between buying a bond and receiving its cash flows (coupon payments and capital repayment) where the weighting is the present value of each of these cash flows.

It is obvious that a bond which pays a high rate of interest in the earlier years will repay the investor a greater part of the return before the final redemption date and hence will have a shorter true length or 'time profile'. An intuitive understanding of duration can be obtained if we compare a three year zero coupon bond with a three year bond bearing a 10% coupon. Zero coupon bonds always have the same duration as their maturity. With the same yield to maturity the zero obviously has the longer duration because all the return accrues in the last year whereas the conventional bond is repaying part of the return from year 1 onwards.

Assuming the bonds offer the same yield to maturity of 12.6% then the zero coupon bond will have been bought at 70 while the 10% coupon bond will have been purchased at 93.8.[3]

$$\text{Duration} = \frac{\text{Present Value} \times \text{Average length of}}{\text{Price of the bond}}$$

Example 3.5   Duration – zero coupon bond

$$\text{Duration} = \frac{3 \times \dfrac{100}{(1.126)^3}}{70}$$

$$= 3 \text{ Years}$$

Example 3.6   Duration – 10% coupon bond

$$\text{Duration} = \frac{1 \times \dfrac{10}{(1.126)} + 2 \times \dfrac{10}{(1.126)^2} + 3 \times \dfrac{110}{(1.126)^3}}{93.8}$$

$$= 2.72 \text{ Years}$$

Having established the method by which the duration of a bond is determined what is the point of it?

It has been pointed out above that low coupon bonds and those with a longer maturity tend to exhibit greater volatility to a given change in yield. Thus bonds which *combine* these two characteristics will clearly be more volatile than bonds which combine the opposite features – a high coupon and a short maturity.

But what about bonds which mix these characteristics? For example how would we rank the volatility of a high coupon/long maturity bond versus a low coupon/short maturity? Which is the more volatile with regard to yield changes?

This is what the duration of bonds is able to tell us. It gives an unequivocal criterion for ranking the volatility of bonds because it takes account of the time pattern and size of the monetary flows. The longer the duration of a bond the more sensitive to a change in yield its price will be. Bonds with the same duration (whatever their maturity and coupon) will tend to have the same sensitivity to changes in their redemption yields. Essentially therefore duration gives us a single measure of this sensitivity.

5 THE BOND MARKET IN THE UK

The bond market in the UK is focused on London's International Stock Exchange. In fact, of the 7000 plus securities with a listing in 1989 nearly half consisted of various types of bonds. In addition there were just over 1000 preference shares so that getting on for two-thirds (4349) of all securities comprise fixed interest securities.

There is an extremely active market in UK government bonds where daily turnover at £4billion exceeds turnover in the equity market by over two to one. On the other hand the Stock Exchange estimates that whole of the *non-gilt fixed interest* sector accounts for only 2% of daily turnover – less than £100m (ISE 1989). In other words except for the fairly recent growth in the issue of Eurosterling bonds the market has tended to become very inactive almost to the point of being moribund.

In terms of domestic bond issues there are something over 1000 corporate issues of debentures and loan stock and a small number of local authority stocks. The reasons for the demise of the corporate bond market relate to the reluctance of UK companies to issue fixed interest debt during the 1970s when high and unstable rates of interest acted as something of a deterrent. In the 1980s under the influence of the bull market in equities companies looked even less to issue debt and finally for large well known corporates the more easily accessible highly competitive Euromarkets provided a speedier and frequently cheaper alternative.

New Issues

The issue of fixed interest corporate debt is normally carried out in the same way as the issue of equity. In some cases a Placing might be the chosen technique as it is frequently the least expensive method. Alternatively an Offer-for-sale can be undertaken by inviting the public to subscribe either at a fixed price or via a Tender process.

The pricing of an issue is not easy – too high a price and the bonds will be difficult to sell – too low a price means that the company has foregone capital that it could otherwise have had. Clearly the gross redemption yield is crucial as it can be readily compared with other such yields. Company bonds are less liquid and also carry greater credit risk than does government paper of the same maturity. Hence a favoured method of pricing is to design the offer so as to give the investor a gross redemption yield above that available on a comparable gilt. The margin is expressed as so many *basis points* (ie hundredths of a percent) and will obviously have to be larger the greater the perceived degree of credit risk. Unlike the US bond market there has been no formal rating of corporate debt issues in the UK and until the market shows some sign of reviving it seems unlikely that rating services will be required in the near future.

The secondary market in fixed interest securities has certain similarities to the operation of the equity market but it is much less active. Hence between three and four hundred of the most actively traded issues are displayed on market makers' screens but only in the 'gamma' category where prices and bargain size are indicative only. Dealing is carried out over the phone. As the rest of the fixed interest securities are traded infrequently market makers allocate them to the 'delta' classification ie they do not appear on SEAQ instead they appear on the simpler viewdata system TOPIC.

UK Government Issues

Gilt edged securities are bonds issued by the British government and traded in London. Unlike some other types of debt they are not secured against real assets: the investor must rely on the government to fulfil its promise to pay the interest and to redeem the issue when its maturity date falls due. As the risk of default is extremely remote gilt-edged are regarded as carrying the highest degree of security in the market.

In common with many other capital markets the gilt-edged market has experienced profound changes in the last few years. These changes have affected both the structure of the market and its operational context. Before dealing with these matters however we need to examine certain key facets of the market to establish some notion of its size and significance.

In view of the media attention that the equity sector receives it frequently comes as rather a surprise to learn that the gilt edged market has traditionally accounted for by far the larger proportion of Stock Exchange activity. Even with a shrinking number of gilts in issue and considerably enlarged equity sector nearly two thirds of the turnover of the Stock Exchange is attributable to trading in gilts.

Table 3.1 gives an indication of the breakdown of turnover in very broad categories and it is quite clear that even at the top of the bull market in equities in 1987 when retail interest in the gilts market was particularly quiet nonetheless that sector accounted for over 50% of the Exchange's turnover.

TABLE 3.1 International Stock Exchange turnover (£m) by major category of security, 1980–9 (Percentage shares are given in parentheses)

	Gilts	Equities	Other	Total
1980	151 698.2 (77.3)	30 801.4 (15.7)	13 790.3 (7.0)	196 289.9
1981	146 055.6 (76.6)	32 386.7 (17.0)	12 224.2 (6.4)	190 666.5
1982	203 389.0 (78.3)	37 414.0 (14.4)	18 941.4 (7.3)	259 744.4
1983	210 755.5 (73.3)	56 131.0 (19.5)	20 700.3 (7.2)	287 586.8
1984	268 679.2 (73.7)	73 119.1 (20.0)	22 877.4 (6.3)	364 675.7
1985	261 529.0 (67.0)	105 554.3 (27.0)	23 391.1 (6.0)	390 474.4
1986	424 414.8 (65.7)	181 211.4 (28.0)	40 639.0 (6.3)	646 265.2
1987*	574 477.8 (62.5)	283 073.3 (30.8)	62 289.1 (6.7)	919 839.9
1988*	547 300.8 (69.4)	191 7207 (24.3)	49 299.0 (6.3)	788 320.5
1989*	531 528.5 (62.0)	264 228.2 (30.7)	62 746.0 (7.3)	858 502.7

*Customer business only – omits intra-market trading.
ISE, *Quality of Markets Quarterly Review*, Summer 1990.

The equity sector has also over this period been boosted by successive privatisations.

The scale of activity conducted by the gilts market reflects the presence of the major investing institutions. Although gilts are purchased by many small investors it is really the institutional investors which dominate. This is evidenced by the average bargain size shown in Table 3.2. Thus in the last four to five years the average gilts bargain has been between eighteen and twenty nine times larger than the average equity bargain. Pension funds, insurance companies and the banks are all active participants in the gilts market as it is sufficiently large and varied in terms of issue size, maturity structure and liquidity to appeal to very different investor groups. As with other fixed interest securities gilts are differentiated according to their maturity and their coupon. Indeed gilts are identified less by their names which tend to be rather uninspiring than by these two characteristics: for example Exchequer 12% 1998 are simply referred to as 12's of '98; Treasury 10.5% 1999 as 10$\frac{1}{2}$'s of '99.

TABLE 3.2   Average bargain size by value (£), ISE 1980–9

	Gilts (a)	Equities (b)	Ratio (a)/(b)
1980	152 230	7280	20.9
1981	153 826	8211	18.7
1982	188 941	9635	19.6
1983	243 002	11 876	20.5
1984	316 373	15 080	21.7
1985	345 315	18 958	18.2
1986	532 454	23 723	22.5
1987*	796 841	29 683	29.1
1988*	894 768	31 715	28.2
1989*	1 060 425	36 148	29.3

*Customer business only – excludes intra-market trading.
ISE, *Quality of Markets Quarterly Review*, Summer 1990.

(i)   Maturity

The following classification is conventionally used to categorise the range of gilts in the market.

(a)   *Shorts*: the ISE's definition of short dated gilts are those with less than seven years to redemption. This end of the gilts market tends to be of particular interest to the banks and the building societies given their relatively short-term liabilities.

(b)   *Mediums*: these have maturities between seven and fifteen years and are of interest to insurance companies and pension funds – both of which have rather longer term liabilities.

(c)   *Longs*: the term here is over fifteen years and they are of major interest to pension funds as they have access to assets which can be matched to their long-term liabilities.

(d)   *Irredeemables*: these are bonds which carry no final redemption date. An individual will be willing to purchase an irredeemable security where there is a *secondary* market as this allows the buyer to sell the irredeemable to a third party and it assures a degree of liquidity.

(ii)   Coupon

Coupons can be classified as low, medium or high. This is impressionistic rather than objectively precise as it depends to some degree on the prevailing level of interest rates. A low coupon would be in the range 5% or less while a high coupon might be 9% and greater.

In the vast majority of cases it is paid on a semi-annual basis at half the stated coupon. The frequency of payment is of course an important feature of any bond as 10% paid once a year is in fact a lower return than 5% paid every six months because the half coupon receivable after six months can itself be reinvested for the remainder of the year.

Generally the coupon is fixed throughout the life of the bond but it is possible to have gilts and other bonds with a 'variable' coupon. UK governments issued variable coupon bonds in the 1970s but there are none in existence at the moment. However in the Eurobond markets there are considerable volumes of Floating Rate Notes (FRNs) outstanding.

(iii) Redemption value

This tends to be fixed in nominal terms but there are variations. One of the major innovations was the issue of index linked gilts in the UK in 1981.

It was thought initially that they would be favoured by pension funds which needed inflation-proofed assets to match their liabilities which were increasingly inflation geared. They offer a small coupon (usually 2% or 2.5%) and this plus the final redemption capital value are adjusted for movements in the Retail Price Index (RPI).

The price of these can fluctuate just like any other gilt as it depends on a variety of factors – their price *vis-à-vis* other stock, the expected trend in inflation and the behaviour of interest rates.

They work as follows:

Example 3.7   Index Linked Bonds

2% Index Linked Treasury 1992 redeemable Mar.1992 and interest paid on 23 Mar.–23 Sept.

The RPI figure on which calculations take place is always lagged by 8 months. Thus eight months prior to the issue $RPI = 97.8$ (calculated in relation to the Jan. 1987 rebasing of the index then standing at 394.5 at 100).

Interest due	23.3.88	23.9.88
based on RPI recorded in	July 1987	January 1988
which was	101.8	103.3
So the Index ratio is	$\dfrac{101.8}{97.8}$	$\dfrac{103.3}{97.8}$
ie	1.04	1.056
Amount payable	£1.04	£1.056
Repayment value is given by	£100 $\times$ $\dfrac{\text{RPI March 1992}}{97.8}$	

Capital Markets

Accrued interest on gilts

All gilts are quoted at a 'clean' price ie without the accrued interest. However they are still sold on a 'cum coupon' basis until they go 'ex coupon': ie the buyer is required to pay the seller the accrued interest. Interest accrues from the day following the *last* interest payment to the date when the stock goes 'ex coupon': this is 37 days before the *next* interest payment falls due.

Example 3.8

Purchase Date	Gilt	Interest Payable	Accrued Interest
1 Oct.	Treasury 12% 1995	25 July	$£12 \times \dfrac{68}{365} = £2.24$

In the ex coupon period prior to the interest payment date the gilt is dealt in *minus* the interest for each day up to the payment date.

6 THE OPERATION OF THE GILT-EDGED MARKET

Unlike the 'account' system for delivery and settlement which operates in London's equity market the purchase and sale of gilts takes place on a twenty-four hour basis: settlement takes place on the next business day after the transaction has been agreed. This makes for a very high degree of liquidity for holders of gilts especially when compared with the equity market. In addition it is a very deep market: the number of market makers and the sheer scale of most issues allows institutions to deal in substantial amounts without necessarily moving the market against them.[4]

Prior to 1986 the gilts market consisted of a handful of jobbers – some half dozen – specialising in the sector. As with jobbing operations in the equity sector firms were partnerships and not heavily capitalised. This inhibited their capacity to finance very large holdings of stock on their own account. This would not have mattered in a market consisting largely of private clients dealing in relatively small amounts nor if the investing institutions simply bought and held to maturity. But as the market became the province of institutions wishing periodically to restructure their portfolios by switching between different stocks, the position of the undercapitalised jobbing firms was difficult: they did not have sufficient dedicated capital to maintain large enough inventories to handle the much larger average bargain size of more active corporate customers. This would obviously tend to undermine the liquidity of the market.

Thus for example in the late 1950s the non-bank financial institutions (building societies, insurance companies, pension funds etc.) held less than 20% of marketable debt; by the beginning of the 1970s this figure had become over 35% and in 1989 they owned over 45% of the total. It is also quite clear from Table 3.2 that bargains were becoming much larger. In fact the table understates the average bargain size for the institutions as it is calculated on *all* transactions including deals done for private clients.

To enable the jobbers to deal with the increasing volumes of business and hence to stabilise market conditions two mechanisms were available. In the first place there existed several money brokers which were able to facilitate the trading process by lending the jobber the necessary gilts or cash to match a sale or a purchase. Suppose a jobber sold gilts which he did not at that moment hold it was possible to obtain them by borrowing from an officially recognised 'money broker' using the cash as collateral. Alternatively in buying a large volume of stocks the jobber was able to borrow cash from the same source using the gilts as security. The money brokers in turn were able to obtain cash or stocks as and when necessary from other financial institutions. In effect then the jobbers had a sort of buffer which allowed them to transact much larger bargains than their own independent resources would permit. This meant that they did not need a large capital base to carry substantial volumes of particular issues on their own account.

In addition to this 'private sector' mechanism the authorities also behaved so as to underpin the operation of the market – via the Government Broker which since the early part of the 19th Century had been a single firm – Mullens and Co. In effect the Government Broker acted in an agency capacity for the Issue Department of the Bank of England. Given the commitment to stability and liquidity the Issue Department was readily prepared to sell and/or buy stock from jobbers as the occasion demanded. In effect the Issue Department was acting as a 'jobber of last resort'.[5]

The Primary Market and the Secondary Market

As with other securities it is possible to identify a primary and a secondary market for gilts. The Bank of England is the authority responsible for issuing gilts in the primary market on behalf of the government. In addition the Bank is responsible for managing the structure of existing debt in the secondary market. Unlike most borrowers governments do not issue debt simply to finance spending programmes although that is clearly the most important reason. Governments may also sell gilts in the conduct of monetary policy – in order to reduce the amount of money in the system. This has the effect of reducing the banking system's capacity to create credit: by selling gilts the government exchanges the amount of money in the banking system for longer run IOUs. Banks are therefore forced to contract their lending further as a consequence of this fall in their liquid assets.

Should the government wish to pursue an expansionary monetary policy it would of course buy gilts.

In pursuing its role in the primary market the Bank has employed a number of methods in issuing government stock depending upon market conditions, for example the most common device was a fixed price *Offer for Sale*. This involves issuing a prospectus in the press inviting direct subscriptions by application. If the offer is not fully taken up by the market it can be bought up by the Issue Department of the Bank. Thus government borrowing is underwritten by the Department ie it guarantees that the government will always get its 'cash'. The stock taken up may later be sold into the market as conditions allow. This is known as a 'tap' issue.

As the objectives of economic policy changed during the early 1970s, greater emphasis was placed on inflation control and the authorities began to pay more attention to monetary targets as opposed to stable interest rates. This implied greater variability of gilt prices as these fluctuate inversely with movements in interest rates. The new approach was not compatible with continuous management of the market which meant that there would no longer be the same level of intervention and support for gilt-edged jobbers.

The viability of the market structure in such variable conditions was already in question and the experience of the mid to late 1970s placed even greater strains on the jobbers. The expansion of government borrowing as a result of increased public spending made the gilts market more and more important as a way of funding the Public Sector Borrowing Requirement. Hence the *supply* of gilt edged stocks increased rapidly. At the same time inflation accelerated into double figures and therefore the *demand* for fixed interest securities of all kinds began to fall – in particular the demand for gilts suffered acutely.

Indeed so unattractive did gilts appear in the 1976–7 period that the City was accused by left wing opinion at the time of having indulged in an 'investment strike' against the government. Certainly the institutions which make up the largest customers of the gilt-edged market were in an unenviable position: they had the duty to protect client positions at a time when the prospective returns on government paper were undermined by accelerating inflation.

Whatever the merits or otherwise of such an accusation the fact of the matter was that the authorities were forced to change the nature of some new issues and their issuing practices in several ways to attract buyers. Tender issues, partly paid issues, convertible gilts, variable rate stock and in 1981 Index Linked Gilts were introduced. The latter were designed to cope with inflation risk but as inflation came under control the attractiveness of conventional issues carrying a high coupon in excess of going rates of inflation reasserted itself.

As monetarist notions about the most effective way of controlling the economy took centre stage in the 1980s the consequences were clear: greater interest rate variability and therefore greater price volatility in the gilts market would ensue. The conventional fixed price Offer for Sale had been replaced by some Tender-style issues in the previous decade largely because some fixed price issues had been oversubscribed. The government therefore had used a modified form of the technique as it also retained a minimum tender price. Also, in the event that the issue was under subscribed, the Issue Department stepped in to take off the residue as a tap stock. Thus the authorities had employed the price tender system but retained the 'comfort blanket' of the Issue Department.

This was quite contrary to the monetarist approach to financing public spending. The latter required the authorities to cover its deficits by borrowing from the non-bank sector and to make use of the Tender style financing while not taking any unsold stock into the issue department (as that would imply easing monetary conditions). However an unsupported use of the Tender procedure meant offering the stock to the market with no minimum price and letting the market decide what price it was prepared to pay to take a given volume of gilts. In effect this would be the equivalent of conducting a sale by auction – the technique employed in the US Treasury Bond market. The existing structure of the gilt-edged market and its jobbers were lacking in the scale of capital resources to deal with such a hands-off Tender/Auction approach and the price volatility which such a system involves. As discussions were already under way about the need for changes in the equity market, the government and the Stock Exchange decided to alter the nature of the gilt-edged market at the same time and therefore to reform both markets together.

More capital would be a crucial part of a reformed system and in so far as certain large and well capitalised foreign firms had already indicated a wish to be involved with the gilts market, it would have to be opened to these 'interlopers'.

The New Market

The gilt-edged market structure introduced in 1986 is modelled in many important respects on its counterpart in the USA – the Treasury Bond Market. In the latter case some forty primary market makers are active in a market which can vary from six to ten times larger than the gilts market and competitive bidding is commonplace – to the advantage of the issuing authorities. Unlike London however the market has not traditionally been located in one of the main floor exchanges but is mainly an Over the Counter market.

London's gilt-edged market has changed dramatically since 'Big Bang'. The former distinction between broker and jobber has disappeared and a new organisation, the broker-dealer has emerged. These new firms are recognised as Gilt Edged Market Makers (GEMMs) by the Bank of England and undertake to make a continuous market in gilt-edged stocks. They deal directly with investors or with other brokers on an agency basis. The role of the Government Broker as an intermediary between the authorities and the market has been abandoned and the GEMM's have direct access to the Bank. The role of the money brokers has been retained and their numbers increased while a new layer to the market – the Inter Dealer Broker – has been borrowed from the example of the US Treasury bond market.

The Market Makers

Initially close to fifty firms were interested in becoming Gilt Edged Market Makers but in the event the Bank accepted only twenty-nine. A variety of pressures have since reduced the numbers to below twenty. Even with these reduced numbers however it is hard not to conclude that the market has too much capacity: particularly compared to the T-Bond market in the USA.

While the GEMMs are committed to offering prices in stated bargain sizes on a continuous basis there is no obligation for market makers to display their prices on the SEAQ system although many have in fact provided this service. Price quotations and bargain sizes are obtained by telephone as any prices displayed on the screen need only be indicative and larger clients can negotiate. This new market structure is supposed to deliver competition and liquidity. While some degree of specialisation may eventually emerge the Bank of England and the Stock Exchange clearly expect market makers to deal in a wide range of gilts. Detailed supervision is carried out by the Bank as to matters of capital adequacy, risk exposure etc. while market makers are registered with the Stock Exchange and therefore subject to regulations from this quarter as well.

In exchange for taking on their role GEMMs obtain a number of privileges among which are: favourable tax treatment of dividends; the right to deal directly with the Bank in terms of making outright bids for stock held by the authorities and the right if necessary to borrow money from the Bank in the event that normal sources are not available. The fact of being a recognised GEMM implies a credit status which will allow them to borrow funds elsewhere at cheaper rates than they could otherwise obtain.

Inter Dealer Brokers

Given the number of market makers in the new system the government has achieved its objective of stimulating an intense degree of competition and at the same time individual market makers have enlarged the size of their books. A higher degree of risk has shifted to market makers than was the case in the former system. A mechanism which enables that extra risk to be reduced is provided by the Inter Dealer Brokers (IDB) – an idea imported from the US. The function of the IDB is to act as a sort of anonymous notice board through which GEMMs are able to indicate a willingness to sell or buy a stock without disclosing their identity to competitors. Thus if a market maker buys a substantial quantity of a gilt which establishes a long position it is possible to unwind the position by 'advertising' the availability of the stock via the IDB. A GEMM which is short of the same stock can indicate a willingness to buy and the transaction can be effected to the satisfaction of both parties.

Two firms carry out this role, their numbers having come down from four in 1989. Matching of bids and offers in this fashion enables the IDB to enhance the liquidity of the market as GEMMs are more easily able to obtain or offload a stock by a redistribution of it on an intra-market basis. As of 1990 this arrangement is available only to designated GEMMs although it is always possible that other participants could be allowed to make use of the IDB facility at some future date. This seems unlikely and would be resisted at present as the profitability of the GEMMs has been under pressure and allowing others (fair weather dealers) to join the IDB system would divert turnover away from the committed GEMMs with further deleterious effects on their profits.

Money Brokers

An enlarged number of Money Brokers, nine in all, enhance the liquidity of the market by operating in a similar fashion to their activities prior to Big Bang. The lending of stock and/or money as required by the market maker provides a second layer to the market which enhances its liquidity. In return for this function the money brokers carry the status of approved borrowers and lenders which gives them exemption from possible Capital Gains Tax which may arise out of their activity. Supervision is carried out by the Bank of England.

Evaluating the New Structure

The first point to note is that it has proved difficult for participants to make profits. This partly reflects the increased competition but also relates to the changed environment within which the market is forced to operate.

Dealers in the gilt-edged market make profits in three possible ways:

1. By the difference between 'bid and offer' prices which they quote when buying and selling stock;
2. By charging commissions on their sales;

3. Finally by 'taking a position' in particular stocks depending on which
    way they feel the market might move. This of course is the most
    speculative of ways of making profits and can be particularly dangerous
    if market movements are misjudged.

Cumulative gross losses across the whole market were estimated to be
approximately £190m over the period 1986–8 (Bank of England, Feb. 1989).
As a result there has been a steady stream of withdrawals from market
making and the number of GEMMs has fallen below twenty. The position
may well have stabilised by the end of 1989 as aggregate operating losses for
market making were only £12m and this figure included the results of firms
which had pulled out of the market during that year.

A number of reasons can be adduced to explain the contraction: the new
structure is considerably more costly than previous arrangements (costs were
put at £150m v. £15m) partly as a result of the over-optimistic expansion of
capacity. On the revenue side the greater degree of competition has had a
dramatic impact. Prior to Big Bang average commission on institutional
business was between 0.05% (shorts) and 0.08% (mediums and longs)
whereas since then most activity conducted on behalf of the institutions
takes place on a net basis ie without commission. This pressure on
commissions was expected of course while dealing spreads have narrowed
and as a result the Bank of England estimated overall reductions in dealing
costs to be between 56% and 72%.

In addition the fall in the general level of turnover and activity in the
market as a whole has put further pressure on all concerned. Indeed it should
be pointed out that in 1988 and 1989 nearly half of all turnover reported in
gilts took place on an intra-market basis. If these trends were to continue
market makers would find that less profits would accrue from margins
earned via dealing with their clients and they would be forced to rely on
position taking in particular stocks. In other words if business remains thin
then the dealers may resort to a more speculative policy than may have been
the case hitherto. Thus it would come as no surprise to see further
withdrawals.

A further problem for the gilt-edged market has been the turnround in the
government's finances. The move into considerable budgetary surplus has
meant that there has been a dearth of gilt-edged while the authorities enjoyed
a Public Sector Debt Repayment (PSDR).[6] A budget surplus in the region
of £14billion (1988–9) which was fully funded implies that the Bank became
a net buyer of gilts thereby reducing the range of products available to the
market makers. This has had a negative impact on what was the more
profitable side of the business – new issues – and consequently depressed
potential profits further. In addition the policy of government appears to be
one of reducing the average maturity of outstanding debt by operating in the
long end of the maturity spectrum. As a result this has tended to invert the

yield curve. In late 1989 the yield on medium and high coupon bonds was more than 1.3% (130 basis points) below that on short dated gilts – the result of buying longer dated gilts while increasing short-term interest rates.

If budget surpluses continue to be a common feature of UK finances while a strategy of redemptions in the longer end of the maturity structure is maintained, it is possible that the investing institutions will be driven toward foreign and Euromarkets in order to assuage their appetite for long dated fixed interest securities. On the other hand the situation may lead to the revival of the *domestic* bond market. If the government is no longer a net borrower in the markets then the arguments which surfaced in the 1970s about the public sector 'crowding out' private borrowers will no longer apply and there is more room for high quality corporate borrowers. Corporate debt is however unlikely to prove a good substitute for the high credit quality and deep liquidity market in gilts.

In any case a continued surplus is improbable – it has been artificially boosted by privatisation proceeds which will naturally diminish and a recession in the economy would rapidly drive the fiscal surplus into deficit.

Local Authority Issues

Local authorities in the UK issue bonds which have a maturity of just over a year (one year and six days) termed 'yearlings'. Minimum denominations of £1000 are normally the rule. These carry a fixed semi-annual coupon set so that the yield is generally in excess of that currently available on gilt-edged. There are also longer dated local authority stocks offering a fixed semi-annual coupon and running through the maturity spectrum in a similar way to gilt-edged (ie shorts, mediums, longs and irredeemables).

International Bonds

Issues of sterling denominated Eurobonds have increased dramatically in the 1980s from only £500m in 1984 to nearly £17billion in 1988 when they accounted for 13% of new Euromarket issues. The increased activity came about as a result of several factors. For example the 1984 Finance Act made it possible for UK companies to pay coupons on Eurobonds without deduction of withholding tax. Previously a British company wanting to issue Eurobonds without deduction of tax on the coupon at source had to operate through offshore subsidiaries and this made for a more cumbersome procedure. In addition however customer demand for sterling Eurobonds was stimulated by foreign perception of the state of the UK economy and the performance of the pound. By 1989 however the Euro-Sterling market was no longer in such favour and new issues barely reached two thirds of the previous year's volume.

There are also Bulldog bonds – Sterling denominated debt raised in the UK by foreign borrowers. This market has been tapped by a variety of issuers: governments, supranationals and corporates but on the whole tends to be dominated by sovereign borrowers. However the market remains relatively small with only £4billion outstanding and in 1988–9 only some £435m appeared as new issues (*Euromoney*, Jan. 1990). Like gilts they pay a semi-annual coupon but they are similar to Eurobonds in so far as they are bearer bonds.

7 THE BOND MARKET IN THE USA

The market for debt in the United States is extremely large, active and heterogeneous. It encompasses various sorts of issuers:

o The federal authorities issue Treasury notes and bonds directly and also indirectly by guaranteeing bonds issued by federal agencies such as the Federal National Mortgage Association or the Government National Mortgage Association;
o Other tiers of local government ie state and municipal authorities and even school districts issue various types of debt such as general obligation bonds, revenue bonds, industrial revenue bonds and the like;
o The corporate sector issues a wide range of both short and long term debt on an active basis – Commercial Paper, Medium Term Notes and long dated bonds;
o Finally there are foreign issuers which issue 'Yankee' bonds as a major alternative to issuing dollar denominated Eurobonds.

Federal Securities

The market for US Treasury securities is the largest and most liquid market for government debt in the world. Table 3.3 gives some indication of recent levels of transactions on a daily basis.

TABLE 3.3   US Government Securities – dealers' transactions* (average daily turnover $m), 1986–9

1986	95 444
1987	110 050
1988	101 624
1989	121 453

* Measured as both sales and purchases.
Federal Reserve Bulletin, 1989.

Short dated bills (those with less than a year to maturity) comprise between 30 to 35% of the total, the rest is accounted for by Treasury notes and bonds.

The market has been fuelled in the 1980s by the massive budget deficits which have characterised US public finances. Federal debt was some $530 billion in 1975 and by 1989 had grown to $2684 billion with a further $514 billion in contingent liabilities as a result of the government acting as guarantor to the debt issued by a variety of federal agencies. Treasury notes are simply coupon bearing bonds with maturities between one and ten years while Treasury bonds – T-bonds, as they are colloquially called, have maturities of between 10 and 30 years.

Prices are quoted as a percentage of par with a nominal value of $1000 – thus a quote of 98 implies an actual price of $980. In addition unlike ordinary shares, T-bonds are normally traded in fractions of thirty-seconds (on occasion sixty–fourths) rather than eighths.

The Treasury bond market can be thought of as comprising two layers:

o A regulated primary market consisting of approximately 40 primary dealerships regulated in the first instance by the Federal Reserve Board;[7]
o A larger less closely supervised set of secondary dealerships which trade bonds on an OTC basis to end investors.

The Federal Reserve Board[7] regulates the market for T-bonds – setting trading standards and imposing capital requirements. In addition it organises new issues on behalf of the US government: the normal process is to offer bonds to primary dealers on an auction basis.

Most primary dealerships are American but foreign houses have also established a presence, most recently the Japanese. A crucial feature of the market and one which was adopted for the UK gilts market is the role of inter-dealer brokers. In 1989 some six brokers fulfilled this role (Bollenbacher, 1988). In effect this is an intra-market device which allows a market maker to restructure his portfolio by anonymous bids and/or offers. Anonymity is important as no dealer wishes to convey too much information about the position of the firm's book to other market makers.

As of the time of writing there is an extensive investigation of the structure and operation of the primary market being carried out by Congress's General Accounting Office which is likely to open the market up still further.

Federal Agency Debt

Essentially this arises from bodies appointed by the US government which authorises them to issue bonds in order to attract capital to carry out specific tasks. Some issuers such as the Department of Defense, the Tennessee Valley Authority or the Federal Housing Administration are part of the apparatus of government while others such as the Student Loans Marketing Association are federally 'sponsored'. Where agencies are part of the government their paper carries the usual 'full faith and credit' of the federal authorities but where they are private 'sponsored' organisations the debt issued carries an *implicit* guarantee with regard to their interest and principal.

Possibly the most well known agencies are to be found in the housing sector – the Federal Home Loan Banks for example had paper outstanding of nearly $140 billion in 1989 while the Federal National Mortgage Association has outstandings of over $100 billion. The securities issued by federal agencies are long established, and well known in the US by retail as well as institutional investors.[8]

There has however been a proliferation of these agencies: they are also found in the agricultural sector, in bank deposit insurance and in the area of trade finance. More recently because of the major crisis facing American Savings and Loan Associations (the equivalent of UK building societies) the federal authorities have established a new body – the Resolution Trust – charged with trying to solve the problems of the troubled 'Thrifts'. It is uncertain what the precise extent of this commitment will be (BIS, 1989) but some estimates suggest that it may involve taking over and liquidating up to $100 billion worth of properties by the mid 1990s. If so this constitutes another major factor in quasi-government borrowing.

Municipal and State Borrowers

Local government borrowers – state and municipal authorities – issue fixed interest securities on a very large scale in the US market. They are highly favoured as they offer considerable tax advantages eg the coupon is exempt from federal income tax and in addition they are free of local income tax to residents of the issuing authority. The net of tax yield therefore makes these securities very attractive to higher rate tax payers. This frequently means that the coupon on these bonds can be as much as 2% (200 basis points) less than debt carrying a similar degree of credit risk. The market therefore is highly competitive and the annual rate of issuance has grown enormously. From approximately $48 billion in 1980 it had grown to some $214 billion by 1985 and fallen back approximately $108 billion by the end of the decade (*Federal Reserve Bulletin*, 1989). Total outstandings were in excess of $1200 billion by 1989.

Corporate Issuers

Unlike the UK's corporate bond market the US market has been extraordinarily active in the 1980s. With the growth of the so-called 'junk bond' phenomenon and the use of debt to pursue highly leveraged buy-outs, in the view of some observers the market may have been hyper-active! The value of public offerings of new issues quadrupled between 1980 and 1988 from $41 billion to $222 billion – and these figures do not include private placements – which comprised for example a further $90 billion in 1988. Bond issuance was particularly intense in the mid 1980s when takeovers financed by debt were a favoured technique. Unlike the UK, corporate issuers in the US appear to have favoured debt finance over equities with over 80% of new issues being accounted for by bonds (see Table 3.4).

TABLE 3.4 **New security issues – US corporations, 1987–9 ($ millions)**

	All Issues	Bonds	Common Stock
1986	423 726	355 293	68 433
1987	392 156	325 648	66 508
1988	264 987	222 531	42 456

Federal Reserve Bulletin, 1989.

Corporate issues are supervised by the Securities and Exchange Commission and while bonds are generally exchange listed they tend to be traded rather more in the Over the Counter market as is the case with federal and municipal bonds. In addition the use of formal rating procedures by Moody's Investor Services and Standard and Poor's Corporation has given the bond market a greater degree of efficiency and transparency than is often the case in OTC markets.

Table 3.5 below gives an example of the rating formulations used by S&P's and Moody's.

These rating categories imply the following:

Prefix A:
Triple 'A' is a first class borrower with undoubted capacity to pay principal and interest. Minor weakness is indicated by AA. A single 'A' credit by itself implies undoubted capacity but nonetheless a degree of susceptibility to adverse changes in circumstances.

Prefix B:
Varies from a strong capacity to pay principal and interest down to weak capacity to pay. Often relates to young companies or to established companies in declining industries. BB implies a low degree of speculative risk while CC implies the highest. Bonds with BB ratings and below are termed 'junk bonds'.

Prefix C:
This implies serious financial difficulty for example no interest is being paid on income bonds.

Prefix D:
This prefix means that the debt is currently in default: payment of interest and/or repayment of principal are in arrears.

TABLE 3.5   Bond rating criteria of major agencies

Standard & Poor's	Moody's	Commentary
AAA	Aaa	Highest quality debt: capacity to repay interest and principal undoubted.
AA	Aa	High quality debt: differs marginally from highest grade.
A	A	High medium debt: strong repayment capacity but may be affected by adverse economic conditions.
BBB	Baa	Medium grade debt: greater possibility of suffering from adverse economic conditions.
BB	Ba	Lower medium grade debt but higher risk of exposure to adverse conditions.
B, CCC, CC	B, Caa, Ca	Debt receiving these grades is speculative with regard to both payment of interest and principal.
C	C	Income bonds where payment of interest is suspended.
D	D	Debt in default: payment of interest and principal in arrears.
NR		No ranking.

Rating is an expensive and time consuming process: the agency conducts a thorough investigation of the borrower and has access to confidential information in forming its view. Ratings may be changed up or down periodically with significant consequences for the issuer and for the price of existing bonds. The factors which help to determine a bond rating will include earnings and balance sheet data, liquidity, the characteristics of the industry and the rank of the borrower in the relevant industry.

The use of formal rating agencies distinguished the US corporate market from other world bond markets for many years although these markets are now developing similar procedures. The sheer size and diversity of the US market made credit rating more urgent in the United States.[9] In addition many institutions – pension funds, college trusts and so on – were restricted to investing in high quality corporate debt. This is termed *investment grade* paper and it is normally triple A or double A rated paper.

The yields on corporate issues, even that of the highest quality, tend to be greater than those on sovereign debt to compensate for the differences in credit risk. The 1980s however saw the growth of an extraordinarily active market in what were variously termed 'high yield', 'below investment grade' or more simply 'junk' bonds. On the rating criteria employed by Standard and Poor's these were BB and below and that of Moody's placed them below Baa.

'Junk' bonds were marked by offering substantial margins (200/250 basis points) above the yield on Treasury bonds and it was argued by those responsible for marketing the bonds that the actual rate of default was in fact less than such a considerable yield margin might suggest. Hence investors were apparently being over compensated for the degree of risk they were being asked to accept. It has been suggested however that in some cases default rates may have been mitigated by rather arcane practices (Bruck 1988).

An accumulation of factors severely damaged the general public's perception of the quality of high yield bonds. First the bankruptcy of a steel producer LTV in 1986 undermined the market and the number of new issues declined as a consequence. Then in the wake of the Ivan Boesky insider trading scandal, the SEC launched a series of investigations into the investment house, Drexel Burnham Lambert, which had been chiefly responsible for the growth of the market. When in 1989 the refusal by Japanese banks to underwrite debt issued as part of an LBO of United Airlines was quickly followed by a default on high yield paper by Campeau Corporation, an even more severe blow was dealt to market confidence. Eventually in February 1990 Drexel Burnham Lambert itself collapsed and the junk bond market was effectively declared moribund.

Yankee Bonds

These have been the traditional way in which non-US sovereign and corporate borrowers have raised dollar borrowings. The emergence of the Euromarkets in the 1960s offered a competitive source of dollar finance. Since the lifting of Interest Equalisation Tax in 1974 issues recovered somewhat and annual volume is in the region of $6 billion to $7 billion. There is a tendency for Yankee bonds to offer a yield margin above that of domestic issuers with the same sort of credit rating. This simply reflects the fact of their foreign status *vis-à-vis* domestic issuers.

8 THE JAPANESE BOND MARKET

The bond market in Japan is the second largest in the world. Issuing activity tends to be dominated by central and local government along with municipal authorities which account for over 90% of new business – corporate issues account for less than 5%. This was not always the case as there was no market in government bonds prior to 1965. As in the USA trading for the vast majority of bonds takes place via Over the Counter dealers.

Issues in the primary market have traditionally been highly regulated with a tight syndicate of the major securities houses and banks being responsible for underwriting and selling the bonds to end investors. In the case of government guaranteed local authority and public corporation issues financial institutions played a rather larger role than the securities houses. Eventually when the central government began to issue its own long term paper in 1966 banks, financial institutions (such as insurance companies) and securities houses were the main subscribers but only the latter were allowed to sell their allocation to the public. Syndication still remains the method for the issue of bonds although there is pressure to introduce a more competitive structure as deregulation continues and as foreign securities houses exert pressure to invade the underwriting cartel.

The secondary market in bonds is very active and has undoubtedly been helped by the development of what is termed 'gensaki' markets ie repurchase or 'repo' markets. Here securities houses suffering from liquidity shortages use their bond inventory to raise funds by selling bonds to non-financial companies with temporary cash surpluses conditional on an agreement to repurchase them with an implicit rate of return. In a sense the 'repo' market acts as an interface between the money market and the bond market and it improves the overall liquidity of the secondary market.

In Japan, unlike the US and the UK, non-residents face a considerable tax deduction of 20% on interest at source. This does not apply to zero coupon bonds which are issued at a discount: in this case the yield accrues as capital gain which is not subject to tax.

Central Government Bonds

As pointed out above until 1965 there was no market in government bonds. Increasing fiscal deficits in the late 1960s and the 1970s as a consequence of oil price increases however led to the issue of various maturities of state debt. There are short term – two to four year bonds, medium term paper of up to ten years and finally long dated bonds of twenty year maturities.

Government bonds normally come in denominations of 100 000 Yen and offer semi-annual coupon rates. Some of the medium term paper is non-coupon bearing and simply sold at a discount so that the yield accrues via capital gain.

Local Authority Bonds

These are issued by district and urban authorities. They comprise only a small proportion of bonds in issue at less than 5%. They are similar to government securities in that they are straight bonds with a maturity structure of one to ten years paying a semi-annual coupon. While they carry the faith and credit of the government as in the UK and the USA they nevertheless normally trade at a minor yield spread over state bonds. They are quoted in minimum denominations of 100 000 Yen.

Other Government Guaranteed Bonds

There are a set of bonds issued by public corporations, government sponsored bodies and quasi-governmental organisations which carry state guarantees as to payment of interest and principal. Some private organisations also have this privilege. Among the more significant are the long term credit banks such as the Nippon Credit Bank and the Industrial Bank of Japan. These are some of the largest banks in the world and were established to channel low interest long term loans to Japanese business. They are allowed to issue five to fifteen year bonds.

As these bonds are guaranteed by the state the banks concerned and similar organisations are able to raise capital at extremely fine rates. This has been a major advantage to Japanese industry which has been able to obtain long term loans via the banking system at low rates of interest.[10]

Corporate Issues

The long term credit banks also issue bonds secured against their own assets and where they do not carry a government guarantee they are simply another species of corporate bond. The longer dated issues tend to offer semi-annual coupons but shorter maturities ie five years or less can be issued at a discount.

Corporate bonds with longer maturities than five years are coupon bearing while those with a shorter maturity of five years or less are normally deep discount bonds. This obviates the payment of withholding tax on the yield which comes as capital gain rather than interest. Corporate issues also come in minimum denominations of 50 000 yen. As they do not carry any state backing they tend to trade at yield margins above government issues.

Except for the activity of the long term credit banks the corporate bond market in Japan was moribund until the mid to late 1980s. This partly reflected the ability of Japanese corporate issuers to achieve cheap funds in the Euromarkets, where because of the performance of the equity market, bonds with convertible options or warrants attached were particularly welcome. It also reflected the cumbersome regulations and procedures surrounding the issue of new bonds in Japan itself as a result of Article 65 of the Securities and Exchange Law. For example this required the use of one of the major securities houses to underwrite bond issues and in addition all but a small number of potential issuers had to obtain collateral guarantees from a bank – the top 70 most creditworthy corporates were exempted and could issue debt without collateral. In addition the registering and filing of prospectuses was a lengthy process which led to a queue to tap the market.

This again contrasts sharply with the Eurobond market where issuing procedures are simpler and faster. The net effect of the restrictions was to make bond issues more expensive than other modes of raising finance and to lead to an underdevelopment of the domestic bond market.

However progressive deregulation of the bond market is making it easier and cheaper to use. After 1987 the number of bond issuers not needing bank guarantees was raised to 170 and some 330 were allowed to issue convertible bonds without arranging collateral. Regulation of the bond market was also relaxed by raising the ceiling on the value of issues undertaken via private placement from 2 billion Yen to 10 billion Yen.

International Bonds

There are two varieties of foreign bonds which are issued in Japan. The first are 'samurai' bonds ie Yen denominated bonds issued by a foreign borrower. These have been allowed since the early 1970s but it was not until the 1980s that the market really developed strongly. In the mid-1980s the 'shogun' bond market was also opened. These are bonds issued in Japan but denominated in foreign currencies. For the most part this has been confined to supranational and sovereign issuers but there have also been a small number of corporate borrowers.

This reflects the extraordinarily strong balance of payments position and the accumulation of foreign currency in Japan since the 1970s.

NOTES

1. In the early 1980s just such a view was taken of bonds issued by the Mexican government – United Mexican States 16.5% 2008. The threat to renege on international debt owed to the Western banking system resulted in the bonds falling to less than half of their nominal value. However with the resolution of its debt problem the bonds were reassessed and stood at a premium of between 15-20% to their nominal value by 1989.
2. Some analysts prefer to use *Yield Ratios* which are obtained by dividing one yield by another. The resulting figure is then monitored to see if the ratio is moving outside its historical boundaries.
3. Yields on zero coupon bonds are found from the following formula

$$\text{Yield} = \sqrt[n]{\frac{100}{\text{Purchase Price}}} - 1$$

   where n = the number of years to maturity.
4. Very large issue sizes are commonplace – of the 111 various stocks quoted in January 1989 some 72 (approximately two-thirds) were for £1000m or more while some 13 are in issue sizes in excess of £2000m.
5. For an excellent and more detailed discussion of the operation of policy in the gilt-edged market during this period see Thomas (1986).

6. Indeed the change in government finances led to some interesting and premature speculation about the possible disappearance of the national debt altogether, an outcome which would imply the demise of the gilt-edged market entirely (*The Economist*, Jan. 14–20 1989). This seems an unlikely train of events as the government would be eliminating a useful device for mixing the way in which it manages the economy: an institution such as the gilt-edged market cannot simply be put together and unscrambled at the whim of the public accounts!

7. The Federal Reserve Board is the central bank in the US banking system. It has greater autonomy than for example the Bank of England but has a rather looser organisational structure.

8. Indeed the bonds of some of these bodies are given fairly whimsical names thus the Federal National Mortgage Association issues bonds known as 'Fanny Maes' and the Student Loans Marketing Association issues 'Sally Maes'.

9. Restrictions on inter-state banking made the financing of investment via banks more difficult for large corporates in the United States and made for greater reliance on the public capital markets.

10. The contrast with the United Kingdom and the United States is interesting here. In the UK and the US the traditional role of banks has been that of extending short to medium term credit facilities to industry. At the same time house purchase is arranged via specialist institutions Building Societies (UK) or Savings and Loans Associations (US) using long term finance – twenty-five to thirty years. It is also treated very liberally in fiscal terms. This appears to be the converse of the Japanese approach and may explain what some would regard as over-investment in housing and under-investment in industry in the UK and the US compared with Japan.

4   International Bond Markets

1   INTRODUCTION

International bond markets bring together borrowers and investors from different national jurisdictions. There are two major varieties of international market:

(i)   Those where a borrower domiciled in one country issues a bond in the capital market of another country – this is conventionally termed a 'foreign' bond;

(ii)   Those where the borrower issues a bond simultaneously in a number of different countries and therefore taps a variety of international investors – this is termed a 'Eurobond'.

Foreign Bonds

Examples of a foreign bond would be where a sovereign borrower such as Denmark decides to issue a bond denominated in sterling in the London market, a supranational agency such as the World Bank issues a dollar bond in New York or a corporate borrower such as BP arranges the issue of a yen-denominated bond in Tokyo. In each case the bond offering is subject to the fiscal, legal and regulatory regime operative in the country of issue. Thus listing and registration requirements, the nature of the prospectus and supporting documentation and perhaps the timing of the issue will all depend upon the practices of the specific capital market which is being tapped.

The vast majority of national capital markets are subject to a variety of controls and do not allow foreign issuers ready access. Of those that do permit such access among the most important are New York, Tokyo, Switzerland, the UK and the Netherlands. Foreign bonds issued in these markets have developed their own nicknames – Yankees, Samurai, Bulldogs, Rembrandts and so on.

Eurobonds

Eurobonds differ from foreign bonds in a number of major respects but the most significant feature is the fact that they are bonds issued simultaneously

114

in many different financial centres. Thus a corporate borrower might make a bond offering denominated in dollars which is placed with Japanese, Swiss, German, American and British financial institutions. Nor does the list of possible subscribers stop there; it may extend to bank trustee departments, insurance companies, pension funds and retail investors in many other countries.

Thus the expression 'Eurobonds' no longer simply applies to issues placed in Europe but has become a generic term to cover any issue which mobilises funds simultaneously from various parts of the world economy.

The Euromarkets are not subject to any specific regulatory framework – unlike domestic capital markets which have been the subject of tight control since the 1930s. As a consequence the Euromarkets have led the way in integrating world financial markets and have been able to take advantage of continuous 'product' innovation in terms of offering procedures and bond features.

There is no single integrated market but a series of markets which overlap and to some extent are able to substitute for each other at the margin. Describing the role and functioning of these markets has therefore become quite difficult: not only have the various 'instruments' by which lending and borrowing are effected become more complex but the rate at which innovative financing techniques are introduced gives any description of the markets an historical flavour.

2   ORIGINS OF THE EUROBOND MARKET

Prior to the emergence of international capital markets corporate organisations and sovereign states were confined to borrowing in national capital markets. If for example ICI wished to take on more debt but did not wish to do so via bank finance it could issue debentures and/or other loan stock in the London market. However if the company required dollars rather than sterling this could have been done by issuing debt instruments in New York.

In either case the issue would have been subject to local regulations and listing requirements, covering matters such as documentation, prospectus information, accounting procedures etc. In addition there were substantial differences in terms of commission and fees for managing an issue. Finally tax regimes and investor preference were different in each case. Hence a decision to raise capital in a foreign market could be both an expensive and a time consuming affair particularly where the borrower's name may be relatively unknown. Until the 1960's therefore a company (even a very large company such as ICI) wishing to raise loan capital faced a narrow range of possibilities.

The Eurobond market came into existence nearly thirty years ago: it arose from the earlier development of the *Euro-Dollar* market. This was itself a result of balance of payments deficits run by the United States in the 1950s and 1960s. Initially the US payments deficit was unproblematical: during the process of post-war reconstruction and recovery the demand for dollars to finance growing levels of trade was considerable. Dollars were required not merely to finance trade directly with the United States but also between third parties as the dollar was universally accepted as a means of payment.[1]

It is a short step from a currency being accepted as the universal medium of exchange to becoming a store of value ie from being a means of facilitating transactions to becoming an asset – a way of holding wealth. Governments and larger corporate organisations initially held *dollar balances* to finance international trade and as part of their international reserve assets. Furthermore it was also quite natural to think in terms of holding such balances in the US thereby obtaining a rate of interest.

In the late 1950s however it also became common to hold such balances on deposit with banks within Europe. It has been argued by some commentators that this was initiated by the Soviet Union: there was some fear on the part of the USSR that its dollar balances held on deposit within the US might be frozen so that they would be unable to use them. Hence rather than leave them on deposit in the US they placed them with London banks.

London's role in the development of the Euromarkets was crucial: despite the small size of the UK economy London was at the time and still remains the largest centre for foreign exchange activity in the world. In addition there were a number of highly innovative securities houses with an international orientation and, perhaps most important of all, domestic regulation of securities markets was light compared with European regulatory regimes. Hence London also became the focal point for the development of the Eurobond market. Despite the emergence of other financial centres as rivals London remains the major location for Eurobond business as evidenced by Table 4.1.

As the balances were denominated in dollars, they would not have any impact on the UK's domestic supply of money until such time as they were converted into sterling: the crucial feature of the deposits then was that they did not count as far as the banks' reserve asset base was defined and *therefore such deposits were not subject to domestic banking regulations.* Banks were not required to maintain a minimum level of reserves against loans and advances denominated in such dollars. (Of course they may well have done so for prudential reasons but this would essentially be a commercial decision.) The distinguishing feature of the Eurodollar market therefore was its freedom from domestic regulation.

Initially the dollars were confined to short term lending in the inter-bank market but with the continuing growth of the deposits they were lent out for longer and longer periods. The material base for a securities market was therefore being established from the supply side all that was required was that some financial institution organise borrowers from the demand side to

TABLE 4.1 Location of members of the Association of International Bond Dealers, by centre

	All firms	Reporting dealers*
UK	209	80
Switzerland	152	2
Luxembourg	67	6
Germany	66	1
Hong Kong	45	1
Netherlands	55	3
US	40	–
France	44	7
Belgium	37	3
Other	196	11
Total	911	114

*Those reporting prices on a daily basis.
Bank of England Quarterly Bulletin, Nov. 1989.

tap this potential. This was accomplished by Warburg's, the British merchant bank which lead-managed the first Eurodollar bond issue for Autostrade, the operator of toll motorways in Italy. The bonds carried a fixed coupon with a fifteen year maturity and were denominated in units of $250 although denominations of $1000 and more are now more common. The bonds were issued in bearer form and the coupon was free of withholding tax. These conditions still pertain and it has even become commonplace for the issuer to assure the investor that the coupon will be adjusted upward if a withholding tax is introduced. In latter years the market has become the province of institutional investors although periodically retail investors are drawn into the market by top class names and attractively packaged issues.

The evolution of the Eurobond market was given its largest single boost when in 1963, the Kennedy administration, worried about the continuing payments deficits, imposed an Interest Equalisation Tax (IET) on bonds issued by foreign borrowers in the US market. Until that time New York had proved a highly competitive source of capital and 'Yankee' bonds had become a major form of international borrowing. The effect of the IET however was to make debt issues in the US more expensive and to improve the competitiveness of European capital markets. Further impetus was imparted by the Johnson administration which attempted to staunch the outflow of dollars by encouraging US firms to finance their foreign investment abroad rather than via the domestic market. Many American multinational companies turned to the Euromarkets thereby increasing the range and quality of potential borrowers.

While these measures stimulated the demand for Eurodollar financing, the US authorities had also inadvertently added to the supply. A fairly obscure device imposed on the banking system in the 1930s by the Federal Reserve Board – Regulation Q – placed ceilings on the interest rates banks could offer on dollar deposits in the US. Dollar deposits in Europe however were not subject to this regulation and hence European banks and the subsidiaries of American banks in Europe were able to offer higher deposit rates to attract dollars.

The Eurobond market has grown enormously over the past twenty seven years and despite periodic shocks the market has displayed considerable resilience.

Table 4.2 illustrates the growth in the value of bonds issued annually over an extended period. While it shows quite clearly the spectacular growth and overall size of the market we should not leave the impression that it has been steady uninterrupted process. Setbacks have occurred periodically as events such as the oil crises in the 1970s, the international debt crisis of the 1980s and the collapse of equity markets in 1987 have all depressed issuing activity.

TABLE 4.2   Growth of the Eurobond market, 1963–89

	Annual Issuance ($m)
1963	147
1968	3085
1973	3709
1978	12 009
1983	47 573
1985	163 800
1986	221 700
1987	177 100
1988	225 400
1989	258 900

Euromoney, 1990.

It should be emphasised that the market's difficulties, perhaps with the exception of the Perpetual Notes crisis in the mid 1980s (*The Economist*, May 16 1986) have mainly arisen from external shocks. It has been estimated that over the period 1963–84 only about $800 million out of a total of approximately $550 billion Eurobonds were subject to servicing problems ie some 0.0015% (Kerr, 1984). While further minor problems were reported in 1987 (*Bank of England Quarterly Bulletin*, May 1987, p. 236) it would seem that the Eurobond market has in fact been more successful in terms of risk assessment than has been the case in other segments of the international financial system. This is particularly true when compared with bank finance:

the syndicated credits market experienced major problems in the recovery of debt from underdeveloped and Eastern European countries in the early to mid 1980s and there was a fierce contraction in activity although as Table 4.3 indicates there has been a substantial recovery since.

TABLE 4.3 International syndicated credits, 1980–9 ($ billion)

1980	82.8	1985	19.0
1981	100.9	1986	29.6
1982	88.2	1987	88.7
1983	38.0	1988	101.8
1984	30.1	1989	149.0

Bank of England Quarterly Bulletin, Nov. 1989.

While the US dollar was the currency on which the foundations of the international bond markets were established it has since been joined by over sixteen other currencies. The other major international bond sectors are: Swiss francs, German marks, Japanese yen, UK pounds, Dutch guilders and Canadian dollars. In addition Eurobonds have been denominated in French francs, Australian, New Zealand and Hong Kong dollars, Danish, Swedish and Norwegian kroner, Austrian schillings and a number of Middle Eastern currencies. Bonds have also been issued in composite currencies such as the European Currency Unit (ECU). Tables 4.4(a) and 4.4(b) indicate issuing activity and outstandings of international bonds in various currencies in the late 1980s.

The US dollar clearly remains the most significant of the various currencies however: in only three years since 1963 has it accounted for less than half the value of bond issues (1978 at 46%; 1987 36% and 1988 37%). For much of the period up to 60% to 80% of bond issues were dollar denominated and by the end of 1988 approximately 65% of the cumulative amount had been issued in dollars.

The dominant position of the dollar seems to be waning however as is evidenced from the pattern of recent issuing activity. Thus for example by 1990 dollar issues accounted for less than 30% of the total volume of issuance activity. Although the dollar remains the most widely used medium of exchange and unit of account in international transactions, there are two formidable problems militating against it: the size and persistence of the US balance of payments deficit and the fact that in the 1980s the United States became the world's largest debtor nation (at the end of 1988 the net external assets of the US were estimated at *minus* $544b (Bank of England, 1989)). In effect the system is in the process of change from the dollar led standard of two decades ago to a multicurrency standard with investors switching from one to the other market as they seek to escape the effects of adverse currency movements.

TABLE 4.4(a) Currency composition of new issues in the International Bond Market, 1985–8

	Gross New Issues $billion			
	1985	1986	1987	1988
US dollar	98.6 (60%)	121.6 (55%)	63.3 (36%)	83.0 (37%)
Swiss franc	14.6	23.1	24.1	26.7
Japanese yen	12.3	22.3	24.8	20.4
German mark	11.3	16.3	15.3	23.6
UK pound	6.4	11.4	15.2	23.4
ECU	7.5	7.0	7.6	11.3
Other	13.1	20.0	26.8	37.0
Total	163.8	221.7	177.1	225.4

Bank for International Settlements, *Annual Report*, 1989.

TABLE 4.4(b) Currency composition of the International Bond Market – Outstanding Stocks, 1982–8

	1982	1985	1987	1988
US dollar	145.5 (56%)	314.8 (57%)	425.8 (43%)	469.9 (43%)
Swiss franc	42.6	78.6	157.8	139.3
Japanese yen	16.5	42.8	122.2	132.7
German mark	31.4	50.6	99.2	103.7
UK pound	4.6	19.1	54.8	73.4
ECU	3.2	16.5	41.0	46.5
Other	15.3	34.3	90.0	119.9
Total	259.1	556.7	990.8	1 085.4

Bank for International Settlements, *Annual Report*, 1989.

3 THE PRIMARY MARKET

This section of the market deals with the issue of new bonds. Issues are handled or lead-managed by a major international securities house such as Crédit Suisse First Boston, Deutsche Bank or more recently Nomura Securities. The absence of major UK institutions except Warburg's (ranked 14 in lead managing issues in 1989 see Table 4.8 below) is explained by the fact that while legal and financial expertise was important in the early days this advantage was soon overcome and it became more important to have *placing power* – the ability to sell a new issue to a large client base.

New issues involve a detailed procedure which covers matters such as drawing up the prospectus, credit rating the borrower, assessing the coupon, determining the issue price, setting up the network of underwriters and/or selling group members etc. The primary market is rather less demanding in terms of issue requirements than national capital markets which have traditionally seen themselves as the guardian of the less sophisticated retail investor. Euromarket dealers however see themselves as serving a wholesale market of professional investors. As a consequence, users of the market tend to have a more 'robust' view of investor protection.[2]

The market has acquired a reputation for speed and efficiency which has given it a competitive edge when compared with domestic bond markets. For example it is not unusual for an issue to go ahead and for prospectus details to be completed later. In addition the presence of very large securities houses has meant that issuing practices have changed over the years. Initially the lead manager put together a syndicate of underwriters and a selling group which would agree to take certain quantities of the bond and sell them to end investors. A fee would be charged to the borrower for each of these separate functions although clearly the underwriters might also comprise part of the selling group thereby receiving two sets of fees while the lead manager might appear in all three guises and receive the appropriate fees accordingly.

However the practice evolved where in many cases the lead manager short circuited the syndication procedure and took over the whole of the issue as a so-called 'bought deal' and then distributed tranches to the selling group. This guaranteed that the borrower could more easily time the offering and could also raise the capital on extremely fine terms because of the degree of competition for lead management mandates.

The fees involved in managing and underwriting Eurobond issues vary somewhat with the maturity of the bond – being higher for longer dated paper – and the credit status of the issuer (the 'name'). They are normally based on a percentage of the principal issued and are actually paid via *discounts* to the price. For example if a Eurobond with a face value of $1000 is issued at par, it will be described as issued at 100 (ie 100% of its nominal value). If it is reported as issued at 97.5% then it is below par and so on. However the proceeds which the issuer receives are not determined by the issue price. Instead the agreement might specify that the issuer on a seven year bond will receive 97.5% of the nominal value in which case the 2.5% ($25) discount represents the gross spread from which the various expenses and costs must be met. It also provides the margin from which the lead manager is able to offer discounts on the face value of the bond to underwriters and the selling group.

For example the following may represent the way the spread is allocated

Total

$1000 − $977.5 = $22.5   (2.25%)

Lead managers fee

$982.5 − $977.5 = $5

Underwriters' commission

$987.5 − $982.5 = $5

Selling commission

$1000 − $987.5 = $12.5

This fee structure assumes that the bond is in fact sold at par in the market. A major problem with the Eurobond markets in recent years is that it has been difficult for the lead manager to make sure that the bonds are indeed sold to the final investor at their par value. Given that the bonds are bearer securities there is little to prevent an underwriter or a member of the selling group from selling below par and thus reducing the total gross spread received by the underwriting group. If the bonds were registered securities as is the case in the US corporate market for example it would be simple to identify the 'offending' parties and to exclude them from future syndication.

The inability of Eurobond markets to maintain similar discipline in a large syndicate has meant that the pricing process has been highly uncertain and price stabilisation procedures have been developed by lead managers. This simply acts as a price support mechanism: it provides a bid price which builds in a floor below an issue which may be trading poorly. This effectively protects underwriters by establishing a calculable loss should they be unable to sell the issue: they can sell it back to the lead manager via a third party and protect their anonymity.

The fee structure in the primary market is *officially* set out in Table 4.5.

Table 4.5   Eurobond Issues – fee structure as a percentage of principal amount

Maturity (years)	3	5	7	10 +
Management fee	0.125/0.25	0.25/0.375	0.25/0.5	1.25/1.5
Underwriting commission	0.25	0.375	0.375/0.5	0.375/0.5
Selling commission	1.0/1.125	1.0/1.25	1.0/1.25	1.25/1.5
Total	1.375/1.625	1.625/2.0	1.625/2.25	2.875/3.5

However given the sharpening competition in international financial markets and the degree of overcapacity in the Euromarkets these fees and commissions have frequently not applied.

In 1989 however there were signs of the market moving back toward a tighter degree of control of offering practices: the technique of fixed price re-offering along the American model was used for a number of deals. Here the underwriting syndicate agrees to take the bonds and to sell them on to end investors at their face value without any further discounting of the price. This involves smaller syndicates and greater discipline in the selling group.

Determining the Yield

Clearly one of the most important features of any bond is the promise of a particular return or yield as *ceteris paribus* this is what makes the instrument attractive. As the yield is the outcome of the coupon and the price paid for the security they depend upon a number of features.

(i) The credit status of the issuer

This depends on the 'rating' given to the issuer. Sovereign borrowers and supranational bodies such as the World Bank or the European Investment Bank are given the highest rating and hence are able to borrow at the lowest yields. The novelty of the 'name' may also be important as the market appears to have a preference for well known and well established borrowers.

(ii) Maturity of the bond

Longer maturities tend to offer higher yields but this is not invariably the case as the yield curve may exhibit a hump toward the shorter end of the spectrum in which case longer dated paper may well offer lower yields.

(iii) Issue Size

The larger an issue is, the more of it in absolute terms is likely to be actively traded. If only a small amount of a given issue is traded then there exists a 'thin' market and considerable price changes are likely to occur in the secondary market. Issue size is perceived as likely to enhance the bond's liquidity in the secondary market hence lower yields may be obtained in the primary market.

(iv)   Currency of the bond

Currency instability induced by political factors, balance of payments difficulties, inflation and/or movements in relative interest rates will raise the yield that has to be offered to prospective investors.

(v)   Other features

The existence of particular features such as conversion options, warrants, early redemption etc will tend to affect the yield.

(vi)   Market conditions

The supply and demand for comparable issues will help to determine the yield. There have been instances where borrowers have issued too much paper and the market may be reluctant to absorb more unless it is offered a sharply increased yield.

The Rating Procedure

Credit rating is extremely important as it will affect the markets' perception of the issue and therefore influence the yield. While credit rating has been a long established part of the US investment scene its appearance in Europe has been relatively recent.

The two most widely known and respected rating agencies are both American – Standard & Poor's (S&P) and Moody's Investment Service – and have been recently (1987) joined by Euroratings based in London. National regulators in Japan, the UK and elsewhere have also begun to pay closer attention to rating criteria and this has led to a considerable growth in the activity of rating agencies (*The Banker*, July 1988).

Furthermore one would expect to see this continue: given the processes of *securitisation* (ie the packaging of debt into saleable instruments) and *disintermediation* (the tendency for borrowers and lenders to be in direct contact rather than via the banking mechanism) established lenders such as pension funds or insurance companies will rely on rating agencies more and more. The alternative is to develop in-house credit assessment facilities of the type usually confined to banks.

Institutional and retail investors therefore are guided in their investment decisions by the particular rating grade which a bond issue attracts. Hence the failure to achieve a given grading may result in a higher yield being required either via a higher coupon or by a discounted price.

Similarly any factors which lead to a re-rating of a particular borrower will effect the price of its paper. Thus in July 1989 the launching of a leveraged (debt financed) take-over bid for the UK conglomerate BAT led to a last minute decision to withdraw or 'pull' a scheduled $400 million Eurobond issue. This issue had been launched on June 6 and was due for completion on July 17 when the underwriters were to hand over funds to BAT. Despite a degree of opposition from the lead manager Crédit Suisse First Boston, BAT's management insisted on withdrawal as the price of the bond had fallen by some 5% after the announcement of the bid. Furthermore other BAT bonds experienced a fall in price.

The experience has been a salutary one and has made investors more conscious of the need to protect their investment via the use of more restrictive covenants. Instead of the simple 'negative pledge' which has been a common feature of most Eurobonds there is now a move toward more protective devices such as limiting the amount of debt (eg to no more than 1.5 times the company's capital and reserves) or the type of debt (eg not more than 40% to be secured against the company's assets). In the event of such covenants being breached the bond holders may be able to redeem their bonds at par (*The Treasurer*, Jul.–Aug. 1989).

See p14

It may be helpful to summarize the differences between Eurobonds and domestically issued bonds (see Table 4.6). While this comparison relates to the United Kingdom similar sorts of differences would be observed between Eurobonds and the American corporate bond market.

TABLE 4.6   Comparison of Eurobond and UK domestic bond markets

	Domestic Market	Eurobond Market
Instrument	Normally Registered	Normally bearer but option to be registered
Security/ Covenants	Often secured or with detailed restrictive covenants	Usually unsecured but carrying a negative pledge.
Tax	Coupon paid net of UK income tax	Coupon paid gross
Interest	Semi-annual payments	Normally annual
Issuing houses	UK merchant banks and stockbrokers	UK and overseas banks/ securities houses
Listing	London	Usually London or Luxembourg
Placing	Placed at a fixed price on a specific day	Placed over a period and at varying prices
Secondary market	London Stock Exchange day after issue	Over the Counter trading by issuing banks
Investors	Mainly domestic	Domestic and overseas

Bank of England Quarterly Bulletin, Feb. 1988, p.63.

As a matter of common practice Eurobonds are usually listed on either the London Stock Exchange or the Luxembourg Exchange. Despite this however secondary market trading is conducted via the Over the Counter market provided by major banks and securities houses.

4 THE SECONDARY MARKET

The secondary market is an important adjunct to the effective operation of the primary market because it is the vehicle by which liquidity is supposedly assured to the bond-holder. This is not to say that the primary market would not function but it is clearly less attractive to potential investors if a given bond has little or no prospect of offering a degree of liquidity after the new issue is complete.

The existence of a secondary market also enables the pricing of new bonds to be assessed according to yields on comparable 'seasoned' issues already trading. This is referred to as 'pricing off the secondary market'. As with the primary market in Eurobonds, there is no trading floor in the secondary market – it is an Over the Counter market – trading normally takes place via the telephone with confirmation via telex. There has been some pressure to move to a screen based system such as the NASDAQ/SEAQ system which is used in the United States and the UK but while there is an order matching system in operation called TRAX and dealers appear prepared to display indicative quotes they have been reluctant to display firm quotes. There are three major reasons for this reluctance to move toward a more transparent market:

(i) First it limits the discretion that traders may wish to retain for offering special terms to particular customers.

(ii) Second there is a reluctance on the part of larger houses to act as a buffer stock – 'using our liquidity'- for smaller fair weather dealers.

(iii) Third there is the technical problem of updating firm prices rapidly. In equity markets this is simpler as prices of different shares react differently according to industry news, company announcements and so on. By contrast all bond prices tend to adjust simultaneously as a result of interest rate changes, announcements about money supply growth, inflation figures and so on. Thus a securities house which is trading many hundreds of bonds may find it extraordinarily difficult to change firm prices rapidly enough to protect its position.

Some observers take the view that a more transparent market (via screen-based trading) would enhance confidence in the secondary market and would improve liquidity by stimulating turnover. The fact remains however that screen-based trading was voted down in 1987 by members of the Association of International Bond Dealers which organises participants in the secondary market.

The Association of International Bond Dealers (AIBD)

The AIBD was established in the late 1960s and has more than 900 members in almost 40 countries. It has been instrumental in helping to bring an element of order into the Euromarkets. Nevertheless it has been pointed out that 'bad trading habits continue to abound' (Gallant, 1988) and expressions such as 'buccanneering spirit', 'spivvy practices' and 'cowboy operators' have been used in the past to convey the periodic behaviour of market participants (*The Economist*, May 16 1986).

The influence of the AIBD is only advisory however with the threat of exclusion from membership being the ultimate sanction. Within these constraints it has played a number of roles including acting as a source of information on outstanding issues and attempting to regulate market practices by developing rules and procedures which facilitate the operation of the market. Thus matters such as dealing practices, techniques for calculating accrued interest, determining value dates, settlement and so on are part of the AIBD's rule book.

The freedom from official regulation in London which has partly been responsible for the growth of the Euromarkets was threatened in 1986 by new UK legislation (The Financial Services Act 1986). Initial reaction suggested that the market would respond by moving elsewhere. Given that London plays host to nearly 25% of AIBD members this would have had a considerable impact on employment and value added in the financial sector. Even more significantly in the eyes of some commentators it would have relegated London to the second division of world financial centres.

In the event a rather less stringent supervisory regime was considered desirable. Consequently the AIBD has been classified as a *Designated Investment Exchange* within the UK by the Securities and Investment Board. Designated Investment Exchanges face a less restrictive environment for example in regard to capital adequacy and reporting requirements than is implied in the category of a *Recognised Investment Exchange*. Of course it remains true that the investment houses which are mainly responsible for Euromarket activity are covered by membership of the other Self Regulatory Organisation (SRO) such as the Securities Association but effectively their 'offshore activities' have been preserved.

The Dealing Mechanism

Quotations are done in terms of a bid/offer spread for specified size of bargain and the size of the spread reflects the degree of liquidity of a particular issue as well as the dealer's own position.

Trading is usually carried out in minimum lot sizes of ten bonds so that each lot is generally worth $10 000. However as indicated earlier the minimum denomination of bonds may vary, for example $5000 and $10 000 denominations are not unusual.

In the secondary market dealers attempt to make money in two ways:

1. *The dealing spread.* This varies depending upon the nature of the bond (for example fixed rate issues have a larger spread than floating rate paper) and the degree of liquidity. Generally spreads are around 0.5% for liquid issues and may widen to 1% – 2% for less active issues. The spreads will be adjusted according to the size of the transaction – 'the ticket'.

2. *The dealer's position.* This is the difference between the cost of buying the bonds in the first place and the price at which they can be sold. Thus a dealer may decide to buy in a substantial volume of a particular bond (to 'go long' or 'increase his book') because he feels that it will be in considerable demand such that a marked increase in the price is expected. In this case the profit made comes about because of the 'position' he has taken in that particular security. Of course should he get the price movement wrong then a considerable loss may be incurred. For example should a company be re-rated downward a trader would face a substantial loss on any of that company's paper he holds on his book.

Prices are quoted 'clean' but the bonds are sold on a cum coupon basis – previous owners of the bond must be paid their share of the interest coupon by the person acquiring the security from them. Accrued interest is calculated not on the basis of the trading day (ie the day of the transaction) but on the *value* day which is seven calendar days after the trade. Calculation of accrued interest also assumes a 360 day year and in the vast majority of cases a single coupon is payable annually.

Example 4.1

100 bonds ($100 000 nominal) of an issue are sold on December 15 (value day is therefore December 22) at a price of 96.0%. The issue carries a coupon of 7.5% payable annually on November 13.

Principal ($100 000) × Price (96.0%)	= $96 000
Accrued interest 39 days ($100 000 × 0.075 × $\frac{39}{360}$) =	$812.5
Amount paid to Seller	= $96 812.5

After calculating the amounts payable/receivable the office responsible for settlement informs the appropriate clearing systems – Euroclear (in Brussels) or Cedel (in Luxembourg) – and gives instructions for the payment and delivery of the securities. This normally involves a transfer between customer accounts: bonds are not handled physically but instead remain within the clearing systems for security reasons.

5 TYPES OF EUROBOND – BOND FEATURES

Bonds vary according to their particular characteristics but we shall start with conventional bonds – the so-called 'straight' or 'vanilla' issues. We have already discussed this sort of bond in the context of the gilt-edged market: the differences between the Euromarket and the gilts market relate to the frequency of the coupon, the liquidity of the instruments and the potential credit risk. Allowing for these differences the analytical features of fixed rate bonds remain similar.

In recent years the maturity structure for Eurobonds appears to have shortened considerably. Maturities in excess of fifteen years were not unexceptional in the 1960s but much shorter maturities of three to five years are now much more common. This is a consequence of much more volatile interest rates and rates of inflation experienced in the 1970s and 1980s.

Bond prices fluctuate in the secondary market because of four main factors: technical influences; interest rates; currency characteristics and bond features.

(i) Technical factors

Bond prices are affected by particular market practices. For example in the case of a small or thinly traded issue dealers may go 'short' and borrow the bonds as a consequence of a purchase by end investors (borrowing facilities are provided by the clearing houses). This can cause abrupt price rises as they later attempt to cover their positions. Dealers who are unable to cover their positions however then face a 'buy in' notice. According to AIBD rules in the event of a trader failing to deliver securities within twenty-one days of a sale, the customer (who may well be another AIBD member firm) can issue a buy in notice which gives the trader a further fourteen days to make good. If the seller still fails to deliver then the buyer can instruct a different AIBD member firm to buy the bonds in the market at whatever price is necessary and present the original seller with the bill for the difference.

Deliberate 'ramping' or 'cornering' of an issue whereby one or a few dealers attempts to build up an overwhelming position in in order to push up prices and make a profit out of other dealers who have gone short are not unknown and this can create extra volatility in market prices (Gallant, 1988).

(ii) Interest rates

If the general level of interest rates changes for a particular currency then bond price levels will tend to adjust so that all securities of a given maturity and quality offer a comparable return. The impact of interest rate movements will be similar to the way gilts react – ie if a general rise in interest rates occurs will induce investors to move out of the old lower yield bonds thereby depressing their price.

(iii)   Currency factors

This obviously has an impact on the price of bonds: if the underlying currency in which a bond is denominated loses value relative to other major currencies then investors based in these other currencies will find both the coupon and the redemption value less attractive on translation. This will undermine a source of demand for such bonds and depress its price. Thus where bonds are denominated in US dollars then Swiss or German clients may be reluctant to buy bonds should they suspect that the trend in the value of the dollar is likely to be weaker. This is because the bonds will involve a capital loss in Swiss franc or Deutsche Mark terms.

A variety of techniques have evolved to cope with this problem of exchange rate risk. The simplest is to offer an exceptionally high yield. But in other cases the issuer has fixed the final exchange rate at redemption according to the spot rate when the initial offering is made. This covers the downside risk but it also means that the investor does not gain from any possible *strengthening* in the underlying currency. Given the extra element of risk it is obvious that the yield which this type of bond must offer to prospective investors has to be greater for weaker than for stronger currencies. Thus Eurosterling and Australian dollar bonds have both been high yield bonds.

(iv)   Other characteristics – 'bells and whistles'

If a bond carries a particular feature there may be price effects related to changes in that feature eg if the bond has the option to convert into the issuer's equity and the latter performs exceptionally well this will influence the bond price.

As competition has become fiercer new sorts of bonds have been introduced to cater for different sorts of investor and to minimise the coupon payable by the borrower. Hence there is now a whole range of hybrid bonds – instruments which embody a mix of characteristics. The make-up of issues over the past five years is illustrated in Table 4.7 below. It is quite clear that equity related convertibles and warrants have been expanding more rapidly than any other sector of the market.

(a)   Floating rate notes (FRNs)

These differ from conventional bonds in so far as they do not offer a fixed coupon. Instead the issue promises to pay the investor a return which varies with a key or bench mark interest rate. In most cases the interest rate chosen is the London Inter Bank Offered Rate (Libor). This is the rate which banks

TABLE 4.7   Total international financing activity ($ billion), 1985–9

	1985	1986	1987	1988	1989
Fixed rate bonds					
Straights	96.69	146.0	117.2	160.0	149.3
Equity related	11.6	26.7	43.2	41.8	85.1
of which					
Warrants	4.3	19.2	25.2	29.7	69.6
Convertibles	7.3	7.5	17.6	12.1	15.6
Bonds with non-equity warrants (gold, currency debt)	na	na	8.2	1.2	0.5
Total Fixed Rate	107.8	172.4	163.6	202.9	234.9
Floating rate notes	55.9	47.8	12.0	23.5	24.2
Euronote facilities	50.3	70.7	73.2	79.1	64.5
Syndicated Credits	19.0	29.8	88.8	99.4	148.4
Total	233.0	320.7	337.6	405.0	472.0

Bank of England Quarterly Bulletin, May 1990.

in London will quote for other banks wishing to borrow from them. Thus in the case of a specific Eurobond the coupon may well be $^1/_2$% above Libor – for example Citicorp has a dollar bond in issue maturing in 1998 carrying a coupon $^1/_4$% above the six month offered rate. Indeed particularly good names may be able to issue bonds with a coupon which is at or below Libor. Nor need Libor be the only reference rate FRNs have been issued with the coupon tied to the US Treasury Bill rate.

Floating Rate Notes are especially attractive to institutions which want to hold assets which are comparatively free of interest rate risk. Unlike the capital value of straight bonds which varies inversely with interest rates, that of FRNs does not because changes in the yield are achieved via fluctuations in the floating coupon. Such bonds therefore may be particularly attractive to risk averse monetary institutions which offer their depositors a variable rate of return – banks therefore would be prime customers for such issues.

(b)   Drop Lock Bonds

These are essentially floating rate bonds with a fixed floor. The floating rate converts into a fixed coupon should the bench mark rate fall below a specified level. Both parties will then be locked into this fixed rate until redemption. As interest rates have become more volatile during the 1980s these bonds have no longer become so attractive to potential investors.

(c) Cap and collar (minimax) bonds

These are simply variations on the droplock bond. It is possible to issue bonds with a 'cap' where the issuer imposes a ceiling on the floating rate or with a collar which means that *both* a floor and a ceiling on the floating coupon are provided. Clearly a cap protects a borrower from too high a level of interest rates and investors would obviously look for a higher spread above the relevant reference rate as compensation.

(d) Zero coupon bonds

Euro zeros offer no coupon at all to the investor. They made their initial appearance in a 1981 offer by Pepsico. Obviously in offering no coupon such bonds will only command investor interest if they are at a discount to their par value. They are therefore sold at a discount (usually a deep discount) to their nominal value so that on redemption the investor receives a substantial capital gain. The yield therefore may be more attractive to certain classes of investor who want capital gains and not necessarily income.

(e) Dual currency bonds

These vary in form but in the majority of cases the principal of the bond is denominated in one currency – say dollars – while the coupon is payable in another (eg Swiss francs). The issuer of such a bond may be a corporate borrower wishing to obtain dollars to support a US (or other venture) but with substantial Swiss franc earnings which are available to service the debt. The investor on the other hand is effectively taking on a degree of currency risk depending upon the behaviour of exchange rates.

(f) Multi-currency bonds

The increased volatility of currency exchange rates since the 1970s gave particular impetus to the development of a number of ways of hedging investments. In an attempt to minimize the effects of such currency fluctuations some bonds have been issued in artificial units – eg European Currency Units and bonds denominated in the Special Drawing Rights of members of the International Monetary Fund. The mix of currencies which make up the value of the bond is usually determined by some form of agreed international criteria but in principle there would be nothing to prevent an issuer denominating a bond in *any* mix of currencies. The barrier would simply be investor perceptions of such an offering.

The ECU bond appears to have become the most successful of these composite currency bonds and since the early 1980s the equivalent of nearly $25 billion have been issued. In addition the growth of the bond has been remarkable – between 1981 and 1988 the value of offerings increased from approximately $300 million to some $11.3 billion. In June 1988 the European Commission issued an ECU500 million bond which will undoubtedly provide a benchmark against which other issues can be assessed.[3]

The advantage of such bonds is their ability to reduce exposure to currency risk inherent in a bond denominated in only one currency. Thus a company which perhaps has a number of revenue flows denominated in different currencies might find it easier to hold ECU denominated instruments than to set up a hedge in each of currency seperately. This may be particularly true of currencies where hedging is not easily accomplished.

(g) Convertible bonds

Various types of convertible bond have been issued. Some give the investor the right to convert into another fixed coupon bond and therefore the value of the conversion will depend upon how interest rates change: where the rate of interest falls the ability to switch into another fixed rate instrument may add to the attraction of the original bond. If interest rates rise the investor need not exercise the conversion. However problems may arise where conversion can be forced ie if the bond is 'callable'.

Equity convertibles issued by corporate borrowers give the investor the right to convert into the equity of the issuer (or in some cases the equity of a subsidiary). As a result these bonds tend to offer a lower coupon to prospective investors than is the case for straight bonds. The upside performance of the bond depends on the fortunes of the underlying equity. The strength of the Japanese equity market has made Japanese corporates anxious to use equity convertibles. They suffered badly in the aftermath of the 1987 Crash in equity markets but issuing activity picked up in 1988 and 1989 as equity markets recovered only to fall again in 1990.

(h) Eurobonds with warrants

These bonds with warrants attached give the investor, in addition to the coupon, the right to purchase additional fixed rate bonds or equity or even currency at a specified price on or before a particular future date. Unlike the convertible bonds referred to above the exercise of the warrant requires the investor to come up with more cash. In the case of convertible bonds on the other hand there is simply an exchange of one form of capital for another.

Warrants which require the subscription of more money on exercise are similar to a long-term call option. In the case of equity warrants a rise in the price of the underlying equity will tend to make the warrant more valuable. In the case of bond warrants the important factor will be changes in the rate of interest: as a fall in the rate of interest increases bond prices the warrant will become more valuable in the event of falling interest rates because it confers the right to buy the bond at a fixed price. Rising interest rates will of course have the opposite effect – depressing the value of the warrant.

The effect of adding warrants to a bond issue allows the borrower to shave the coupon somewhat or to sell the bond at a better price. The investor may hold the warrant to take advantage of its terms or, as warrants are generally detachable, they may be sold in a secondary market. On the downside – if the underlying equity does not rise in price or interest rates rise sharply a given warrant may not be worth exercising and the investor will have received coupon less than could otherwise have been obtained. In 1988–9 there have been several issues of bonds with money back warrants: if the underlying equity does not rise as expected then the warrants will not expire valueless; instead the issuer will buy them back.

The Japanese role in bond issues with equity warrants has been very marked until recently. So for example out of a total of nearly 450 such offerings between 1963 and 1987 over 330 were from Japanese issuers ie more than 73%. During the same period the cumulative value of such issues came to some $38.4 billion of which the Japanese accounted for $25.2 billion or more than 65% (Fisher, 1987).

This dominance in equity linked issues has been one of the key factors explaining the rise of Japanese Eurobond houses as lead managers.

Table 4.8 gives an indication of the performance of various securities houses in the Eurobond market.

It is clear from Table 4.8 that Japanese houses have indeed been capturing the lion's share in the underwriting of new issues in recent years: a comparison of their respective rankings over the period 1985 to 1988 bears this out quite clearly. Much of this is explicable in terms of the size of their capital base, their placing power and the ability to lead manage equity linked bonds in the context of a rising stock market in Tokyo. Whether this dominance can be sustained in more adverse conditions is difficult to answer and will be tested as Tokyo Stock Exchange (TSE) enters a bear phase. It does appear that the Japanese presence is unlikely to be ephemeral however.

Other Financing Techniques in the Euromarkets

Euronotes

Euronotes are not in themselves a particularly novel instrument: they are simply short term promissory notes issued by non-bank borrowers or a certificate of deposit (CD) by banks. The real novelty lies in the way issuing techniques have changed. The result is that larger companies now have available a wider range of short term financing instruments which are additional to and frequently cheaper than traditional bank borrowing. Until 1986 the most common form in which short term finance was arranged was via a note issuance facility (NIF) or a revolving underwriting facility (RUF) but since then a market in eurocommercial paper (ECP) has also emerged.

TABLE 4.8 Eurobond lead managers

Manager	1988				1987	1986	1985
	$b	Rank	Issues	%	Rank	Rank	Rank
Nomura	17.68	1	135	10.30	1	2	8
CSFB	13.89	2	82	8.09	2	1	1
Deutsche Bank	12.23	3	84	7.12	3	3	5
Daiwa	9.43	4	80	5.49	6	5	11
Yamaichi	7.27	5	61	4.24	5	12	20
Nikko	6.87	6	61	4.00	4	10	25
Merrill Lynch	5.95	7	32	3.47			
J.P. Morgan	5.60	8	34	3.26			
Banque Paribas	5.52	9	45	3.22			
Ind. Bk of Japan	5.50	10	48	3.21			
UBS	5.45	11	47	3.17			
Bankers Trust	5.34	12	49	3.11			
Salomon Bros	4.92	13	31	2.87			
Warburg Secs.	4.54	14	23	2.65			
Goldman Sachs	3.88	15	25	2.26			
Dresdner Bank	3.80	16	24	2.21			
Morgan Stanley	3.62	17	30	2.11			
Commerzbank	3.45	18	30	2.01			
Swiss Bank Corp.	2.81	19	25	1.64			
Hambros Bank	2.26	20	46	1.56			
Total	173.08		1481				

Financial Times, 3 Jan. 1989 & IDD Information Services.

NIFs and RUFs

These are arrangements which cover the medium term under which borrowers can issue short term paper in their own name as market conditions permit. The notes issued generally have a maturity of three to six months. There is no coupon with such paper, instead it is issued at a discount to its face value and the return accrues when the notes mature. The notes are distinguished by the fact that they are guaranteed by a bank or more frequently a group of banks. The latter receives fees for an agreement to underwrite the issue by being prepared to purchase any unsold notes or by providing a stand-by line of credit.

Multi-option facilities (MOFs)

Multi-option facilities are variations on NIFs: they are arrangements whereby several possibilities for obtaining finance are made available to the borrower. They include note issuance facilities, short and medium term credits sometimes with the added twist that they can be drawn down in a mix of different currencies.

Eurocommercial paper

Eurocommercial paper (ECP) has been aptly described as 'tap issues of short term notes without the backing – or the cost – of a revolving underwriting facility' (Gallant, 1988 p.46).

Essentially commercial paper consists of short term notes offered on a continuous basis with a maturity of between 7 and 365 days. Most ECP business is focussed on the 30–180 day period. Older issues carried a coupon but it is now customary for the notes to offer no coupon. In addition the notes come in bearer form.

This paper with very short maturities and no bank guarantee is a very recent addition to the armoury of financing techniques in the Euromarkets yet it has been a feature of the American scene since as far back as the nineteenth century (Topping, 1987).

The Eurocommercial paper market has been growing extremely quickly and by the end of 1988 over $51 billion of total ECP programmes had been announced: in particular it is of increasing significance for institutional investors. ECP derived from the underwritten Euronote market (NIFs and RUFs) and the market in syndicated credits of the early 1980s.[4] Originally these Euronotes were perceived as an alternative to the syndicated credits market arranged for borrowers by banks in the early 1980s. The Euronote facility is distributed via a tender panel and utilised by the issuer whenever the finance is required.

By 1984–5 newer varieties of programme were being announced and these differed quite markedly from the previous arrangements: not only were they not underwritten by the banks but in addition the issuer simply appointed a small group of banks and dealers to act as placing agents distributing the notes on a 'best efforts' basis. This minimises the underwriting fees but the corresponding difficulty of course is that the issuer has no guarantee that finance will come through in the event that the market becomes bearish.

While ECP bears many similarities to its US counterpart there are two substantial differences. First US commercial paper is backed up by strong bank credit lines and is rated by a major agency in a similar manner to bond issues. This contrasts with ECP practice where there are no explicit bank credit lines and no credit ratings. Second the US commercial paper market usually deals with shorter maturities.

The growth of ECP programmes has been substantial in recent years and it can be argued that this rash of innovation has been yet another consequence of increasing securitisation of capital markets in the 1980s.[5] In particular given the travails of the banks in terms of the overhang of Third World Debt allied to declining profitability, some corporate borrowers have been perceived as more credit worthy than the banks themselves.

This has in turn allowed *disintermediation* to occur as top quality borrowers have realised that they can obtain cheaper credit by borrowing directly in their own names rather than use bank as an intermediary. (Volvo or IBM for example may be regarded as better quality names than BankAmerica.) Meanwhile the dismantling of restrictions on the issuance of short term paper in Europe has altered the balance of advantage *vis-à-vis* the US commercial paper market. In the past top class European names for example BP and British Telecom could only use the US market where, given their foreign status, they were often required to pay a risk premium compared to similar US domestic issuers.

A number of other features have combined to give ECP an advantage over traditional underwritten Euronote facilities. For example not only can top line issuers raise funds without the kind of support which committed facilities require (thereby saving underwriting fees) they can also obtain rather more rapid and flexible access to finance as compared with mobilising a tender panel.

Interestingly there has as yet been no major development of secondary market activity in commercial paper markets generally. One might expect this to be the case for the US market given the very short maturity structure of the paper but in other CP markets the practice seems to be that dealers stand ready to buy back paper from their client base. It seems to be much more common to hold the paper to maturity.

Euro Medium Term Notes (EMTNs)

This segment of the Euro markets commenced activity in late 1970s. In a sense the Euro Medium Term Note market is simply an extension of Euro Commercial Paper to maturities longer than nine months but unlike ECP the notes carry a coupon. In both cases the role of banks as intermediary lending bodies is cut out and the borrower is able to obtain cheaper funds while the investor might also achieve a higher return. The notes are 'continuously offered' which also means that the issuer has greater flexibility compared with a conventional bond offering. This allows a more opportunistic approach to exploiting investor funds because while such notes are described as continuously offered, they do not have to be, the borrower can issue from time to time to take advantage of a particular interest rate window.

The expression 'Medium Term' is rather elastic however and was derived from the US MTN market. This was effectively established by the car finance companies such as Ford as a way of raising liabilities to match the two to three year loans they were making. Nevertheless maturities of up to five years and beyond have been established in the United States. In Europe by contrast the majority of issues has been for maturities of less than two and a half years with the longest maturity being 5 years. These longer maturities are overlapping with the shorter end of the bond market proper.

In addition the size of programmes has been surprisingly large – while the smallest has been $50m, in 1987 GMAC expanded an initial programme of $1 billion to $3 billion. The implication is of course that the market is characterised by sufficient liquidity to assure investor confidence. Finally EMTNs appear to be somewhat simpler than Eurocommercial paper in so far as there is a single co-ordinating agent and all programmes pay their interest on a single payment date selected by the issuer.

Table 4.9 below is indicative of recent developments in this area.

TABLE 4.9   Announced Euronote facilities ($ billion), 1986–9

	1986	1987	1988	1989
ECP/ECDs	17.8	46.3	52.7	47.9
NIFs/RUFs	47.6	15.2	10.5	6.6
MTNs	5.5	12.0	16.1	11.8
Total	70.9	73.5	79.3	66.3

Bank of England Quarterly Bulletin, May 1990.

It is quite clear that the ECP/ECD (Eurocommercial paper/Euro Certificate of Deposit) markets have grown rapidly and to some extent at the expense of the underwritten facilities (NIFs and RUFs). This appears to support the notion that in general, trends in capital markets tend to be moving in the direction of disintermediation.

Thus far in examining the Eurobond market we have assumed that issuers structure their borrowing in order to meet their own specific requirements. Thus a corporate borrower wishing to obtain Yen at a fixed rate simply issues a bond under advice from the lead manager which would achieve that end. This however is a rather simple view of the world: the Eurobond market is much more flexible than this. It may be possible to obtain the required Yen more cheaply by issuing a bond denominated in another currency eg US dollars and swapping the proceeds with a counterparty.

6 SWAPS

One of the most significant innovations to have emerged in the Euromarkets in the last decade has been growth in the international market in swaps. These operate in various ways but essentially allow a borrower in one capital market to obtain access to another via a counterparty to the swap.

Swaps are akin to *back to back* loans which emerged many years ago as a way of getting around stringent capital market controls. In the 1950s a UK based company wishing to invest in the United States might obtain the necessary dollars by arranging to lend the equivalent amount in sterling to a subsidiary of the American company. The exchange rate would be at the spot rate and the interest payable would of course have to be negotiated between the co-operating entities. *Parallel* loans operate in a somewhat similar way but in this case a British firm lends sterling to the UK subsidiary of an American company, while the American parent lends dollars to the UK company's subsidiary.

These arrangements are tailor-made and hence relatively inflexible as they suffer from what economists call 'the double coincidence of wants' ie a UK company wanting dollars would have to find a US company that at the same time wants pounds.

Much of the growth of Eurobond issuing activity in recent years has been fuelled by organisations wishing to take advantage of swaps of one sort or another. Indeed it has been argued that the vast majority of new issues of Eurobonds in the 1980s were motivated by the desire to arrange interest rate or currency swaps (Bowe, 1988; Das, 1989).

Swaps offer two major advantages to potential borrowers:

o Reallocating risk: they are a mechanism by which certain types of uncertainty can be reduced or eliminated by allowing companies to alter the profile of liabilities or income flows;
o Arbitrage: they offer an opportunity for borrowers to take advantage of discrepancies which exist in different capital markets to gain effective access to a particular market so as to lower the effective rate of borrowing. These discrepancies might relate to interest rate disparities, tax regimes, currency problems or regulatory differences.

Currency Swaps

(i) Straight swaps

A straight currency swap simply involves the exchange of different currencies at a particular rate of exchange combined with an agreement to pay the currencies back at the same exchange rate at some future date. Given that interest rates may be different in the two countries concerned there will be an agreement to build into the arrangement the payment of interest by one party to the other. For example if company Z exchanges £1m for $155m with company Y and sterling assets offer an interest differential of 3% then the party receiving the sterling (company Y) may agree to pay £30 000 to compensate Z for interest foregone.

(ii)   Currency debt swaps

Here the companies concerned issue fixed rate debt in currencies which they can each access. They then swap the proceeds and assume each other's obligations for the interest and repayment of principal. This then goes further than the straight swap as each party agrees to take on the periodic interest payments due on the foreign debt.

Interest Rate Swaps

These can take two forms: a 'vanilla' or plain swap where fixed rate interest payments are exchanged for floating rate payments; or a 'basis' swap where floating rate payments determined in relation different bases are swapped eg US prime lending rate *vis-à-vis* the London Interbank Offered Rate (LIBOR).

In the case of vanilla interest rate swaps one borrower issues fixed rate debt while the other borrows floating rate debt and they then exchange their interest rate payments.

This can be illustrated by the diagram in fig. 4.1. Here each party is borrowing the same volume of funds with the same maturity from different lenders. One party however issues fixed rate debt while the other issues floating rate debt and they then proceed to exchange the interest payments.

Example 4.1

Suppose company A prefers floating rate debt while company B wishes to obtain fixed rate finance. But company A has sufficiently high ratings to be able to borrow at 10% fixed *or* at LIBOR. Company B on the other hand is not so highly rated and as a consequence can only borrow at 13% *or* at LIBOR plus 1%. It is possible to envisage a mutually beneficial trade which can be accomplished as follows.

They each borrow the same volume of funds – company A issues a fixed rate bond at 10% while company B issues a floating rate note at LIBOR plus 1%.

Company B now makes coupon payments to A at 11% while company A makes LIBOR payments to B.

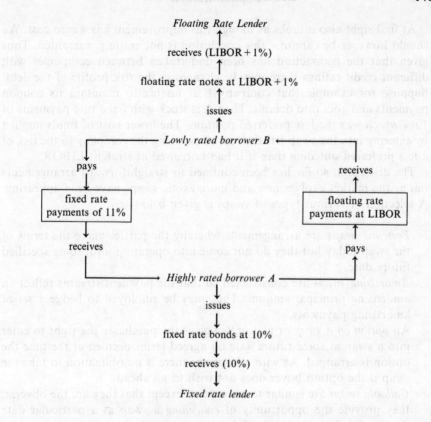

Floating Rate Lender

receives (LIBOR + 1%)

floating rate notes at LIBOR + 1%

issues

—— *Lowly rated borrower B* ←——

pays   receives

| fixed rate payments of 11% | | floating rate payments at LIBOR |

receives   pays

——→ *Highly rated borrower A* ——

issues

fixed rate bonds at 10%

receives (10%)

Fixed rate lender

Figure 4.1 Interest rate swap

1. B's position is now as follows:

    Net interest on the debt = (LIBOR + 1%) + (11%) − LIBOR

    = 12%

Which is a better rate than the 13% that would be involved in a fixed rate issue to the market.

2. A's position is as follows:

    Net interest on the debt = (10%) − (11%) + LIBOR

    = LIBOR − 1%

Which clearly means that the company has been able to obtain floating rate funds at below the going LIBOR.

At first sight also it looks as though this improvement has a zero cost. We should however be careful – this conclusion is not entirely warranted. Thus given that the transaction has been undertaken between companies with different credit ratings there may be changes in the risk profile of the debt. Suppose for example that company B is unable to maintain its coupon payments and goes into default. Then A is stuck with fixed rate payments of 10% which was the less preferred position. The lower cost of funds implied by entering into the swap has the cost of exposing the company to the risk of a less preferred outcome than if it had borrowed at straight LIBOR.

The discussion so far has been confined to straightforward arrangements but as the market evolves new and more exotic swaps have been appearing. A selection of various types of swaps is given below:

o *Forward swaps* are arrangements whereby the parties agree the terms of the swap today but they do not come into operation until some specified future date.

o *Amortising swaps* are constructed so that the payment streams reflect an amortising principal amount. They may be employed to hedge a set of amortising payments.

o An *option on a swap* or a *swaption* gives the purchaser the right to enter into a swap at some future date on agreed terms decided at the time the option is arranged. As with all options there is no obligation to take the swap if the option buyer does not wish to go ahead.

o *Callable swaps* are similar to a swaption except that they are the obverse: they provide the opportunity of *cancelling* a swap at a particular date during the operational life of the arrangement.

o *Index swaps* involve payments which may vary because they are calculated with respect to the behaviour of particular indices. These might be share indices or even general price indices such as the Retail Price Index.

Institutions in the Swaps Market

Swaps tend to be discussed in the context of direct relations between the end-users. The role of international banks in the development of a market has clearly been extremely important however.[6] Initially banks simply acted as *agents* – bringing interested parties together and setting up the details of the transaction for a fee. As the volume of business has grown, banks and securities houses have taken on the role of intermediary – acting as guarantor for the payments of both parties and in some instances becoming market makers in swap deals by taking a swap directly onto their own book prior to finding the other side of the swap. Banks now act as principals in their own right – directly participating in swaps and maintaining open positions which might be periodically closed as opportunities arise. In acting as principals they are assuming new risks and although the record of default has so far been extremely small it is always there.

A factor which has led the banks to involve themselves in these various activities is that they count as so-called off-balance sheet transactions because in effect they are *contingent* liabilities and only become real in the event of certain outcomes. However as became evident in 1989 the swaps market remains fraught with danger as is shown in the dubious legal status of swaps entered into with certain UK local authorities acting as counter parties.

Swaps are an example of financial engineering: the construction of a different stream of payments (debt, interest or foreign currency) than the original borrowing. They allow borrowers to alter or mix their obligations into a more preferred format. The blossoming of this market in the 1980s coincided with the expansion of a whole series of *derivative* markets offering financial contracts based on an underlying security. These markets also offer 'financial engineering' and the promise to control or assume risk as desired.

NOTES

1. A similar sort of status was conferred on Sterling in the nineteenth century when it was the currency which was the main international means of payment.
2. An interesting discussion of some of the sharper practices found in the secondary market is provided in Gallant (1988).
3. The valuation of cocktail bonds is problematical and has been the subject of discussion between various issuing houses – see *The Banker* Nov. 1988.
4. Some ECP programmes were arranged in the late 1960s and early 1970s but the market did not take off in any substantial way.
5. A variety of countries now have their own individual commercial paper markets. Thus for example the French authorities gave permission for a commercial paper market in December 1985 while the Bank of England laid down the conditions for Sterling Commercial Paper in March 1986. These in fact came after similar sorts of liberalisation in the early 1980s by economies as diverse as Spain, Norway, Australia, Sweden and the Netherlands.
6. Indeed some banks advertise their expertise in developing interest rate or currency swaps for example Bankers Trust, Salomon Brothers, First Boston, Citicorp and Morgan Guaranty have been important innovators in this area.

5 Markets for Derivatives

1 INTRODUCTION

Conventional markets facilitate the trading of financial securities: this simply involves the exchange of ownership rights between seller and buyer. As pointed out earlier this assures holders that their investment retains some degree of liquidity because such securities are listed and therefore bought and sold on an organised exchange.

There are also a range of markets in which trading occurs not in the underlying commodity or security itself but in instruments 'derived' from the underlying commodity or security. These are the markets for *futures* and *options*. They are probably most highly developed in the United States. The Chicago Board of Trade (CBOT) for example has operated a futures market for commodities since the 1860s and now offers a range of futures contracts on financial instruments. Similarly the Chicago Mercantile Exchange (CME) provides a market, the International Money Market (IMM), in futures for various foreign currencies. The Chicago Board Options Exchange (CBOE) was established in 1973 and is the most famous example of a *traded* options market.

Since then similar markets have emerged with in other financial centres such as London, New York, Tokyo, Paris and Amsterdam. Indeed these markets are still in the process of evolution. For example in July 1990 an agreement was reached to merge the London International Financial Futures Exchange (LIFFE) with the London Traded Options Market (LTOM) to form the London Derivatives Exchange (LDE).

Markets in futures and options emerged because of the existence of uncertainty about future prices of commodities and financial securities. They work by splitting off one of the key features of securities and commodities – their price volatility. When an investor looks at a possible investment one of the major points of interest is the range of potential price fluctuation. For some investors this may be precisely the most important feature of the security or commodity as they hope to take advantage of such movements. For others exposure to large price variations is a matter they wish to avoid. Futures markets and options therefore allow the *risk averse* investor who

144

does not wish to carry these risks to minimise his exposure and to pass them on to someone else: a counter-party who is willing to bear such risk. In other words, for a premium, these markets allow hedgers to avoid risk by transferring it to speculators who are willing to bear risk.

In addition however futures markets also fulfill a 'price discovery' role (Siegel and Siegel, 1990): because futures markets are a way of distilling and conveying information about forward spot prices they improve investors' capacity to judge market *expectations* about forward spot prices.

Risk transfer and price discovery are not simply a function of futures markets however. For example for an investor fearing a considerable fall in market values, the risk transfer process can be achieved without futures markets by simply selling shares outright or even selling short ('within the account' in the UK or 'against the box' in the US). In this way the buyers of the securities bear the risk. Similarly price discovery occurs in any market: ie the spot price summarises a great deal of information about the future prospects of the company – indeed in efficient markets *all* such information is embedded in the spot price. Futures markets however are said to increase the efficacy of risk transfer and price discovery because the costs of futures transactions are generally below those of spot markets.

Before discussing these particular markets in detail we will look at the related notion of 'forward markets' as these are somewhat simpler to grasp.

2 FORWARD MARKETS

Forward markets grew out of attempts by manufacturers and other users of a commodity to avoid the instability of commodity prices. Primitive examples of such techniques termed 'arrivals' trading were to be found in the late eighteenth century in the Liverpool Cotton Exchange: here buyers and sellers would strike an agreement over price, quantity and possible delivery date of the commodity while it was still at sea. Provided the ship arrived within the delivery date and the cargo met the quality and quantity specifications the previously agreed arrangements would be concluded by payment and the taking of delivery. More sophisticated arrangements are now extensively used in foreign exchange dealings and many internationally traded commodities such as cocoa, rubber, grain, coffee and so on. When would a forward market be used and for what purpose?

A simple example may help to illustrate the essential idea. Assume that in February a food manufacturer negotiates an order to supply a large retail chain with freeze dried coffee. The first order is very large and is to commence as from the following December because the retailer has an existing contract with another producer which does not finish until then. If furthermore to obtain the order the manufacturer has quoted a fixed price contract then an obvious problem arises: what happens if between February and December there is a failure of the coffee crop and coffee prices increase sharply? The effect of this unexpected occurrence may be to wipe out the food manufacturer's prospective profit. Of course should a bumper harvest occur, an unexpected fall in coffee prices will result in a fortuitous increase in profit.

The manufacturer faces a number of possible courses of action:

1. He could go into the market in the present and buy the coffee at the 'spot' price but he would have to face the expense of storing it either in a raw or manufactured state until some months later when it is due for delivery to the final customer. This in itself has an opportunity cost in the form of storage space and the loss of interest that could otherwise have accrued on the capital tied up in stocks. He could instead wait and purchase the coffee nearer to the date when he has to start the manufacturing process. In this case the manufacturer carries a risk that the price of the commodity will move against him. Other 'normal' risks such as the possibility of industrial relations going wrong or the plant breaking down are problems he may be able to do something about – they are within his sphere of influence and he may be able to exert some degree of control. In the absence of forward markets the manufacturer would simply have to carry the risk of price fluctuations himself unless he can persuade the final customer to bear some of it by negotiating a more flexible price arrangement.

2. If forward markets exist however the food manufacturer can buy the coffee in the forward market. This secures the necessary volume at a fixed price today (ie in February) and depending upon the time scale of the contract he does not need to take delivery until later in the year. Nor does he have to pay for it until that time. In this way the manufacturer will have fixed the price he is required to pay and need not worry about it thereafter. Of course the likelihood is that he will be paying more for it than the current spot price but this may be regarded as a small penalty to avoid a much larger risk. The counter-party to the transaction now carries the risk of an adverse movement in the price. If prices rise his position will be a losing one as he will have to deliver the coffee at a price lower than the price it actually reaches on the relevant future date. On the other hand should prices fall his position will be profitable because he will be getting a higher price for the coffee than he would have obtained selling it at the spot price on that future date.

These sorts of transactions whereby a seller contracts to deliver a precisely defined amount of a specific item on some future date at a price fixed in the present have been part of commercial life for many years. Devotees of Shakespeare will recall that he uses a similar concept in *The Merchant of Venice* where the denouement of the play turns precisely on the specificity of the forward contract!

3 FUTURES MARKETS

Forward markets are used by companies and individuals who wish to carry out transactions in the physical commodity: the seller normally intends to deliver and the buyer to take delivery of the commodity in question. As a consequence, forward contracts are specific or custom made to the requirements of the buyer and seller. If however the markets were simply confined to end users they would not be very liquid and considerable price fluctuations would occur from time to time. However liquidity and efficiency can be enhanced if the market allows the participation of individuals and/or organisations which are not necessarily interested in the underlying commodity but are simply willing to take a view and speculate on potential price changes.[1]

Futures markets therefore have evolved in order to facilitate this participation. These markets trade *contracts* to buy and sell commodities at various future dates. The contracts may be based on physical commodities such as rubber, cotton, cocoa, copper and so on or they may be financial commodities such as bond futures. Futures markets unlike forward markets however are based on a standardised contract. This indicates both quantity and quality.

Example 5.1

o The *coffee* contract is denominated in lots of 5 tonnes net weight of specified coffee: there are different types of coffee, the major contract traded in London is in Robusta which is most suitable for producing the various instant blends. New York on the other hand trades in the higher quality Arabica.
o The *cocoa* contract is based on lots of 10 tonnes;
o In London there is a long gilt future contract based a notional gilt with a 9% coupon at £50 000 nominal· traded on the London International Financial Futures Exchange (LIFFE);
o There is a long bond contract with a coupon of 8% based on $100 000 notional US Treasury bond traded in both London (LIFFE) and Chicago (CBOT).

In other words whereas in *forward* markets (for foreign exchange, coffee and so on) any particular quantity can be bought and sold forward and the price locked in until the seller delivers the quantity to the buyer, in *futures* markets standard lots are defined. For example as the cocoa contact is based on lots of 10 tonnes and the gilts contract is for £50 000 nominal, ten contracts in cocoa would represent 100 tonnes of the underlying commodity and ten gilts contracts would represent £500 000 nominal. The contract is revalued day by day with gains or losses being credited or debited to the client's account or 'marked to market' as it is called. In addition the vast majority of futures contracts are usually closed out by making transaction in the opposite direction before delivery needs to be made.

But how does this help the dealers in the underlying commodity and how does it facilitate the reallocation of risk? Let us examine two possibilities, one relating to a physical commodity and the other to financial futures.

Example 5.2

Recall our food manufacturer who, in February, agreed to a fixed price contract for delivery of the goods in December. He has has effectively sold the coffee forward at a fixed price.

Futures contracts in coffee are sold in lots of five tonnes and in February the price quoted for coffee in the November futures is £1050 per tonne hence each contract will cost

$$5 \times £1050 = £5250$$

Ignoring transactions costs his position would look like this

February
Sell 50 tonnes at £1000 per tonne	£50 000
Buy ten November contracts at £5250 per contract	£52 500

If by October the price of coffee rises to £1100 per tonne this will increase the value of his November contract and the position will resemble the following

October
Buy 50 tonnes at £1100 per tonne	£55 000
Sell ten November contracts at £5750	£57 500
Loss on physical transactions	−£5000
Gain on futures contracts	+£5000

The loss in the physical market is £5000. Because of his fixed price contract the manufacturer has effectively sold the coffee to the retailer in advance of paying for it and taking delivery himself. If by October coffee prices have risen to £1100 per tonne it would cost £55 000 to acquire the necessary quantity to fulfil his order. This is the sort of risk we referred to earlier and the loss results from not 'hedging' the potential price movement.

However a more perceptive manufacturer would perhaps have made use of the facilities provided by the futures market and have set up an offsetting transaction. The rise in the coffee price in the cash market will have made the five futures contracts more valuable and in this case their sale would realise a profit which exactly offsets the loss in the physical market (£57 500–£52 500).[2]

The above example relates to an internationally traded commodity. It is also possible to to see the operation of futures markets as they relate to financial factors. As we are aware from the earlier discussion the price of gilts and other fixed interest securities tends to fluctuate inversely to changes in the rate of interest: they are susceptible to interest rate risk. If an investor holds a portfolio of gilt-edged stock and fears a fall in price as a result of a rise in interest rates what are the possible courses of action available? Is there some way of avoiding or hedging this risk?

Unlike the commodity or foreign exchange markets there is no *forward* market in gilts so this particular route is unavailable. The investor is not able to sell his portfolio forward and thereby fix the price today. It is possible of course to alter the mix of the portfolio in favour of gilts which are less volatile with respect to the rate of interest. Alternatively he could sell his portfolio today in the hope of buying it back after the rise in interest rates takes place or simply switch into other securities which are not so interest rate dependent.

Prior to the emergence of financial futures these were the possible ways of attempting to cope with interest rate risk. Since the early 1980s however with the opening of the London International Financial Futures Exchange (LIFFE) a further possibility has been available in the London markets.

Assume that a company has a temporary cash surplus of £500 000 which will not be required until three months time. It would be possible to place the money in gilt-edged for a while in order to take advantage of a favourable yield but the company treasurer may be dissuaded by the possibility of an upward hike in interest rates which would reduce the price of the stock and involve a capital loss. The existence of a futures market would help to minimise the potential capital loss.

Example 5.3

March	Buy gilts	£500 000
	Sell ten June gilts contracts	£500 000
June	Sell gilts	£450 000
	Repurchase June gilts contracts	£450 000
	Loss on cash transaction	−£50 000
	Gain on futures transaction	+£50 000

The June gilts contract is bought back just prior to its maturity. The loss on the gilts themselves is offset by the fact that the futures contracts have already been sold in March for a price greater than the price at which the contracts are repurchased in June. If our investor had got the movement in interest rates entirely wrong and they fall, the rising value of the gilts in the spot market would now be offset by a loss in the futures contract.

The example given above is deliberately simplified to emphasise the nature of the hedging process where the individual is simply trying to protect a position against potential loss but there are a number of complications which should be recognised. Not only have we not taken into account the various transactions costs but it is not always possible to match exactly the futures contract with the asset to be hedged. Ideally the investor needs to buy and sell futures which match his portfolio but if it is not possible to get an exact match, an imperfect hedge may have to be arranged.

In the case of an individual who wishes to set up a bond hedge in the UK, at the time of writing, there were two contracts available standardised on £50 000 worth of two notional gilts: a long contract with a 9% coupon and a medium contract also with a 9% coupon. Such a procedure at first sight seems rather puzzling – why use an artificial, 'invented' gilt which is not traded? Why not use a real gilt which could then be delivered as necessary when the contract expires ?

An artificial or contrived gilt is needed in order to enlarge the scope of the market as much as possible. If the contract were to be based on an actual gilt it would suffer from the fact that the amount of the gilt actually in issue and traded regularly is likely be small compared to the volume of trading in the futures contract.[3] This would obviously have adverse consequences for the liquidity of the futures contract. Therefore an artificial gilt has been devised and a series of real gilts which closely resemble this notional one can be used to effect delivery – these are so-called *deliverable* gilts. Thus for the long gilt contract, LIFFE designates real gilts with a maturity of between fifteen and twenty-five years as allowable surrogates. These can therefore be delivered to meet a futures contract. The real gilt is of course likely to be characterised by a different maturity and/or coupon from the artificial gilt so the amount of it delivered to meet the contract has to be adjusted accordingly.

The adjustment is carried out by via the following procedure:

a. Find out what would be the price of the particular deliverable gilt on a yield to redemption of 9%
b. Divide 'a' by the price of the 9% notional gilt on a yield to redemption of 9% (ie £100).

The ratio of 'a' to 'b' constitutes a conversion or adjustment factor which is applied to the deliverable gilt. This means of course that different quantities will be delivered depending upon the particular coupon/maturity characteristics in question. It further means that there may be one particular 'cheapest to deliver' gilt which can be bought in the spot market to meet the delivery on the futures contract.

So far the discussion has proceeded on the assumption that the user of the futures market wishes to hedge or to make/take delivery of the underlying commodity. However the user may or may not hold or wish to deliver the underlying security – the market may be used for straightforward speculation.

Our previous focus has been on the price of the contract close to expiry date, let us see how movements in the contract are dealt with on a day to day basis. The gilts contract (like the US Treasury bond contract) is priced as a percentage of the par value of the bond and price movements or 'ticks' are $^1/_{32}$ of a percent. Thus a quote of 96-26 means $96\,^{26}/_{32}$ percent of par. This price is not payable to anyone but simply the variable which constitutes the base for calculating losses and gains. The buyer of the contract is hoping to see this price go up and the seller is hoping to see it go down. In effect then it is simply a vehicle around which participants can take positions to bet on its possible movements.

Assume the investor is bullish about the rate of interest and expects that it will fall. Therefore he hopes to see a rise in the value of gilt-edged stock and the futures contract based on that stock.

Example 5.4

Suppose that the investor buys a £50 000 gilt contract at $96\,^{26}/_{32}$ and by the end of the trading period the price has moved to $96\,^{29}/_{32}$ the position will look like this

$$£\,(96\,^{29}/_{32} - 96\,^{26}/_{32})\,(0.01)\,(50\,000) = £\,(^3/_{32})\,(0.01)\,(50\,000)$$

$$£\,(^3/_{32})\,(0.01)\,(50\,000) = £\,46.875$$

Each 'tick' in the gilts contract is therefore worth £15.625.[4]

In this case at the end of the trading day the account stands some £46.875 to the good and will be credited accordingly. If the individual had bought ten such contracts then his gain would have been £468.75.

But for every buyer of a futures contract there must be a counter-party who in this case would face a loss. Note though there does not have to be an exact match: if our buyer had taken ten contracts, there could be for example three counter-parties – one seller of five contracts, one of three contracts and one of two. Their positions would then look like the following

A. $\quad 5 \times £\,(96\,^{26}/_{32} - 96\,^{29}/_{32})\,(0.01)\,(50\,000) = -£234.375$

B. $\quad 3 \times £\,(96\,^{26}/_{32} - 96\,^{29}/_{32})\,(0.01)\,(50\,000) = -£140.625$

C. $\quad 2 \times £\,(96\,^{26}/_{32} - 96\,^{29}/_{32})\,(0.01)\,(50\,000) = -£\,93.75$

Capital Markets

Losses are debited against the relevant accounts and the individuals concerned may face a call for more cash margin to support their position.

Net of transactions costs the gains of the buyer (the person going 'long' on the contract) exactly match the aggregate losses of the sellers (those going 'short' on the contract).

Individuals who wish to participate in these markets can only do so via a futures broker, called in the USA, a futures commission merchant (FCM). Such a broker acts as an agent or intermediary who transmits buy and sell orders on behalf of clients for a commission. Commissions were originally fixed as a percentage of the value of the transaction but now they are a fee and subject to negotiation and competition (Courtney and Bettelheim, 1986). The client's orders are transmitted to the floor of the exchange by the broker or FCM. Exchange members may take on a number of roles: some are just brokers acting as a conduit for outside orders and paid a commission for their services; others are traders dealing exclusively for their own account; and finally there are some who broker-dealers who trade for clients *and* their own account.

Orders are executed in a location termed a trading 'pit' by members of the exchange via an open outcry auction. Open outcry is the *required* technique because that way all orders are exposed to market participants. It is also feasible because of the precise standardisation of the contract which distinguishes a futures market. This 'homogeneity' of the product means that traders do not have to be concerned about the quality or characteristics of any particular trade (or trader) merely the contract's price and quantity.

Futures exchanges are currently centralised floor exchanges as one might expect given the *open outcry* method of trading. Nevertheless various exchanges have been trying to develop an electronic market which will allow screen trading. A number of variants are under discussion or development. For example the Chicago Mercantile Exchange (CME) has been actively promoting a system called Globex. This was due to go live in 1990 and the CME has been attempting to get other exchanges to list their products at the close of the business day. Globex is an electronic system for matching orders. This contrasts with LIFFE's Automated Pit Trading (APT) system which came into operation at the end of November 1989. In effect LIFFE has attempted to develop a screen-based version of the open outcry method of trading: instead of bids and offers being called and signalled physically each trader is identified on the screen by a symbol with his initials and the identity of his brokerage house. As bids and offers are made the trader's identifying symbol light up in different colours – blue and pink – indicating the number of contracts he wishes to deal in.

The key feature of APT is that it models the floor trading because the system is transparent and interactive ie the screens are able to communicate with each other almost instantaneously. Indeed with Automated Pit Trading response times are very short: it will take only 0.2 of a second between the input of new information and the system's response. This is very much faster than Globex which will take between five and six seconds and is sufficiently rapid to allow APT to process some 100 transactions per second which is much greater than is the case on the trading floor. Other technological developments can be foreseen which will not only allow the routing, processing and clearing of orders but may also maintain a degree of regulatory oversight over market dealings.

While doubts remain in certain quarters about the use of electronic trading there can be no doubt that the march of technology is unstoppable. As well as CME's Globex and LIFFE's APT, the Chicago Board of Trade is developing a system called Aurora. This is closer to the APT structure but it has been long delayed and much more costly to develop. There is some possibility that the Globex and Aurora systems may eventually be merged but this would seem some way off.

How can buyers and/or seller be assured that the counter-party will not default on the contract? After all without such an assurance the reputation of the market will suffer as will liquidity and turnover. Buyers and sellers are able to ignore the likelihood of default as ultimately it is not an individual client or counter-party who guarantees that the contract will be honoured but the clearing house (association) itself. In effect the clearing house becomes a principal for each contract. In London for example, the International Commodities Clearing House (ICCH) performs this role for traders in cocoa, coffee, potatoes and so on while the LIFFE performs it for financial futures. Obviously however this only applies to deals undertaken for clients by 'bona fide' members of the clearing house.

The existence of a guarantor of last resort, albeit the most important single feature underpinning each market, does not preclude other devices designed to minimise the problem of default by clients. One such device used to reduce the possibility of default (and hence to try to assure the integrity of the trade) is for futures brokers to demand collateral either in the form of securities or a cash margin (a cash deposit) from clients on whose behalf they are acting. Minimum margins are usually imposed by the relevant authorities and take the form of an initial margin paid when a contract is opened and a 'variation' margin which is altered as and when the contract price changes. The level of these margins is affected by factors such as the charges which the relevant clearing house imposes and the price volatility of the particular contract. As the value of the futures contract varies the client will find that his account is credited or debited depending upon whether the price has moved in his favour or against him. If he loses there will be a call for extra margin to support the contract if he gains then he can take the profits. Furthermore these adjustments are made or '*marked to market*' ie on a day by day basis.

It is this combination of dealing on margin and daily settlement which constitutes both the attractions and dangers of futures markets. If margin requirements are set at 10% which is not untypical in the futures markets an individual who has placed £5000 with a broker can support a contact with a total value of £50 000 and this can produce spectacular gains and losses.

Example 5.5

Total Contract Value (TCV)		Margin @ 10%	
	£50 000		£5000
5% Price Move	± £ 2500	Change in Margin Position	± £2500
		Gain or Loss	± 50%

The gain or loss relates to the total value of the contract and while it only represents 5% of that value this translates into a 50% profit or loss when compared to the individual's margin. In like manner a 2% change in the value of the underlying contract produces a 20% change in relation to the individual's current margin position. The degree of leverage is of course directly determined by size of these margin requirements.

Given the inherent volatility of commodity prices such dramatic shifts in the position are quite feasible and this adds an extra dimension to the risks involved in futures trading. As indicated above when the market moves against the individual there will be a call for extra margin in order to maintain the position as the alternative is simply to offset the contract or to get out. The system of daily settlement or 'marking to market' means that unless the individual responds promptly to the demand for extra margin the broker may be required to liquidate the position. This again has the effect of putting pressure on less sophisticated clients who are given little time to reflect on whether or not they wish to continue to support a losing position.

The essential point about futures markets therefore is that they provide a vehicle by which investors can reduce the risk arising from fluctuations in the price of the underlying commodity or financial asset. In the case of fixed interest assets a financial futures market helps to control exposure to interest rate risk. However for every investor relieved of risk in this way there is another individual or organisation prepared to take on that risk by selling futures contracts on commodities or financial assets that they do not have. Such a speculator is hoping to close his futures contract at a profit by, for example, buying it back more cheaply *after* an interest rate rise or selling a contract previously bought at a lower price because prices in the spot market have since risen.

Thus in our earlier example of the coffee importer if we assume that the counterparty to his future contract is a speculator the position would be as follows

February
    Sells ten November contracts at £5250 per contract   £52 500

October
    Buys ten November contracts at £5750   £57 500

In this example the speculator has lost and contrary to public belief speculators do lose periodically. They cannot of course lose indefinitely and hence Friedman for example has argued that ultimately the efficient speculators survive. Furthermore there is also the argument which is linked to the efficient markets hypothesis that they cannot necessarily win indefinitely. In the view of many economists the speculator therefore is fulfilling a useful function in the sense that he is relieving the end user – manufacturer or the processor – of one or more elements of risk involved in production activity.

However a major problem remains: even if the rate of return to speculation does not vary greatly from the average there appears to be a tendency to focus not on the average rate of return but the exceptional. Hence it has been relatively easy to induce the greedy but gullible into dealing in these more arcane and by definition riskier pursuits (Bosworth-Davies, 1988).

Regulation

The structure of regulation in futures markets gives an impression of being both rigorous and comprehensive: thus the markets are based in recognised Exchanges for example the Chicago Board of Trade (CBOT) and the London International Financial Futures Exchange (LIFFE). Brokers and traders are governed by a series of regulatory layers which, in addition to the exchanges themselves, include legally constituted bodies such as the Securities and Investment Board in the UK or the Commodity Futures Trading Commission in the US as well as self regulatory organisations such the Association of Future Dealers and Brokers (AFDB) in the UK and the National Futures Association (NFA) in the US (Bettelheim and Courtney, 1986).

The apparently impressive battery of regulatory bodies has not been sufficient to keep all malpractice at bay as became clear in 1989 when after two years of investigation over 250 traders in Chicago were served with sub-poenas by the FBI alleging market abuses (*The Economist*, Jan. 28 1989). Similarly in the UK accusations about the conduct of futures brokers and their desire to maximise commission income without too much concern for the client's position have surfaced from time to time. Complaints have not only been concerned with illegal activities: there is also the use of high pressure sales techniques deployed against clients whose financial sophistication is limited and a battery of alleged sharp practices in the management of client accounts (Bosworth-Davies, 1988).

The management of client accounts has been the cause of recent dispute between regulatory agencies in the US and the UK (*The Economist*, Sept. 2 1989). In the United States broker-traders have been required to segregate client accounts from their own accounts under regulations imposed by the Commodity Futures Trading Commission. In the United Kingdom on the other hand it was standard practice until 1986 for broker-traders to conduct business without segregating their clients' and their own accounts. Nor were contracts time-stamped so that it was almost impossible for clients to identify dealings on their behalf from those of the firm itself!

This lack of elementary protection gave opportunities to the unscrupulous to make use of intra-day price changes to trade and allocate poorer results to clients while keeping profitable deals for the 'house' account. This is no longer the case in the United Kingdom where all futures markets except the London Metal Exchange (LME) maintain segregation of client accounts. Hence in the case of the London International Financial Futures and London Futures and Options Exchange (FOX) practice now conforms much more closely American practice.

The LME however which has a substantial US based clientele argues that given its particular clearing mechanism there is no necessity for such segregation. This is because unlike other futures exchange clients are not required to post daily cash variation margins with a clearing house as contract prices change. When market prices move in particular ways the clearing house uses bank guarantees instead of an extra margin call from clients. Accounts are finally settled only when contracts expire.

This argument has not been readily accepted by the Commodity Futures Trading Commission (CFTC) which argues that where the American clientele is concerned deals must be regulated by the Commission unless the foreign brokers are covered by equivalent rules to its own.

4 TRADITIONAL OPTIONS

An option simply gives the holder the right to buy or sell a commodity or a financial security at a fixed price some time in the future. Notice the option confers the right to buy or sell the item in question: *there is no obligation to exercise that right.* Thus should the holder wish he or she can simply abandon the option with no further commitment.

Traditional or conventional options have existed for many years on many of the world's major exchanges. The buyer of an option faces two sets of charges: first a premium payable to the individual or organisation selling the option; second as options are arranged by a broker there will be a commission charged to the buyer. In London traditional options have a life of three months. They can in theory be negotiated on any shares but they tend to be confined to a relatively restricted number of fairly well known companies.

Options come in two major varieties: there are Call options and Put options. Call options give the right to buy or 'call' the shares at a fixed price and therefore are of obvious interest to individuals who feel that the price of the underlying shares is going to rise. 'Put' options confer the right to sell at a fixed price and therefore are of more interest to those who feel that the market price is going to *fall*. In this case should they prove correct they are in a position to profit from the opportunity to sell shares at a higher price than they cost in the market.

But who can they buy these shares from at a fixed price in a rising market and who can they sell the shares to at a fixed price in a falling market? The counter-party to either of these transactions is the so-called *writer* of the option and they stand ready to deliver the shares should a call be exercised or to buy the shares at the agreed price when a put is exercised. The writer receives a premium for writing the option and of course may hope or expect that the option will not be exercised ie that the price rise or fall will not result in the holder taking the option up.

Table 5.1 below indicates a selection of conventional call options which were available in London in the Spring of 1989. It is noticeable that in the majority of cases the call rate is between 7% to 8% of the underlying share price although slightly higher ratios are observable for marginally second line issues such as Midland Bank and Morgan Grenfell both of which had a rather difficult time in the previous three or four years. Amstrad is well out of line and the investor would be paying a substantial premium in relation to

TABLE 5.1   Call rates available for traditional options, 10 May 1989

Company	Call rate	Share price	$\dfrac{\text{Call price}}{\text{Share price}}$ (%)
Amstrad	18p	109p	16.5
Barclays	34p	457p	7.4
British Petroleum	21p	281^1/$_2$p	7.5
British Telecom	21p	268p	7.8
ICI	85p	1214p	7.0
Jaguar	22p	294p	7.5
Morgan Grenfell	28p	285p	9.8
Midland Bank	35p	346p	10.1
TSB	9p	109p	8.3

the underlying share price in 'giving for the call' in this case. Puts tend to be slightly cheaper than calls. It is possible to obtain a 'double' which allows the buyer to exercise a put or a call depending upon what happens to the underlying price but these are relatively rare and cost at least half as much again as the call rate.

Under what circumstances would an option be taken up? Assume the investor is aware that a certain sum of money eg £15 000 will be available two months from today and that he or she is interested in Jaguar's shares. They currently stand at 294p but the investor feels that they may move upward over the next two or three months because of expectations over a weakening dollar or because of the possibility of a takeover bid. If the investor waits until the funds are available it may be too late: the market may have moved and the shares may no longer be the bargain they were. The following course of action may be contemplated: the purchase of options on Jaguar shares today will lock in the price of the shares at the current price and then when the funds are available it is possible to exercise the option obtaining the shares reasonably close to today's price. Assume the investor has sufficient funds to hand to take an option on 5000 Jaguar shares the transaction will be as follows

5000 Jaguar @ 22p = £1100

This however excludes the broker's commission which is based not on the value of the options but on the value of the shares *whether or not the bargain is exercised*. Fixed commission rates were dismantled as a result of Big Bang in 1986 but assuming that the old commission structure were applicable the cost to the investor would be

1.65% of £14 700 (5000 × 294p) = £242.55

Hence ignoring Stamp Tax and Value Added Tax (which in this case would add a further £110) the total cost of the options comes to £1342.55.

In London traditional options are treated like equities in so far as the normal account period for settlement applies.

When the funds become available the exercise of the option will cost

5000 Jaguar @ 294p = £14 700

The overall cost is £16 042.55 or approximately 321p per share.

If, within the three month time period, the Jaguar share price were to move to levels beyond this then clearly the decision to use the options has been fully justified – the investor has protected the original position. He or she would simply inform the broker and the options would be exercised on the next 'options declaration day' which is always the last Thursday of the account. Indeed if the underlying price moves through the 321p break-even level the investor can exercise the options and sell them immediately informing the broker that he or she is 'closing against options'. The transaction will be executed without having to pay the extra £14 700 which exercising them would have involved: the investor will simply receive any profit.

For example if the price reaches 360p the investor will face the following opportunity

Cost of acquiring 5000 shares via the options = −£16 042.55

Sale of shares realises 5000 × 360p = +£18 000.00

Profit = +£1957.45

There are no further charges involved in exercising options as the investor has already paid full commission and other charges when taking the options initially. Also when *closing* against options the individual is buying and selling within the account so there are no commissions charged on sale of the shares.

If however the investor's expectations are over-optimistic and the share price does *not* rise then there is a problem. If for example the share price falls and stays below the exercise price of 294p to say 280p then it is pointless exercising the options as the shares can be bought more cheaply in the market. This would be the worst possible scenario and the investor's £1,342.55 is lost if a decision is made to abandon the position. If the fall in price is not too drastic then it may be worth exercising the options anyway as any dividends, rights or bonus issues which are declared from the date when the options are purchased will then accrue to the investor. In addition losses made on options are allowable provided that they have actually been exercised.

It is clear however that some investors may wish to use options not as a way of fixing the price of shares for potential future purchase but instead to undertake a limited speculation. If the individual only had £1350 and no promise of future funds the above strategy of using call options offers the chance of a gain of £1957.45. While the price of the share rises from 294p to 360p ie a gain of 22% the options will have produced a gain of 45% ie

£1957.45
£1342.55

Suppose however that the share price does rise as expected but does not reach the break-even 321p? Say for example it settles at 315p and the expiration of the three months is approaching. The choice faced by the individual is

1. Exercise the options, buy the shares at 294p and retain them in the hope that they will continue to perform reasonably well;
2. Finally close out – exercising the options and selling them simultaneously.

If the latter course is undertaken the position will be

Cost of acquiring 5000 Jaguar shares via the options	=	−£16 042.55
Sale of 5000 shares @ 315p	=	+£15 750.00
Loss	=	−£292.55

It is in fact worth exercising the options even if the share price does not reach the break-even point provided it rises beyond the original exercise price because this limits the extent of the loss.

Put options work in the opposite direction thus suppose the individual felt that Jaguar were in fact more likely to fall then the following might be a possible scenario if the put options were to cost 18p on an exercise price of 294p.

5000 × 18p	=	£900.00
Add		
Commission costs @ 1.65% of value of underlying bargain	=	£242.55
Total outlay	=	£1142.55
Cost per share	=	23p

The break-even point therefore

$$(294p - 23p) = 271p.$$

For this strategy to be profitable a price of 271p or less has to come about. For example should Jaguar's price fall to 250p the exercise of the put will have the following outcome.

Sell 5000 shares @ 294p	=	+£14 700.00
Cost of the options	=	−£1142.55
Cost of shares @ 250p	=	−£12 500.00
Profit	=	+£1057.45

Each of the above positions is discussed from the perspective of the buyer of the relevant option. What about the position of the counter-party – the writer of the option? Institutions tend to dominate this aspect of option trading as they are more likely to own shares in sufficient quantities. It can be viewed as a useful source of income and a way of locking in gains which have already accrued.

Assume the Jaguar shares were originally acquired at 196p and the holder is satisfied with the 50% gain which has since accrued. A decision to sell at 294p is one possible course of action but an alternative is to write options.

A writer of the above call options on Jaguar would receive 22p per share ie £1100 on the 5000 shares. In the event that the options remain unexercised at the end of the three month period another set of options can be written on the shares and in this way extra income can be generated. As the individual concerned is already content with the 294p then he or she will not mind should the options be exercised as the 50% gain will have been locked in and in addition the options will have resulted in an effective price of 316p.

The point about dealing in options as opposed to short selling is that the downside risk is predictable and limited to the outlay on the options.[5] A bearish investor who buys put options as described above can abandon the options should the price of the underlying shares rise instead of falling. A loss of £1342.55 would be incurred but this is the maximum extent of the loss. A short sale however commits the individual to deliver shares which have already been sold and there is therefore a potentially unlimited risk.

Suppose that the investor expects the price of Jaguar to fall and therefore decides to sell 5000 shares short then the following indicates a possible scenario in the event of a price increase.

Sell 5000 @ 294p	+£14 700.00
Subtract commission @ 1.65% of the value of the underlying bargain	−£242.55
Proceeds	+£14 457.45

Assume the price of Jaguar moves up from 294p then when the short seller has to make delivery he will be facing a losing position. Indeed should the price rise to 360p the investor would face the following outcome in attempting to cover the short position

Buy 5000 @ 360p	−£18 000.00
Net loss	−£ 3542.55

An upward movement in the share price to 316p (7.5%) is sufficient to incur losses which wipe out the option money. The short seller faces an unlimited potential for losses as theoretically there is no upside limit to a price move.

5 TRADED OPTIONS

This takes the idea of a conventional option and turns it into a standardised format. In the case of traditional options the buyer has one of two choices: exercise if the price moves favourably or allow the option to expire unexercised. By contrast traded options present a third possibility: they are negotiable and can be bought and sold several times prior to the expiry date. The option contract is itself a tradable security which adds an extra element of flexibility and liquidity. Of more than sixty options which are available in London, all but one are based on the extremely well known and heavily traded equities. The exception is an option based on the FT-SE 100 share index (the Footsie).

Traded options also differ from traditional options in a number of other ways:

1. Instead of there being only a single exercise price for the option there usually three exercise prices;
2. There are also a number of expiry dates fixed at intervals of three months. All options are placed on one of three cycles;

(a) January, April, July, October.
(b) February, May, August, November.
(c) March, June, September, December.

The longest life a traded option can have is 9 months so that there can only be three expiry dates on offer at any time. For example take a share assigned to the cycle (b) above. *During* February there will be available – the (about to expire) February options, and the May and August options. On 1st March the market will create a November series to take the place of the now expired February series. When the May options expire on 31st a new February will be added and so on.

The Footsie is the exception to this rule as it offers much shorter expiry dates only one, two, three and four months ahead.

3. There is a minimum unit of trading – a contract – normally set at 1000 shares. Hence when taking traded options (giving for the call or put) the investor will for example talk in terms of a specific number of 'contracts'.

The relatively large size of the contract reflects the preference for low priced shares in the London market and it applies to the vast majority of the options. However if the underlying share price is particularly 'heavy' the unit of trading may be adjusted downward to 100. This is the normal unit of trading in the US.

With the existence of three expiry dates and three exercise prices there are, at any one time, for a given share *nine* possible positions that can be taken in call options and the same number in put options.

TABLE 5.2 Call and put premia for traded options – an example

		Calls			Puts		
		Jul.	Oct.	Jan.	Jul.	Oct.	Jan.
ICI	1150	107	129	162	13	27	33
(1216p)	1200	77	95	132	28	44	52
	1250	43	68	105	55	70	75
Ultramar	280	47	57	70	3	6	8
(316p)	300	32	43	54	8	11	15
	330	13	25	36	21	26	28

This example illustrates two possibilities – a heavily priced share ICI and a more lowly priced share Ultramar.

Immediately below the name of the share is the underlying price as reported on the previous day. Normally three exercise or striking prices are determined: one below, one above and one close to the current market price.

Each option therefore has two sources of value: intrinsic value and time value.

Intrinsic Value

In the case of Ultramar with the actual price standing at 316p two options are 'in the money' in the sense that they stand *below* the current price and one is 'out of the money' at 330p.[6] Options which are 'in the money' such as the 280p series are said have an intrinsic value of 36p (the actual price minus the option's exercise price ie 316p − 280p) while the 300p series has an intrinsic value of only 16p (316p − 300p).

The 'out of the money option' at 330p has no intrinsic value. Clearly the latter is the most speculative option as the price of the underlying share may never get to this level. Hence this will be the cheapest of the options. The existence of a range of exercise prices therefore provides the investor with the possibility of choosing a more or less conservative position.

Time Value

At each exercise price the investor can choose one of three expiry dates – July, October or January. Obviously the longer the expiry date the more valuable a given option will be because there is a longer period of time within which the underlying share price can move in the necessary direction. 'Out of the money' options only have time value whereas 'in the money' options have both time and intrinsic value. Time value declines as the expiry date approaches so that there is continuous downward pressure on the price of all the option series from this factor.

The option premiums which are shown in bold in Table 5.2 are quoted on a *per share* basis so that taking a single contract in the Ultramar July 300 calls will cost

(32p × 1000) = £320 plus expenses.

This gives the holder the right to buy 1000 Ultramar shares for 300p each when they currently stand at 316p. It is an option which is 'in the money'

A single call contract in the Ultramar July 280's would cost

(47p × 1000) = £470 plus expenses.

This is more expensive because it is deeper 'in the money' giving as it does the right to buy the shares at only 280p. This option has a greater 'intrinsic value'.

On the other hand a single call contract on the July 330's will only cost

(13p × 1000) = £130 plus expenses

This particular series is cheaper than the others because it gives the right to buy for 330p shares which currently only stand at 316p. It is obviously the cheapest of the options as it is out of the money.

These option premiums are however only a guide and those appearing in newspapers are normally offer prices ie those at which the investor can buy. As with any security there is a lower price at which the dealer will buy back – the bid price. This spread can be quite substantial calculated as a percentage of the premium – for example spreads of between 10 to 20% have been observed on out of the money options. In the money options can be priced on a similar scale or according to the spread on the underlying security. In addition commission rates can be fairly steep for private individuals – no doubt financial institutions may be able to negotiate cheaper rates. The following were still typical several years after Big Bang:

$2^1/_2$% on the first £5000

$1^1/_2$% on the next £5000

1% on anything above £10 000

A fixed charge of £1.50 per contract is also levied payable to the London Options Clearing House (LOCH). Finally this market does not operate the usual account procedure: it is a cash market and payment is required within twenty-four hours of the deal.

The big advantage that options provide is the potential for gearing. Thus suppose the investor feels that Ultramar's shares which in the middle of May stand at 316p are going to rise sharply over the next two months say to the region of 350p. Let us assume he has sufficient capital to purchase 1000. There are a number of choices which could be made: he could buy the shares themselves and then sell after they appreciate. In which case the gain would be

$$(350p - 316p) \times 1000 = £340$$

less expenses on buying *and* selling the shares. Under the old fixed commission rates and allowing for tax this would have cost nearly £160.00. Ignoring these expenses for the time being the percentage gain on the shares themselves is

$$\frac{350 - 316}{316} = 10.75\%$$

The alternative may be to take a single call contract on July 300 series. This would cost approximately £320.00 (32p × 1000). If the underlying share price then rose to 350p the investor would have the right to buy the shares at 300p and sell at 350p ie a gain of some 50p or 18p more than his present premium. In theory the premium should rise to reflect this now more valuable option and the gain will be in the region of

$$\frac{50 - 32}{32} = 56\%$$

Markets are rarely perfect, however, and one would not expect the option premiums to mirror exactly the change in the price of the underlying share. In addition given what we have said earlier about bid/offer spreads and so on it is clear that the actual gain might be considerably less. However this does not change the fundamental feature of traded options that they are going to exhibit larger percentage changes in their value as the underlying share price changes.

So far we have looked at only one of the possible option series, how would we expect the premiums of the other series to react?

Table 5.3 illustrates the degree of change that would theoretically occur to the premium as each options series expires at different closing prices in the underlying security. It is clear that the least risky position is in the July 280's; these are deepest in the money and have therefore the largest intrinsic value. If the underlying share price is 320p at expiry then given that the shares can be bought for 280p there remains an intrinsic value of 40p and the loss on the original offer premium is only 7p. In the case of the July 300s however a

TABLE 5.3   Change in option premia in relation to share price at expiry

Option Series	Offer Price	Share Price at Expiry		
		320	350	370
July 280	47	− 7 (15%)	+23 (49%)	+43 (91%)
July 300	32	−12 (37%)	+18 (56%)	+32 (100%)
July 330	13	−13 (100%)	+ 7 (54%)	+27 (208%)

price of 320 at expiry implies an intrinsic value of 20p and this is a loss of 12p on the original premium of 32p. Each of the values for gain or loss is calculated in the same fashion. Those options which have some intrinsic value offer a lower risk/reward ratio and therefore despite involving the largest cash commitment they represent the most conservative strategy.

What is noticeable is that the July 330's which are out of the money offer the greatest potential gains from moves in the underlying share price beyond the exercise price and of course they suffer the greatest potential loss if the share price does not rise as expected. Thus these offer the highest risk/reward ratio and involve a smaller initial cash outlay.

Of course this is a deliberately stylised example, in the real world share prices will fluctuate day by day and therefore the price of the traded options will likewise fluctuate. It is worth reiterating therefore that the investor is not locked in to any particular strategy. He does not need to hold the options until they expire: he is in a position to take advantage of a sudden rapid rise in price by selling or alternatively if the price of the underlying security falls it may be judicious to cut one's losses and sell the options at a lower price now rather than wait around in the hope that the share price will recover.

The essential point remains however that in the money options expose the investor to less risk than out of the money options. The counter party to the buyer of traded options is the seller or 'writer' of them. There are two possible approaches here.

Covered Option Writing

To become a writer of options the individual must own at least 1000 shares in one of the traded options. These are then registered in the name of a bank nominee and pledged to the London Options Clearing House. Having done that the writer then chooses an expiry date and exercise price and instructs the broker to write the relevant options. As this is a cash market the proceeds (the bid price minus the commission) are available within several days.

The particular series chosen depends on what view the writer has about the movement in the share price and whether or not he is keen to retain the shares. Let us examine the possibilities. Assume that the investor holds enough shares in Ultramar to write options in them. It is the middle of May and the individual is simply considering the July options. The following may represent the bid prices facing the writer

	July	Oct	Jan
Ultramar 280	43	52	63
300	29	39	48
(316) 330	11	22	31

If the individual expects the shares to remain fairly static between the present and the end of July then he could decide to write the 330's in the hope that they will remain out of the money. If his expectations are borne out the calls will expire without being exercised and he not only receives 11p × 1000 (minus costs) but he is in a position to write more options and generate further cash. He is protected all the way up to 341p (330p + 11p).

If the writer is bearish about the shares' prospects in the short term then the 280's may be the most attractive possibility as they offer a substantial premium and if the individual's expectations are borne out he will not be exercised. If he is wrong and the price moves the other way then he will almost certainly be exercised but he will have the compensation of realising 323p (280p + 43p). In both cases described above the option writer actually owns the underlying securities and is therefore in a position to deliver them if the buyer of the call option decides to exercise. It is possible however for the writer to go 'naked' and write options on shares that he does not actually have.

This is a highly speculative strategy because while the buyer of options has a *right* to call or put shares at a fixed price, the writer (seller) of options is incurring an *obligation*: he must deliver the underlying securities if a call is exercised or take delivery of the securities if a put is exercised.

Thus if a holder of call options exercises his option the writer will have to go into the market to acquire the shares at *whatever* the market price may be to meet his obligation.

Taking our earlier example of Ultramar July 330's, the writer may feel that there is little chance of the share reaching these levels and therefore write ten option contacts without owning the shares. If the shares were now to surge to 370 then he will almost certainly be exercised and face a loss (ignoring costs) of

$$(10 \times 1000 \times 370) - (10 \times 1000 \times [330 + 11]) = £2900$$

Theoretically the loss is open-ended as the underlying share price could go to almost any level.

The writer of naked options is required to lodge a 'margin' with LOCH of cash equivalent to 25% of the value of the underlying security and as with futures this margin is adjusted to take into account the degree to which the option series is in or out of the money. Greater margin is required when the option is in the money and less if the option is out, as in the former case the possibility of being exercised is greater than in the latter case.

Writing Put Options

Effectively the individual is selling the right to sell at a fixed price. This therefore means that he is obliged to take delivery of the underlying security at an agreed price and in return for taking on this obligation the writer receives the put premium. This particular approach is difficult to make sense of until one realises that it would appeal to a person who is optimistic about a share's prospects. Thus say the investor decided to write puts in Ultramar the following possibilities were available as of May 1989

Puts

		July	Oct	Jan
Ultramar (316)	280	3	6	8
	300	8½	11	15
	330	21	26	28

If the investor takes the view that the share is likely to rise or stay the same over the next six months then by writing puts in the October 300 series a premium of 11p per share is available and for as long as the share price stays above this level he will not be exercised.

On the other hand if the individual actually wants to buy Ultramar but feels that the current market price at 316p is a little on the high side then by writing the January 300's the individual will have generated some short term income and in the meantime should the market price fall below the striking price exercise will occur so that he will have to take delivery of the shares at 300p. As long as the share price falls no lower than 285p (300p − 15p) the individual has obtained the share at what may be considered a satisfactory price. On the other hand if the share price continues to rise beyond current levels then the investor will have missed the boat but at least has some compensation from the premium!

6 INDEX OPTIONS AND INDEX FUTURES

Thus far we have discussed options in the context of individual shares and the existence of a real underlying security implies that should the buyer of a traded option wish he could exercise the option and thereby obtain the shares.[7] There are in addition however options which are not based on a 'real' security but instead based on an *index* of share prices. Unlike the earlier examples however this option is not exercised on an underlying security. Instead the process of exercise if it occurs is accomplished by a cash transfer equivalent to the intrinsic value of the option ie the difference between the present index value and the exercise price.

At first sight this may seem rather peculiar but remember what gives a traded option its value is the *price* of the underlying share – hence it is possible to conceive of a traded option based on the price of a group of shares. This might appeal to an individual or fund manager wishing to hedge against a fall not in a single share but in a portfolio of shares caused for example by a drop in the whole market.

Assume the investor suspects that the market is going to fall. There are a number of possible strategies that could be considered:

o Liquidate the entire portfolio and move into cash in the hope of buying back once the market adjustment is complete;
o Switch into fixed interest investments on the assumption that they will suffer less or even gain in the event of a downturn in the equity markets.

Whichever of these is chosen there will be transactions costs involved in a wholesale switch in the portfolio and if the market moves contrary to the investor's expectations then there will be an additional opportunity cost involved if the market recovers inducing a rise in the value of the portfolio.

A third alternative therefore might be to make use of the index options: the FT-SE 100 index option might be a suitable way of setting up a hedge.

For example on 15 November 1989 the Footsie was very close to 2200 (it was actually 2202). With a number of rather unsettling experiences such as the 190 point drop on Wall Street on 13 October and the emergence of poor economic news, a London investor might decide that a further fall in share prices of around 10% is likely in the short run say by the end of January 1990. It would be possible for the investor to protect the position either by selling the portfolio (hoping to buy it back later) or by making use of the index option in the following way:

Buy the January FT-SE 2200 puts. If the investor is trying to protect a portfolio of £265 000 it would be necessary to buy some twelve put contracts

$$\text{ie} \quad 2200 \times £10 \times 12 \ = \ £264\,000$$

to be almost completely covered. This is because the contract size is simply shares to the value of £10 multiplied by the level of the index. As the premium for the January puts was 90p the cost of this operation would be (omitting commission expenses):

$$90 \times £10 \times 12 \quad = \quad £10\,800$$

If the index does indeed fall by about 12% to 1950 and the premium on the 2200 puts rises to 300p the result is

$$300 \times £10 \times 12 \quad = \quad £36\,000$$

This constitutes a profit of some

$$£36\,000 - £10\,800 \quad = \quad £25\,200$$

Which is almost sufficient to cover the loss of 10% (£26 400) on the portfolio. The investor still retains the original shares.

If of course the market does not move over the period in question the buyer of the put will have effectively given up some 4% of the original portfolio (£10 800) in purchasing the downside protection of a put. The fact that the index rose to about 2300 by the end of January 1990 means that the investor's portfolio would be worth approximately

$$\frac{2300 \times £265\,000}{2200} \quad = \quad £277\,045$$

ie a gain of some £12 000 – sufficient to offset the original costs of buying the puts.

The point about this strategy is that the alternative route of selling the portfolio outright would clearly have been the incorrect decision

An alternative strategy would be *write* call options on the index on the assumption that the market is going to fall. Hence the premium income would help to compensate for the falling value of the portfolio. In the event that the call writer gets matters wrong then the loss that would result from being exercised can be covered by the higher value of the individual's portfolio.

Index Futures

An index future based on the S&P500 was introduced in 1982 by the Chicago Mercantile Exchange and consistent with the size of the American market this has proved to be the most widely used such contract in world markets. In London a futures contract based on the FT-SE100 is offered by LIFFE.

The S&P500 contract has a series of expiry dates based on the nearest two consecutive months and a quarterly cycle: expiry actually takes place on the third Friday of the relevant month and settlement which takes place in cash depends upon the opening value of the index on that day.[8] In terms of size the contract is $500 multiplied by the level of the index and the size of the 'tick' is $25. With an index value of some 338 as of November 2nd 1989 each futures contract effectively represented the equivalent of a basket of equities worth

$$\$500 \times 338 = \$169\,000$$

Obviously given that most users will be unable to deliver the exact stocks that comprise the S&P500 index the contract is settled by cash transfers from losers to gainers.

One of the features of index futures is that there is a close relationship between the value of the futures contract and the underlying index on which it is based. The link is maintained by the process of arbitrage between the cash and the futures market. By holding a group of shares which reflects the index, the owner obtains a flow of income arising from dividends but on the other hand the investor foregoes a *certain* income that would have come in the form of interest from putting the funds into the money market. However unlike investing in the money market possession of the shares and/or the futures contract gives the investor an opportunity to profit from capital gains or losses arising from movements in the market. A 'fair price' for the futures contract can be calculated from the following equation:

$$P_f = P_i \left(1 + \frac{[r-d].n}{365}\right)$$

where P_f = price of the futures contract;
P_i = price of the index;
r = the relevant money market rate for 'n' days;
d = the dividend rate calculated on an annual basis;
n = the remaining number of days before the contract expires.

There is an irreducible uncertainty embedded in this relationship arising from the fact that 'd' is unknowable and can only be estimated but we might expect the actual price of the futures contract to gravitate toward the best estimate provided by this equation. In any case differences arise between the futures price of the index and the cash price and it is to take advantage of these price differences that certain techniques of *index arbitrage* have arisen.

For example if the current level of the S&P500 is 330 while the fair value of the futures contract is 335p and the actual index futures price is 340p (ie futures stand at a premium to their fair value) the process of selling the futures contract and buying the underlying stocks will tend to close the discrepancy – driving down the price of the futures contract (towards 335p) while simultaneously raising the value of stocks in the cash market (towards 335p).

This process is accomplished via the use of programmed trading and is most efficiently executed by computers (see Chapter 8). The recent development of this phenomenon has led many people to associate the volatility of markets in the 1980s with index arbitrage. In fact, as is obvious from the example, the effect of this form of arbitrage is simply to close the gap between the cash and futures markets and in this way does not itself contribute to large increases in market volatility. Indeed there are some who argue that the futures market reacts more rapidly to economic and political 'news' and in effect 'signals' likely changes to the actual stock market.

Given both the lower cost and the greater liquidity of the futures contract it is in fact easier to take a position with regard to the direction of the market in the futures market than to move into and out of the underlying stock. This in itself may mean that fund managers who wish to hedge against a market fall do not have to sell the actual shares; instead going short on the futures contract may provide the necessary protection. In this sense it may be argued that the futures market acts as a sort of shock absorber and insulates the real market from rather larger movements that otherwise would be experienced. Nevertheless it is possible to argue that a slight increase in the level of volatility has been induced: for example one might envisage circumstances where dealers have two offsetting positions – one in the cash market and the other in the futures market – as expiry dates approach these dealers may let the position in the futures market expire while closing out the position in the actual shares.

In fact however the evidence about the supposed volatility of the market is not clear cut: there seems little correlation between programmed trading and the volatility of the market. Grossman (1988) shows that there is no significant relationship between the intensity of programme trading (as measured by the percentage of total New York Stock Exchange orders accounted for by programme trades) and market volatility as measured by the ratio of daily market highs and lows. The real explanation of market volatility lies not with the existence of futures markets and index arbitrage but with portfolio insurance:

> Index arbitrage and futures markets are not the central issues in understanding large price moves. The central problem is that when large institutions simultaneously attempt to sell stock in order to lock in capital gains, they will fail and stock prices will fall. (Grossman, 1988)

NOTES

1. The forward markets in foreign exchange are exceptionally liquid because of the existence of a considerable number of large banks who are not only end users but also willing to 'take a position' in various currencies.
2. We have assumed for simplicity that the future price varies one for one with the spot price for coffee. If this is not the case then it is possible to calculate the necessary number of contracts by setting up an adjusted hedge – termed a *delta* hedge.
3. This could cause undesirable feedback effects from the futures to the spot market. For example if the value of contracts outstanding is greater than the value of the gilt in the spot market then a speculator who threatens to take delivery of a contract will induce disruptive effects on the pricing process in the spot market. Those people who have sold ('are short') the futures contract will try to buy the real gilt for delivery and this rush to meet their commitments will cause very large movements in the price of the relevant gilt.
4. In like manner each tick in the US Treasury Bond contract is worth $(\frac{1}{32})(0.01)(100\,000) = \$31.25$.
5. A short sale is undertaken when the investor sells shares that he or she does not currently own. The hope is that having sold the shares at a fixed price it will be possible to buy them back for delivery *after* the price falls. Short selling is fairly commonplace in the United States and less so in the UK. However in London such a strategy can of course be undertaken within the 'account'.
6. If the exercise price of one of the option series happened to be equal to the underlying share price this would be described as being 'at the money'.
7. It is also possible to buy options on exchange rates or interest rates. This might be a preferred alternative to buying foreign exchange forward or entering into a forward rate agreement.
8. Termed the 'witching hour' in the USA when on this quarterly expiry date triple witching can take place as futures, options and options on futures expire simultaneously.

6 The Institutional Investors

1 INTRODUCTION

Free market economies are characterised by a vast range of financial institutions. In the past legal barriers (in the US and Japan for example) or self-imposed constraints (in the UK) led certain financial institutions to confine their activities to particular markets. But with the process of deregulation and liberalisation there has been a steady erosion of these lines of demarcation so that more and more institutions now range across different markets offering a variety of financial services. For example in the UK building societies are intruding into territory that was once the preserve of the banks and vice versa. In the US there is intense pressure on the authorities to repeal the Glass-Steagall Act to allow banks to deal in securities to compete with the German and Swiss universal banks which do everything US and UK banks do but in addition are directly involved in underwriting and trading equities and bonds.

But while the barriers to different markets have been crumbling some differences remain: it is still useful for example to distinguish organisations offering a variety of money handling and investment advice services such as banks and building societies from those institutions which have longer term horizons and operate principally in the capital market.

2 INVESTMENT INSTITUTIONS

The investment institutions are classified into four major categories – insurance companies, pension funds, unit trusts and investment trusts.[1] They are similar to deposit taking institutions in so far as they aggregate savings from a variety of sources and apply them to various outlets. They differ from deposit takers in so far as they do not necessarily offer a specific rate of interest and they do not guarantee the value of the investment. Instead the return will depend on how well the underlying investments perform. They invest in different types of assets – money market instruments, equities, fixed interest securities, property, and even, in the case of some pension funds, fine art.

Investment institutions also tend to operate over a much longer time horizon and in the case of insurance companies and pension funds a great deal of the savings flow they mobilise takes the form of contractual commitments. While unit trusts and investment trusts have traditionally been more geared toward lump sum investment they also have schemes which allow for regular savings plans.

One of the most significant features of capital markets over the last thirty years has been the rise of the institutional investors. This phenomenon has been a characteristic of nearly all capitalist economies and is particularly marked in those economies with well developed stock markets. The growth of institutional ownership has led one commentator to describe the system as 'money manager capitalism' (Kregel, 1988).

In the UK the programme of privatisation implemented during the 1980s appeared to have halted the process by greatly expanding the number of individual investors but the collapse in share prices in 1987 quelled the enthusiasm of many first time investors and the trend toward institutional dominance re-asserted itself. Table 6.1 illustrates changes in the holdings of ordinary shares in the UK over the period 1963-89.

Between 1963 and 1981 the decline in individual shareholdings was mirrored by the growth of the insurance companies and pension funds which together accounted for over 47% of the total. The rise in the pension funds over the period was extraordinary resulting in about a fourfold increase in their share of the total.

TABLE 6.1 Percentage distribution of shareholding by value – UK equities

	1963	1978	1981	1989
Pension Funds	7.0	20.4	26.7	29.0
Insurance Companies	10.6	17.2	20.5	25.0
Investment and Unit Trusts	10.2	13.5	10.7	9.0
Total Institutional	27.8	51.1	57.9	63.0
Persons	58.7	33.2	28.2	18.0
Industrial and Commercial Companies	4.8	4.1	5.1	4.0
Overseas holders	4.4	5.0	3.6	8.0
Other*	4.3	6.6	5.2	7.0
Total %	100.0	100.0	100.0	100.0
£bn	27.0	63.0	92.0	460.0

* Public Sector/Charities etc.
Financial Times, 22 Feb. 1990.
The Stock Exchange Survey of Share Ownership, 1981.
Committee to Review the Functioning of Financial Institutions, Cmnd 7937, 1980.

From 1981 to 1989 the proportion of equities held by the personal sector continued to fall rapidly despite the growth in the *number* of shareholders consequent upon the privatisation programme. In fact however while share ownership became wider it is very thinly spread as over 60% of shareholders own shares in only one company.

By 1989 the institutions accounted for nearly two-thirds of the total. The proportion held by industrial and commercial companies was broadly static while overseas holders were rebuilding their share toward that of twenty-five years before.

In the United States the picture of institutional dominance of equity holdings is not so marked as in the UK. This partly reflects long standing cultural attitudes to individual share ownership but it also reflects the impact of legal provisions which tended to constrain the investment policies of institutions such as pension funds and life insurance companies – limiting their investment in equities and emphasising high quality 'investment grade' bonds. Nevertheless in the US the growing role of the institutions has also been the subject of much discussion since the early 1970s.

Table 6.2 indicates that the proportion of equities held by the institutions has more than doubled in the period 1970 to 1988 from 16.9% to nearly 35% and this growth has occurred mainly at the expense of persons. In other words households have been switching from direct holdings to collective investment vehicles. It is pension funds which are again most significant in this process. By contrast US insurance companies having increased their holdings in the 1970s appear to have allowed their share to diminish marginally in the 1980s. Mutual funds have experienced something of a roller coaster effect with a substantial increase in the 1980s after a marked contraction in the previous decade.

TABLE 6.2 Percentage distribution of shareholding by value – US equities

	1970	1980	1988
Pension Funds	9.5	18.4	25.5
Insurance Companies	2.8	3.7	3.3
Mutual Funds	4.6	2.7	6.0
Total Institutional	16.9	24.8	34.8
Persons	74.0	65.9	54.4
Overseas holders	3.2	4.1	6.4
Other*	5.9	5.2	4.4
Total %	100.0	100.0	100.0
$bn	857.5	1569.0	3117.7

* Non-profit organisations/commercial and savings banks etc.
Derived from Board of Governors of the Federal Reserve System, *Flow of Funds Accounts*, 1989.

Another remarkable feature of the 1970s was a substantial fall the number of individual shareholders. Indeed in April 1973 the Chairman of the NYSE was moved to suggest that 'the individual investor has already acquired the status of an endangered species'. (Seligman, 1982 p. 446)

Contrary to expectations however the 1980s saw a major revival of individual interest and the number of private investors rose very rapidly almost doubling – until by mid-decade over 47 million (20%) of the population held shares directly compared with just over 25 million (12%) ten years previously. This revival was undoubtedly fuelled by the boom in equity markets up until 1987, but it seems unlikely to change the long run trend as the incentive to hold shares via collective savings vehicles remains strong because of their tax advantages and their diversification potential.

In Japan similar trends have been at work: there has been a substantial contraction of individual equity holdings from just over 61% of the total in 1950 to only 23.6% by 1987 (Tagaki, 1989). Over the same period financial institutions – banks and insurance companies excluding investment trusts – increased their holdings from 12.6% to 42.2%. However there is also considerable cross-holding of shares among related corporations in Japan – a phenomenon which is less common in the UK and the US. By the late 1980s these cross-holdings accounted for a further 30.6% of the total – up from 26% in 1950. In other words there has been the same inexorable growth in the significance of institutional/corporate ownership so that by the late 1980s nearly three-quarters of shares were held collectively. There has also been a growing foreign presence from just over 1% of the total in 1960 to nearly 4% by 1987. The vast majority of this is undoubtedly in the portfolios of overseas institutional investors.

Other stock markets do not yet exhibit institutional/corporate dominance to anything like the same degree. In Germany for example the role of pension funds and insurance companies in equity markets has been held back by two factors. First there are legal constraints which have restricted the proportion of capital they can invest in shares to 25%. Secondly pension funds tend to be used predominantly for the internal financing needs of the company granting pension rights hence little escapes to the external capital market. As a consequence pension funds and insurance companies own only 12% of domestic equity (Federation of the German Stock Exchanges, 1988). In other European markets the number of individual shareholders has been rising albeit from an extremely low base: in France for example there were only 4 million shareholders with less than 15% of listed shares at the beginning of the 1980s and this was creeping up toward 5 million owning 18% by 1988–9. Tax incentives introduced in the late 1970s offering relief on income directed to the purchase of equities (up to a ceiling of FF7000 annually) as well as the effect of privatisation of public assets in the 1980s stimulated individual interest in share ownership. But the vehicles for collective investment – Sociétés d'Investissement à Capital Variable

(SICAVs) and the Fonds Communs de Placement (FCPs) investment in which also attract tax breaks – have been growing exceptionally rapidly and are likely to become the preferred mechanisms for private investors.

3 INSURANCE COMPANIES

Insurance comes in two main types – 'general' insurance which is normally taken out on a yearly basis and provides cover against the possibility of loss from a wide range of phenomena such as fire, theft, automobile accidents etc; and 'life' insurance which is a longer term contract offering cover against risk of death, injury, incapacity and so on. In both cases payment depends on the occurrence of some contingent event. Life insurance however is frequently designed to provide an element of investment in the form of capital security plus a long term yield hence it has become common to refer to this arrangement as life *assurance*. In this case the proceeds will certainly be paid out either because death occurs during the period when the policy is in force or because the specified term is complete (eg ten years, twenty years) and the accumulated income derived from investment and reinvestment of the annual premia falls due. The exact sum received by the policy holder will not be so predictable as although there is an element which is guaranteed or 'assured' there is also a variable element which depends upon the performance of the investments chosen by the company.

This part of the insurance business has become so successful that policies are now advertised and sold which barely mention protection on death (not after all the most promising line for sales literature to pursue) instead all the emphasis goes on the saving element in the contract – 'with profits' endowment, unit-linked policies and so on. The growth in this species of insurance was aided in the UK by two major tax advantages in the form of lower corporate taxes on investment income and (prior to 1984) income tax relief on premiums.

Life companies are not simply confined to insurance per se; they are deeply involved in the management of pension funds and other investment media for which they receive fee income.

They are similar to other financial intermediaries: they gather the savings of individuals and families and transfer them to organisations – corporate, public and/or governmental – which have a deficit and need to borrow. Hence insurance companies are significant providers of capital to a variety of markets. The portfolios of the industry are generally spread across a spectrum of different assets with government securities having a major role. Property, ordinary shares, mortgages, loans and cash also play an important part in their asset allocation decisions. Most companies have also built up a considerable volume of assets in foreign markets and as such markets continue to liberalise this is likely to be a permanent feature of their portfolio construction in the future.

An indication of the recent pattern of UK life companies' assets is provided in Tables 6.3 and 6.4. These tables do not take into account cash and short term assets of the companies which are not inconsiderable – for 1988 net short term assets were over £2.8 billion.

It is clear from the Tables 6.3 and 6.4 that government and other public sector securities represent a considerable proportion of invested assets and while this total has been declining in recent years (from 30% to 20%) one would nevertheless expect this to remain an important arena for UK insurance company funds.

TABLE 6.3   UK insurance companies assets at market value (£m), year end 1983–8

	1983	1984	1985	1986	1987	1988
Total of which	106 061	124 874	142 563	174 058	187 457	213 285
Public Sector securities	31 470	33 267	36 112	38 444	42 380	41 642
Company securities of which	48 568	62 404	75 734	101 033	104 454	121 619
Ordinary shares	39 778	50 637	60 996	79 087	79 180	90 915
Unit trust units	3703	5480	7995	13 547	15 125	18 461
Preference shares and Bonds	4920	6287	6743	8399	9649	12 243
Other investments* (Inc. overseas)	26 023	29 203	30 717	34 581	40 623	50 024

* Overseas government securities/Mortgages/Loans/Fixed Assets etc.
Business Statistics, MQ5, 3rd Quarter 1989.

TABLE 6.4   Distribution of UK insurance companies assets, at year end (%)*

	1983	1984	1985	1986	1987	1988
Public Sector securities	30	27	25	22	24	20
Company securities	46	50	53	58	56	57
Other investments	24	23	22	20	21	23

* Numbers have been rounded up.

Since the 1960s and the so-called 'cult of the equity' there has been a shift in allocation towards equities – and this has continued in the 1980s: ordinary shares were some 37.5% of total assets in 1983 and by 1986 some 45%. This of course partly reflects a bull market which saw equity values rising faster than the other sectors – hence after the 1987 Crash the share of equities fell back to only 42%. However the rise in equity values is only part of the story as clearly there have also been policy decisions to increase the weight of equities in the overall portfolio. By 1987 and 1988 company securities were accounting for nearly two-thirds of the net *investment* undertaken by the companies.

As insurance companies are in competition with other institutions for the savings of potential investors better performance in areas such as 'with profit' endowment or unit linked products becomes an important selling point. In addition equities provide a better inflation hedge over the long run (compared with fixed interest products).

The position in the United States bears some comparison: assets of the life companies nearly doubled over the period 1983–8 from some $655 billion to $1140 billion. By 1988 government paper played a minor and diminishing role at less than 8% whereas company securities accounted for some 56% of the total. Unlike the UK however it is corporate bonds which provide the single largest outlet for insurance company investment accounting for 35% in 1983 and 46% by 1988. This is probably a function of the size and liquidity of the corporate bond market in the United States but in addition it may also reflect legal constraints as to the range of investments which life companies and other institutional investors are permitted to undertake.

4 PENSION FUNDS

Pension funds in the UK and the US have taken over from insurance companies as the largest institutional force in capital markets. For example in the UK they account for almost 30% of equity holdings while total assets are in excess of £200 billion. In the United States at the end of 1988 the corresponding figures were 23% of equity holdings and nearly $1300 billion. This gives them enormous leverage and influence and the fact that the funds may be managed by a relatively small group of merchant banks, insurance companies and/or specialist fund managers has occasioned critical disquiet (Minns, 1980).

Pension schemes come in two varieties: 'pay as you go' schemes and 'funded' schemes. The former are really inter-generational transfer payments in which current pensions (and other benefits) are paid for via the contributions of members of the scheme who are still working – many state schemes operate on this principle. In 'funded' schemes, a fund is accumulated from the contributions of the members of the scheme and in due course the fund itself provides the wherewithal to pay the various benefits.

Funded Schemes

These operate either as *defined benefit* schemes or as a *money purchase* arrangement. Defined benefit schemes promise the member a range of benefits which relate to matters such as final salary, lump sum benefits, life insurance, survivor benefits and the like. The scheme is normally funded so as to achieve these benefits but in the event that resources are deemed to be inadequate the employer frequently underwrites them by increasing contributions accordingly.

Money purchase schemes do not operate by promising a range of specified benefits but instead attempt to accumulate the largest possible fund and then benefits will be purchased from the proceeds of the fund according to how well it has done. Most collective pension schemes are of the defined benefit variety while most personal pensions are money purchase arrangements.

In the case of funded schemes a great deal hangs on the growth of the underlying fund. While contributions add to the value of the fund over time, the prospective pensioner will clearly be better off the more effectively his or her savings are invested.

Pension funds therefore represent a very significant area of long term contractual savings and the tax treatment of pension schemes has traditionally made pensions one of the most attractive areas of personal investment. Not only are contributions free of tax but so too are any capital gains which may be made on the fund's investment. In addition no form of corporation tax applies to the income accruing in the fund. This generous tax treatment goes a long way to explain the astonishing growth in the size of pension funds.

Not only does the funding basis of pensions vary but also they can be managed in a variety of ways. This makes for a further layer of complexity in attempting to evaluate their significance for the economy. Thus many of the larger occupational schemes may be self-managed and simply hire a group of financial advisers on a full or possibly part-time basis, others may be passed over totally to be managed for a fee by a merchant bank via a fund management arm, and yet others, fully insured schemes, may be managed by insurance companies.

Pension funds have a series of prospective liabilities and attempt to match their assets to these liabilities. This implies investing the flow of funds in a manner which obtains a sufficiently high yield to meet their obligations without subjecting the fund to undue risk. In this respect the money purchase funds are a good deal riskier than the defined benefit schemes as in the latter case, as pointed out above, the employer is frequently committed to make good any actuarial deficit. In addition in company pension schemes the fund is legally separate from the financial position of the employer so that if the company goes bankrupt the position of pensioners is protected.[2]

In the case of defined benefit schemes a complicating factor arises in so far as future liabilities are in *real* terms because the benefits are related to wages and salaries near the time of retirement and once the pension is in payment many schemes offer inflation proofing by adjustment of the value of the pension.

The nature of these commitments makes it important for pension schemes to perform better than the rate of inflation and this has consequences for the types of investment that may be judged suitable and the investment policy of the relevant fund.

Tables 6.5 and 6.6 indicate the way in which self administered Pension Fund holdings have changed over the last five years. This is in fact a subset of all pension funds as it does not include those which are managed by insurance companies or specialist fund managers. Nevertheless it provides a useful insight into the investment behaviour of the funds.

TABLE 6.5 Public and private pension fund assets (£m),at year end 1983–8

	1983	1984	1985	1986	1987	1988
Total	107 854	129 438	151 215	182 988	187 580	202 278
of which						
Public Sector securities	22 865	24 716	27 438	28 927	29 321	27 234
Company securities	66 556	84 045	102 442	131 710	134 785	149 585
of which						
Ordinary shares	63 903	80 915	98 916	127 171	129 281	143 479
Unit trust units	793	958	1040	1308	1505	1930
Preference shares and Bonds	1860	2172	2486	3231	3999	4176
Other investments* (Inc overseas)	18 433	20 677	21 335	22 351	23 474	25 459

Business Statistics, MQ5, 3rd Quarter 1989.

It is noticeable that the pattern of asset holding has shifted very markedly toward the corporate sector: government securities still play a significant but declining role in the overall allocation. As is the case for the life companies much of the growth in company securities is a consequence of the rise in the equity values over this period but it is clear evidence from the disposition of new inflows of money that equities receive the lion's share.

This reorientation of pension fund portfolios in the UK away from government securities predates the contraction in the gilts market discussed

TABLE 6.6 Distribution of self-administered pension fund assets, at year end (%)*

	1983	1984	1985	1986	1987	1988
Public Sector securities	21	19	18	16	16	13
Company securities	62	65	68	72	71	74
Other investments	17	16	14	12	13	13

* Numbers have been rounded up.

in Chapter 3 so it reflects 'demand side' rather than 'supply side' factors. Pension funds like insurance companies have also become increasingly involved in global asset allocation and have built up a considerable holding in overseas markets.

5 UNIT TRUSTS

Unit trusts or open-end funds as they are termed in the United States have become an extremely convenient way for individual investors to take a stake in a variety of capital markets.

Unit trusts work by aggregating the savings of individual investors and buying a portfolio of investments. The portfolio is valued daily and units of a given value are sold to investors in proportion to the amount of money they have invested. Unit trusts are 'open ended' in the sense that the size of the fund varies according to the value of the underlying portfolio and the number of units in issue. As money flows into the fund the managers can create more units to meet this demand and use the proceeds to enlarge the underlying portfolio. Similarly if investors wish to cash in part of their holdings the manager will buy back and cancel the units. This may mean that part of the portfolio will be sold but more often the managers will try to match sales against new purchases and use their cash balances changing the portfolio according to the net balance.

Normally investors pay two sorts of charges when investing via unit trusts – a front end charge of 5 to 6% payable only upon initial purchase; and an annual management charge of perhaps 1 to 1.5% of the aggregate value of the trust. The initial charge is used to pay commissions to financial intermediaries involved in selling the trust and partly to cover initial administration. The annual charge goes to the trust's management and largely covers dealing expenses involved in the active management of the underlying portfolio and the units themselves.

The units are sold to the individual at an offer price and bought back on a bid basis. The difference between this offer and bid price is often as much as 6 to 7% so that in effect an investor who bought £1000 worth of units today and sold them tomorrow without any change in the value of the underlying portfolio would only receive about £930.

The formula for calculating the value of the fund in the UK is dictated by the Securities and Investment Board. Theoretically it could allow for a gap as large as 13 to 14% between the bid and offer price. The upper limit – the offer price – is determined by asking what would be the cost of constructing the underlying portfolio as of today from cash and to this is added the trust's initial charge. The lower limit – the bid price – results from estimating the cost of liquidating the trust as it stands on the day.

Not many fund managers feel that this sort of spread would present an attractive opportunity to potential investors. Competition and awareness of investor resistance therefore tend to narrow the spread between the bid and offer price. However the pricing range which the formula permits gives fund managers the opportunity to shift toward the top end or the bottom end according to the state of demand for the units.

The following example may make this clear.

Asset value of unit		£2.00
Maximum permissible spread 14%		
	Offer price	£2.14
	Bid price	£1.86

1. *Pricing on an Offer basis*			
Maximum offer price	£2.14	Investor buys at	£2.14
		Investor sells at	£2.00
		Spread	7%

2. *Pricing on a Bid basis*			
		Spread	7%
		Investor buys at	£2.00
Minimum bid price	£1.86	Investor sells at	£1.86

Clearly while possible it is unlikely that fund managers will switch from one to the other pricing basis very rapidly although this can happen in extreme circumstances such as occurred in October 1987. In fact in this instance the extraordinarily rapid fall in markets made it virtually impossible to calculate the value of the trust and managers were forced to suspend unit redemptions although some investors felt that fund managers were only too pleased to be able to do so.

As share prices vary day by day the underlying value of the portfolio must be recalculated daily to establish the unit price. There are two possible valuation bases – a *historic* pricing base (ie the previous valuation day) or a *forward* pricing base (where the price is presently unknown but will be determined on the next valuation day). The former approach was typical of UK unit trusts until 1988 when the latter approach, common in the USA, was recommended by the SIB. The position is now mixed and either system may be in use. However in the event that markets become volatile and prices move by more than 2%, or if the client has an explicit preference, forward pricing must be employed.

The move to forward pricing was not universally welcomed by the unit trust industry partly because it injects an extra degree of uncertainty into the pricing process but mainly because it removed a possible source of profit for trust managers – operations via the 'box'. Because unit prices were calculated on the basis of previous valuation, managers were in a position to create extra units at times when the price was low or at the bottom of the pricing range. Following a rise in the unit price or a shift to the top end of the bid/offer range these units could be sold to clients rather than newly created units obtained via the trustee. In effect this realised a capital gain for the managers. The profits could then be used to defray expenses and/or cover situations where charges were inadequate in relation to costs. This is not feasible where forward pricing is the rule.

In the UK unit trusts are normally established under Trust Law (as opposed to Company Law) by a management group which will be required to manage the fund's assets in accordance with a 'trust deed'. The deed is examined by the SIB which can refuse authorisation if it is not satisfied. The deed also indicates how the fund is to be managed including such matters as what management charges will be and how units will be priced. In addition it covers other matters such as how investment is to be undertaken eg most funds may only put a limited proportion of their investments into the USM; there are restrictions on the use of financial futures and funds are not normally allowed to invest directly in international commodities.

There is also the added protection of an independent trustee – normally a major bank – appointed to hold the trust's assets. There are something in the order of 1400 unit trusts in the UK and over 2000 mutual funds in the US offering a variety of investment philosophies and orientations. Many trusts confine their investment to the domestic market offering to invest in equities or a mix of equities and fixed income securities, others offer a geographical specialisation by country or by area such as Japan, USA, Australia or Europe, the Pacific, Asia and yet others specialise by sector for example money market funds, smaller companies, recovery stocks, technology, property, commodities and so on.

Thus they encompass a variety of investor preferences including exposure to overseas markets within the context of a reasonably diversified portfolio.

Indeed this is one of the most important selling points which unit trusts are able to offer: they give the smaller investor the opportunity to diversify and therefore to limit the degree of risk to which he or she is exposed. Trusts generally invest in a substantial number of investments, sometimes up to 150–200 but there still remains some degree of risk no matter how well diversified the portfolio may be. In particular of course systematic, market related risk cannot be diversified away. In addition a heavily specialised unit trust offers greater variation in returns as it is deliberately constructed to differentiate itself from the market average. Hence the investor in such a trust should be aware that he or she is being exposed to greater variation in potential return.

Another of the major selling points which is stressed in the promotional material is that of suggesting that unit trusts offer the investor greater market expertise in the selection of shares and the allocation of a portfolio. This has an element of truth in it particularly where international and perhaps other specialist trusts are concerned: clearly when buying into, for example Japanese or Australian companies, some local knowledge is likely to be desirable. However the claim to special expertise should not be overdone – there is little evidence that this translates itself into superior performance in the management of clients' funds.

6   INVESTMENT TRUSTS

These have been around for a much longer period of time than have unit trusts with which they are often confused. They emerged in the nineteenth Century – the first being Foreign and Colonial Investment Trust 1868. However they are not really trusts at all – this is a misnomer: they are trading companies like Amstrad or Texas Instruments but instead of manufacturing and selling specific commodities they use their capital to buy and sell the *shares* of other companies. To this purpose the 200 or so existing investment trusts have floated share capital at some time in the past and used the proceeds to acquire a portfolio of investments the performance of which provides the wherewithal to pay dividends etc. Unlike unit trust therefore they are in American terminology 'closed end' funds because when the value of the underlying portfolio of shares changes this is reflected not in the creation (or withdrawal) of units instead the value of their shares will change.

They offer an advantage similar to unit trusts with regard to the element of diversification they can offer smaller investors. Thus buying say 500 shares in an investment trust means that the individual will be holding an interest in a range of investments.

Take for example an investment in the Fleming Technology Investment Trust: buying shares in this particular trust would have given the investor an indirect stake in over 100 companies including such names as Racal Electronics, Cray Electronics, Cable & Wireless and so on (AITC, 1989).

In the UK investment trusts have suffered *vis-à-vis* unit trusts in the last thirty to forty years because of their inability to advertise.[3] In addition because they are *listed* companies the main route to acquiring shares in such trusts was via a broker and this was a perceived as a cumbersome and forbidding process compared with cutting a coupon from a newspaper or responding to a salesman. On the whole therefore unit trusts have been able to position themselves very effectively as the appropriate vehicle for the risk averse investor who wishes to have part of his or her savings in the equity markets. In addition the existence of contractual saving plans gave the unit trust industry a major marketing advantage. Some investment trusts have also introduced regular saving schemes linked to pension plans and life insurance. Nonetheless investment trusts have tended to lose out *vis-à-vis* unit trusts in attracting new savings.

Investment trusts on the other hand have considerably more room for manoeuvre in terms of their investment policy: as they are conventional companies they are not constrained in the same way as unit trusts. Thus for example they can acquire shares in unquoted companies, invest more heavily in the USM, use options and futures, have a higher proportion of investments overseas and so forth. By contrast the terms of the trust deed impose a legal constraint on a unit trust as to what does and does not qualify as a proper investment.

In addition a unit trust which performs poorly and fails to satisfy investors will face growing net redemptions and this, by reducing the size of the fund, puts pressure on the manager to find a solution fairly quickly. The managers of an investment trust however can alter the composition of the portfolio much more readily: not only is there no deed but shareholder pressure is unlikely to be felt so immediately. Dissatisfied investors sell their equity in the market not back to the trust and the result is simply the substitution of one set of shareholders for another. This, so the argument goes, allows investment trust managers to take the longer view and invest in firms which may have poor short term prospects without worrying that a dip in the share price will generate a shrinkage in the capital invested. As investment trusts are companies they are not confined to issuing equities: they can issue other sorts of capital for example fixed interest bonds may be sold and the proceeds used to expand the share portfolio. They can also issue convertible loan stock and warrants which gives them a great deal of flexibility. Warrants have been particularly favoured in recent years as given their 'promissory' nature they allow trusts to raise fixed interest capital at finer rates. The bullish nature of stock markets in the 1980s led to a considerable growth of issues with warrants attached.

Investment trusts have considerably lower annual management charges than do unit trusts: this is partly explained because unit trusts have larger

Capital Markets

advertising/marketing expenses – it has been estimated that the annual management expenses of investment trusts are between 0.4 and 0.5% of the value of the total assets compared to between 1.25 and 1.5% for unit trusts.

The Discount

A curious feature of investment trusts is the existence of a 'discount' to the net asset value. Recall that in the case of a unit trust the assets of the fund are revalued daily and unit prices are calculated so as to reflect this underlying value. Thus once having subtracted the spread and initial management charge the price of the units will exactly reflect the value of the assets.

This is rarely true in the case of investment trusts. Instead more frequently the shares of the investment trust stand at a discount to the net value of the assets they represent. This rather peculiar result can perhaps be best explained by the use of the simple example in Table 6.7.

TABLE 6.7 Calculating the investment trust discount

		Company X £m	Company Y £m
a.	Market Value of assets	250	740
b.	Liabilities	35	80
c.	Net Assets (a − b)	215	660
d.	Shares in Issue	25m	80m
e.	Value of Net Assets per share (c/d)	860p	825p
f.	Current market price per share	730p	676p
g.	Discount (e − f)	130p	149p

The usual procedure is to express this discount as a percentage of the net asset value hence

h.	$\dfrac{130p \times 100}{730}$	$\dfrac{149p \times 100}{676}$
	17.8%	22%

It is possible but rather less usual for the share price to stand at a premium to the net asset value and of course the discount itself may widen or contract depending upon the behaviour of the share price and the underlying assets.

The existence of the discount is something of a puzzle which is not easily explained: some have pointed to the narrower market for IT shares compared to their underlying portfolio; there is also the fact that some of the income received from investments is not distributed to shareholders either being reinvested or going into management fees. These hardly seem to be very convincing arguments as reinvested income should ultimately increase the assets and income of the trust and management fees are simply too small in relation to the size of the discount.

Despite this proponents of investment trusts emphasise the existence of the discount as a point in their favour compared to unit trusts. In fact the discount is irrelevant to the investor unless it changes over the period when the shares are held. On the other hand the existence of the discount has tempted takeover bids by those wishing to obtain a stake in another target company or who want to realise the value of the underlying assets by selling them in the market.

As with unit trusts, investment trusts may have a number of possible orientations and investment philosophies – growth, income, geographical specialisation, technology – often with a strong overseas orientation as is borne out by the fact that foreign investment accounted for over 45% of holdings in the late 1980s. Up until 1987 the split between domestic and overseas investment had been very broadly equal with perhaps a slight leaning toward the overseas sector. This appears to have been interrupted in 1987 when in common with all the other institutional investors there was a major scaling down of foreign investment as a consequence of the October Crash.

7 INVESTMENT PERFORMANCE

The notion of investment performance is integral to the evaluation of any investment strategy. Unfortunately such an evaluation is not a simple task and there are a number of issues which must be clarified before performance can be assessed.

Most obviously the objectives of the investor have to be clear cut. This allows the investor to ascertain the degree to which the investment vehicle has achieved his objectives. In addition it may make it possible for the investor to compare the performance of portfolios which have similar objectives. Thus an investor whose prime consideration is safety may invest in a portfolio of money market funds and government bonds but should not then complain that his return is below that of a unit trust with an overseas orientation. This is not comparing like with like – the proper comparison is between the return on his chosen portfolio and another which has the same level of risk.

A second reason why it is necessary to clarify the objectives of the investor is the fact that they are not always compatible and a degree of trading-off of one objective for another must be accepted. An obvious case where there may be a trade-off is in relation to return and liquidity: as a general rule one would expect that the greater the liquidity of an investment the lower the rate of return which it offers – conversely the less liquid an investment the greater the return it must promise to get the investor to commit his savings.

In addition of course there is a positive relationship between risk and return: however measured, the greater the riskiness of a given investment the higher the rate of return it must offer in order to induce investors to bear such risk.

Thus there are three key qualities to any investment decision which the investor must consider – liquidity, risk and return. The major problem however is that of specifying acceptable risk for given returns or acceptable returns for a given level of risk.

Institutions are perceived as reducing risk via diversification and increasing returns by particular investment expertise. This is a major selling point in the advertising literature of investment management groups. Given the degree of competition on the part of insurance companies, merchant banks, and specialist fund managers to acquire client funds the ability to demonstrate investment performance is an important promotional ploy in the winning of business. Unfortunately comparisons of investment returns may be made without any mention of relative risk.

In fact a considerable body of empirical evidence suggests that fund managers are not capable of consistently outperforming the main market indexes in the long run. Various academic studies in the UK and the US over the last twenty-five years have indicated that the vast majority of fund managers are unable to provide rates of return which are *consistently* better than broadly based market indexes (Sharpe, 1966; Jensen, 1968; Shawky, 1982; Malkiel, 1985). The proportion varies from study to study but they demonstrate conclusively that 60 to 70 per cent of fund managers are unable to outperform a representative market index such as the Standard & Poor's 500 or the FT-Actuaries All Share Index.

Furthermore even if it were the case that investment fund managers could outperform the market consistently this would not necessarily be to the advantage of the end investor as the abnormal returns might be captured by the fund managers in the form of higher fees and other expenses! In a recent detailed and careful study of mutual fund performance in the US, Grinblatt and Titman (1989) found that 'superior performance may exist, particularly among aggressive growth and growth funds and those funds with the smallest net asset values'. (p. 415)

However the better performing funds were also characterised by the highest expenses so that 'their actual returns, net of all expenses, do not exhibit abnormal performance.' (p. 415)

This leads to a rather depressing conclusion – even when you pick a winner you only get an average return!

Index Linking

Much of the literature critical of performance derives from academic studies in the United States and however unpalatable the early findings were to American fund managers by the mid-1970s funds were advertised which simply offered to construct a portfolio which mirrored a selected market index. Initially the funds in which one could 'buy the market' were only available for large clients such as pension funds but fairly quickly they also became available for ordinary private investors (Malkiel, 1985). Index funds have since grown extremely rapidly and most of the major fund managers in the United States now offer their clients access to one or more such funds. Indeed more than 50% of the top 200 funds in the USA are now index-linked (*The Economist*, Sept. 16 1989).

Initial acceptance of the idea was rather slower in the United Kingdom where there was greater scepticism but the first 'pioneers' began to implement the idea of indexed or passive funds in the early 1980s. There has been a considerable growth since then despite the fact that there are fund managers in the industry who remain unconvinced ('On the Trail of the Index Trackers', *Pensions Management*, April 1989). In 1989 *The Economist* (Sept. 16) reported a survey, conducted by Greenwich Associates, of some 258 pension funds which showed that nearly 20% of their holdings of UK equities were indexed. The same journal pointed out that of 1400 *actively managed* funds, the majority outperformed the FT-Actuaries All Share Index in only three of the ten years between 1978 and 1988.

Nor is it only pension funds which have indexed funds: in 1988 Morgan Grenfell introduced the first index-linked unit trust in the UK and a number of other fund management groups have since followed suit.

The rise of indexing clearly represents an admission by practitioners of the validity of the academic research but it also reflects the fact that index managed funds are less costly in terms of both annual charges and broking commissions – the lower costs are a consequence of the fact that the portfolio tends to be adjusted much less frequently.

Despite protestations from traditionally minded fund managers the idea is one which appears likely to grow, so how exactly do the various arrangements operate? In contrast to the approach by which fund managers choose equities so as to construct a portfolio which outperforms competitors, indexing is a straightforward technique which builds a portfolio in order to approximate a chosen market index. It is not feasible to expect the fund's performance to match the index perfectly so there will usually be an irreducible error which is termed the 'tracking error'. This measures the degree to which the portfolio is expected to deviate from the index – for example plus or minus 0.5%.

There are a number of ways of constructing an index fund for example replication, stratified sampling or optimised sampling – each of which has its protagonists. While there may not be a great deal of difference in the performance of funds which use these methods there may be marginal differences in the fee structure because of the degree of complexity.

In fact the issue of fees and expenses is one of the main advantages of the indexed fund: because the fund is managed in a passive manner there is less turnover of the underlying portfolio hence there are fewer commissions paid. Periodically of course it is necessary to rebalance or restructure the portfolio because the constituent elements in the target index change from time to time. Thus for example privatisations of major state run enterprises bring new and frequently substantial additions to the index. In addition takeover activity, mergers, share buy backs all tend to alter the composition of the relevant market index. But apart from these necessary adjustments there is little or no 'churning' of client funds in the chase for performance.

Management fees for indexed funds are only one third of those charged for an actively managed fund: the average fee tending to be in the region of 0.1% of funds under management compared to the more usual 0.3% for an actively managed portfolio. The effect of these lower fees plus the accumulating empirical evidence comparing the performance of passive versus active management would suggest that indexed funds will continue to grow in the near future.

Tilted Funds

Total passivity still goes against the grain for many fund managers so modifications have been suggested which maintain the key features of indexation yet inject a flavour of the actively managed portfolio to produce variations on the basic method. Thus there are so-called 'tilted' funds or the 'core-periphery' (core-satellite) funds. These attempt to combine the mechanistic approach implied in a fully indexed fund with an element of managerial discretion.

In the tilted approach the majority of the fund is indexed but there is a deliberate attempt to exclude poorer performing sectors or to load up on better areas. For example given what has been said in Chapter 2 about the tendency for smaller firms to deliver a better average return some managers might choose to give this sector a stronger weighting in the portfolio.

Alternatively if the outlook for the electronics sector looks weak the portfolio will reduce the weight of electronics shares. The 'core-periphery' approach is simply a variant of the above: by far the greater part of the portfolio (eg 80/85%) is indexed in the conventional way while the rest is allocated to specialist managers who take a more active line in an attempt to outstrip the competition and raise the overall performance of the fund. This will of course increase management expenses and brokerage fees although if management expenses are performance related it would be possible to mitigate their costs to some degree.

Superficially these approaches have their attractions but ultimately one must remember the evidence about the accuracy of analysts' forecasts (Cragg and Malkiel, 1982). Loading up on the so-called 'performing' sectors and avoiding the 'bad' sectors is only as good as the forecasting ability of the analyst/manager. It might be rather easier to forecast the behaviour of *sectors* as opposed to the earnings of individual firms but the fact that it is possible to be off target in short to medium term forecasting means that a 'tilted' fund might be tilted the wrong way!

8 THE SIGNIFICANCE OF THE INSTITUTIONS

Size

The growth of the institutions has been aided by a combination of familiarity, favourable tax treatment and the attractions of a diversified portfolio which they are able to provide for the individual. In addition of course there is the putative investment expertise which they offer to less knowledgeable investors. But the size and concentration of the investment institutions presents something of a problem for some capital markets: for example, London unlike NASDAQ and the NYSE has a smaller individual client base and is dominated by some 150 institutions. This highly concentrated structure may have a number of unwanted effects. For example the institutions may develop a herd-like mentality where, if some are seen to be reluctant to invest, then others will rapidly follow suit (Peston, *The Independent*, April 10 1989). Hence they may be in a position to influence government policy by for example 'staying on the sidelines' in the gilts market.

A small group of institutions may also give rise to fads and fashions with potentially unhealthy effects on merger activity. For example if the institutions develop an investment philosophy which focusses on a narrow segment of the market, this may drive up those share prices disproportionately. This gives the firms in question greater opportunities to embark on a process of growth by acquisition. In biassing investment decisions toward 'blue chips' or the high tech sector the institutions may produce quite unintended effects on the structure of industry.

In addition there are many economists and industrialists who accuse the institutions of 'short termism' by which they mean the tendency for the institutions to focus on the short run share price behaviour rather than longer term industrial developments. The fact for example that turnover (purchases and sales as a proportion of holdings) rose from some 35% to over 60% between 1981 and 1987 seems to point to a 'churning' of portfolios in an attempt to improve short run performance.

Mergers and Acquisitions

One's judgement of the behaviour of the institutions however is also conditioned by whether or not one regards Mergers and Acquisitions (M&A) activity as a benign or a malign influence on the economy. Indeed for those critics (Minns, 1980) who view takeovers largely as a prelude to 'asset stripping', 'green mailing' and the like, the institutions are prepared to vote with their feet rather too readily and to take a short term gain for their policy-holders or pensioners rather than to hold for the longer term. Hence in this view the influence of the institutions is on the whole negative – by holding large concentrations of shares they facilitate M&A activity as they are in a position to determine the success or failure of takeovers, leveraged buy-outs and so on. However there is also a school of thought which sees takeover activity as being crucial to the efficient operation of a free market economy. The model they have in mind is based on the Darwinian notion of the survival of the fittest. Takeovers perform a useful function by being a constant threat to the less efficient managements that if they fall too far behind in the competitive race then the company will be shifted into the hands of others who are able to extract greater returns. There is an implicit and perhaps unwarranted assumption here that the predator firm is indeed likely to produce a structure which is more efficient. Experience in the United States in the 1980s should make us more wary of this assumption: firms bought out in hostile takeovers have not necessarily been more efficiently managed after the event.

Passivity

A further argument about the behaviour of the institutions is that they are such major shareholders that they should exercise power to bring pressure to bear on incumbent managements in order to achieve greater efficiency (Walker, 1987). On the whole in the UK and to a lesser extent in the US however the institutions are largely passive: they are content to allow managements to carry out their function with little interference except in very unusual circumstances.

It may be said that it is not within the competence of the financial institutions to scrutinise the behaviour of managements as they are not directly knowledgeable about the firm or industry in question. If insurance companies and pension funds were to develop a more proactive policy however and they proved to be demonstrably incompetent then the takeover process can still be brought to bear. Little is lost and much might be gained by the institutions taking a closer interest in the performance of companies whose shares are a part of their portfolios.

Volatility

The issue of whether or not greater concentration of holdings by the institutions might impart extra volatility to markets has become an important issue recently particularly in the United States.

This relates to the interaction of new trading techniques and technology referred to in Chapter 8. It is clear that the trading of blocks of shares and portfolio restructuring on the part of relatively few institutions has the *potential* to increase the volatility of markets and undermine long term liquidity. However the rapid switching of a substantial portfolio is no easy task for a large investment fund as it can be expensive in terms of commissions and it may move the market adversely. Consequently derivative markets, ie futures and options, are advocated as more efficient ways of hedging and/or restructuring a portfolio (see Chapter 8).

On the other hand the use of sophisticated techniques such as portfolio insurance and new instruments such as index futures and options may impart a false sense of security and engender more active trading whilst overlooking the fact that market liquidity is only as good as the counterparties' financial position. The situation in the United Kingdom is not yet as advanced as in the US where such trading strategies have their origin but it will be interesting to watch the behaviour of the Tokyo market where the new techniques made their debut in 1989.

Ironically much of the evidence collected over the past twenty-five years points to the fact that 'buy and hold' strategies normally outperform trading strategies. For this reason one might expect institutional holdings to become more stable but the temptation to enhance performance by the use of sophisticated arbitrage strategies might be too strong. This was shown in the US where investment houses having advertised their abstention from these techniques in the wake of the 1987 Crash were at it again on behalf of their clients by 1988-9.

NOTES

1. Unit trusts and investment trusts are mutual funds (open end funds) and closed end funds in the USA.
2. There has been considerable controversy about the protection which members actually do have under current legal arrangements in the UK (Foley, 1987) and the Occupational Pensions Board has put forward a series of proposals in an attempt to mitigate some of the problems (*Financial Times*, Nov. 1989).
3. Under the Financial Services Act 1986 (Part V, Sec. 160) any company is not allowed to advertise shares for sale unless it has either delivered a formal prospectus to the UK Registrar of Companies or framed the advertisement in such a way that no agreement can be entered into until a prospectus has been delivered. The rather anomalous position of investment trusts is currently under review by the authorities.

7 Regulating Markets

1 INTRODUCTION

Markets have been characterised as mechanisms which harness the pursuit of private gain to social ends. This idea of the market as an 'invisible hand' reconciling individual self-seeking with the social good is encapsulated in one of the most famous quotations in the history of economic ideas:

> It is not from the benevolence of the butcher, the brewer or the baker that we expect our dinner but from their regard for their own self-interest. We address ourselves not to their humanity but to their self-love, and never talk to them of our own necessities but of their advantages. (Smith, 1776, p. 119)

However Smith's argument was tempered by the recognition that *competitive* markets are strictly necessary for the invisible hand to operate without exploiting the consumer and he was well aware that private behaviour frequently carries consequences which have effects going beyond the merely individual. The self interest that constitutes the mainspring for markets to work will if carried to extremes produce effects which may undermine the market itself:

> Social life is impossible unless the pursuit of self-interest is mitigated by respect and compassion for others. A society of unmitigated egoists would knock itself to pieces; a perfectly altruistic individual would soon starve. There is a conflict between contrary tendencies, each of which is necessary to existence and there must be a set of rules to reconcile them. *Moreover, there must be a mechanism to make an individual keep the rules even when they conflict with his immediate advantage* (emphasis added). (Robinson, 1964, p. 10)

Regulation of markets is most frequently justified in terms of protecting the less sophisticated citizen from potential exploitation. It was the political perception of 'market manipulation' in the 1920s and 1930s which gave rise to American securities law and the new regulatory framework in the UK seems to be informed by the notion of 'protecting Aunt Agatha' in the words of Sir Kenneth Berrill former Chairman of the Securities and Investments Board.

The imposition of a framework designed to prevent the emergence of activities which have anti-social consequences however can be justified not merely in terms of protecting the members of the general public but also in terms of protecting the integrity of the market itself. In the context of capital markets, investors will be reluctant to entrust their savings to organisations which have a reputation for sharp practice, incompetence or theft. This is recognised by the fact that frequently market participants will themselves voluntarily construct a set of more or less formal rules designed to minimise abuse. Indeed such self imposed regulation has often predated public or governmental regulation.

The problem in devising a regulatory framework however is to develop a structure which accomplishes two things:

o Allows the market sufficient room to carry out its role while preventing practices which take advantage of the gullible and perhaps bring the market into disrepute thereby undermining its integrity and long term viability;
o Does not inhibit the innovative potential of market participants.

Going too far in the direction of regulation may itself impose costs which are intolerable in relation to the expected benefits. In sum, regulatory regimes tread a difficult line between maintaining the honesty and competence of dealers and stifling the effectiveness of the market.

There seem to be two major approaches to financial regulation:

(i) A framework which places the responsibility for implementing, monitoring and enforcing standards on a legally constituted public body.
(ii) A voluntaristic approach that relies primarily on self-regulation to carry out the same duties as above within a broad legal framework.

In general the former approach has been characteristic of the United States and most European countries while the UK has chosen the latter. In Japan the mix is different again with the Ministry of Finance having a very powerful formal role but preferring a regime of informal control consistent with a social tradition of hierarchy and consensus.

In the UK a tradition of pragmatism, evolution and compromise with existing interests has produced an intricate structure in which firms can find themselves supervised by and reporting to several organisations. Ironically much of the effort that has gone into establishing the present system may have been misplaced as it is quite clear that the single market in Europe in 1992 will drive regulation in the UK toward the more legalistic model. In many ways this will be no loss as there has been a great deal of criticism, not least from within the financial sector itself, of the costs involved in the current structure.

2　THE REGULATORY FRAMEWORK IN THE UK

Prior to the Financial Services Act in 1986 regulation of capital markets in the UK was extraordinarily loose in comparison with other developed economies such as the US and Japan. Indeed it was precisely this mild regulatory regime which led to the majority of Eurobond and Eurodollar activity being focussed on the UK.

In the past observers had often referred to the City as being similar to a 'gentleman's club' as a way of expressing the degree of self-regulation which was practised. The role of the authorities such as the Department of Trade and Industry and the Bank of England was confined to that of only occasional intervention – a regime of winks and nudges combined with periodic admonition.

The various bodies that make up the financial network of the City – the Futures Markets, the Accepting Houses, the Clearing Banks, and so on – tended to formulate their own codes of conduct by which members of the club were supposed to abide. For example the Stock Exchange devised its own rules on takeovers and mergers which had no statutory foundation. The Takeover Panel which is the Exchange's instrument to enforce the code was criticised from a number of quarters as being ineffective particularly as the 1980s produced corporate raiders who were frequently much more concerned about potential enquiries by the Monopolies and Mergers Commission – a statutory body with real, if somewhat cumbersome, powers.[1] Similarly Lloyd's, the insurance broking market, operated its own self regulation and despite a number of major scandals in recent years has been exempted from the Financial Services Act (Hay Davison, 1987), a decision which caused considerable political controversy.

A club's rules will only work effectively however if membership is a reasonably exclusive and therefore valuable privilege: the sanction of expulsion in these circumstances carries both a social stigma and financial penalty. Once there is greater freedom of entry and exit, it becomes much more problematical to discipline people who are not members of the club and care even less about its values.

With the opening up of domestic capital markets to international competition therefore a new, more extensive framework was deemed to be necessary. It was realised that the former mechanisms of control would be ineffective relying as they did on members of the club knowing each other and being willing to abide by the rules rather than incur the obloquy, ostracism and loss of business associated with sharp practice. Hence following the Gower Report on Investor Protection in 1984 the new framework which has been the subject of fierce criticism was established (Seldon, 1988).

Before discussing these criticisms we shall briefly summarise the structure now in place.

The Financial Services Act 1986

This is the legal instrument under which the framework has been established 'to regulate the carrying on of investment business'. In this respect the Act consolidates much existing legislation which had grown up more or less haphazardly and it covers matters as diverse as insider dealing, take-overs, the official listing of securities, and the sale of unlisted securities. The Act also extends regulation to areas of investment business which had been previously been scantily regulated or which had not been subject to regulation at all.

In order to harness the expertise of practitioners the Act also established the category of *Self Regulatory Organisations* (SROs) whose essential role is that of authorising and monitoring individuals and firms in particular segments of the investment business.

The essential idea behind the legislation is to provide a comprehensive structure to ensure that no-one in the UK can carry out investment business without authorisation from one or other of the relevant bodies. Anyone wishing to undertake investment business will have to seek permission from the competent authority and this will be given if it is ascertained that they are 'fit and proper persons'.

For example The Securities Association to which securities houses are affiliated puts applicant firms through a rigorous admission procedure and conducts examinations for registered dealers and traders actually handling the investment activities of the firm.

'Conduct of business rules' designed to provide safeguards for investor protection are also required. Again in the case of the The Securities Association there have to be specific rules for matters such as the relationship between members and clients, advertising, giving advice and recommendations, taking and carrying out orders and the keeping of records. These rules have legal effect so firms may be sued in the event that losses are incurred by an individual as a consequence of failing to meet them. The firm may also be disciplined by The Securities Association.

Finally 'surveillance and monitoring' arrangements are required: for most SRO's this covers matters such as the nature of accounting records, the enforcement of minimum capital requirements and regular reporting of the member's financial position. *Recognised Investment Exchanges* have to make sure that market information is equally available to all users and that the market is 'transparent'. In the case of the International Stock Exchange there is a system of online monitoring which records price, volume and execution times for all bargains. This gives compliance officials the ability to monitor whether execution at the best price has been obtained and whether unusual movements in share prices have occurred.

Should anyone undertake investment business without obtaining authorisation they will be committing a criminal offence and are liable to prosecution under the Act.

The Securities and Investment Board

The Financial Services Act 1986 gives the Secretary of State for Trade and Industry the right to delegate authority to a designated agency. This agency is the Securities and Investments Board (SIB). Unlike the Securities and Exchange Commission in the United States which is a public body the SIB is a *private company* financed by a levy imposed on the investment industry. The Board therefore acts as the regulatory authority to oversee the new framework.

The SIB is empowered to designate organisations which meet specific criteria as Self Regulatory Organisations or Recognised Investment Exchanges. The remit of the SIB is extraordinarily wide, covering everything from in-house pension fund managers to futures and options trading.

(i) Self regulating organisations

There are five SROs thus far covering various aspects of the investment business. These are as follows

(a) *The Securities Association* (TSA) covers securities houses ie firms which buy and sell UK and foreign securities – equities, corporate bonds, gilts, Eurobonds, financial futures and options – as well as corporate finance and investment management and advice.

(b) *Financial Intermediaries, Managers and Brokers Regulatory Association* (FIMBRA) is the organisation for various independent intermediaries and brokers advising on investment products such as life assurance and unit trusts. It also covers the activities of licensed dealers and those providing investment management services for retail clients. FIMBRA was formed by a merger between the National Association of Security Dealers and Investment Managers and the Life and Unit Trust Intermediaries Regulatory Organisation.

(c) *Investment Managers Regulatory Organisation* (IMRO). This authorises investment managers and advisors – particularly those managing institutional funds, collective investment schemes and in-house pension fund managers.

(d) *Life Assurance and Unit Trust Regulatory Organisation* (LAUTRO) deals with life companies and unit trust managers involved in the sale and management of insurance linked investments and unit trusts. Membership of LAUTRO does not in itself authorise the individual or firm to carry on investment business. Life companies must be recognised under insurance company legislation and unit trust management companies will be authorised by one of the other SROs ie FIMBRA or IMRO.

(e) *Association of Futures Brokers and Dealers* authorises firms trading and broking in financial and commodity futures and options or offering investment management and advice related thereto.

In additon to the above organisations there is also a further category of SRO – the recognised professional bodies such as the Institute of Chartered Accountants; the Institute of Actuaries; The Law Society and so on.

To be recognised as an SRO it is necessary for the organisation to submit its rule book to the Securities and Investments Board and also to the Office of Fair Trading. Thus the rules of any SRO have to provide at a minimum the same level of investor protection as do the rules of the SIB itself. In addition the SRO must demonstrate that it can monitor and enforce the rules and that it can ensure that members are 'fit and proper' to undertake investment business as required under the Financial Services Act. Finally there has to be an acceptable procedure for handling complaints.

(ii)   Recognised Investment Exchanges (RIEs)

The RIEs which have been established are essentially existing markets, ie the International Stock Exchange, the London Commodities Exchange, the London Metal Exchange and the London International Financial Futures Exchange. Markets which are not based in the UK can apply for *Designated Investment Exchange* status. This allows them freely to carry on business with UK firms.

RIE status will be granted where the Board is convinced that the particular Exchange has the ability to meet the requirements set out in the Act. This means several things:

(a)   having adequate finance to carry out its duties properly;
(b)   implementing rules which ensure that business can be conducted in 'an orderly matter and so as to provide proper protection for investors';
(c)   demonstrating the existence of arrangements for monitoring and enforcing the rules;
(d)   having 'effective arrangements' for investigating complaints;
(e)   ensuring that clients buying and selling investments dealt with on the exchange are provided with 'proper information for determining their current value';
(f)   recording transactions for reference by the public.

Investment firms are not required to deal only on a recognised exchange but there are strict reporting requirements with respect to 'off-market' transactions in order to maintain adequate investor protection.

The Financial Services Act is primarily concerned with the regulation of *investment* business and comprehensive though it is there remain a number of other pieces of legislation and regulatory bodies which deal with other features of the financial system.

Thus Lloyd's has retained the right to supervise itself and does so under a seperate statute – Lloyd's Act 1982. The Bank of England maintains its role as the watchdog of the banking system, the money markets and the gilt-edged market within the Stock Exchange by for example imposing and monitoring capital adequacy and risk positions. The Department of Trade and Industry has direct responsibility for administering the legal framework for unit trusts and life assurance companies. The DTI is also responsible for prosecuting 'insider trading' but it has been suggested that this will eventually become the responsibility of the Stock Exchange itself (*Financial Times*, 22 June 1989).

Obviously there are areas of overlap and this leads to duplication. It may well be that a firm may find itself in more than one SRO and the requirement to make regular reports to each in turn would clearly be somewhat superfluous: for example, the clearing banks, in addition to being subject to monitoring by the Bank of England, also fall within the scope of the Financial Services Act where their activities touch on investment management and advice. Similarly securities houses which offer pension fund and unit trust management may find themselves straddling two SROs – The Securities Association and the Life Assurance and Unit Trust Regulatory Organisation. Some rationalisation of this overlap is clearly necessary and the process may well be accelerated by the pressure to move toward common financial services provision in the European Community in the 1990s.

The Rationale of Regulation

While the FSA emerged largely as a result of the Gower report on investor protection (1984), there can be little doubt that the system of regulation in the UK would have been the subject of change in any case as a result of the increase in global competition and the deregulation of capital markets. The latter process has been characterised by organisations previously confined to specific functions being allowed to move into each other's natural territory. Changes in legislation have encouraged competition between these previously discrete areas as banks, building societies, finance houses, and fund management organisations vie to offer various sorts of savings accounts, money handling services and market-linked investment products. This blurring of distinctions which is occurring in other developed economies would have brought tremendous strains on the regulatory agencies which existed in the UK and would have made it virtually impossible to continue with the rather haphazard forms of self-regulation which had grown up in many parts of the financial system.

However investor protection is only one possible reason for market regulation. There are other important arguments: for example regulation may be deemed necessary as a way of dealing with 'systemic' failure. In the banking system, failure by one bank may be perceived as a signal that other banks are in trouble and if confidence collapses this may cause a 'run' on the system such as to generate the very outcome which people fear. It is exactly this sort of spectre that haunted the commercial banking system of Western economies in the wake of threatened defaults by Third World debtors.

Regulations which impose minimum capital requirements or offer a degree of deposit insurance may forestall this possibility. Although in the case of deposit insurance it may lead the bank to accept riskier loan portfolios because it is aware that its depositors are 'insured' – this is called 'adverse selection'. The bankruptcy crisis facing hundreds of American Savings and Loan Associations may possibly have been worsened by the fact that insurance covers the depositors in case of failure.

The Costs of Regulation

Regulation is often justified in terms of benefitting the industry but there are a variety of costs associated with regulatory regimes.

(i) Resource costs

These are direct and indirect. The direct cost are the fact that labour and capital are absorbed by the regulatory agency in order to carry out its function.

The indirect costs are those carried by the firms subject to regulation. The process of compliance may demand management time and expertise which could have been more productively used generating revenues in the market instead of accounting for past actions and decisions. The need to maintain specific capital requirements may tie capital up in forms which earn less at the margin than could have been earned if the organisation had complete freedom to choose its own prudential ratios.

Estimates have been made of the likely resource costs of setting up and running the UK's system by Lomax (in Seldon, 1988) in which he argues that the total annual cost could amount to as much as £100m. Goodhart has suggested that it may well be more than this (in Seldon, 1988).

(ii)   Compensation funds

The existence of a compensation fund is a one-off transfer which is effectively levied on the constituent firms. In itself it need not represent a cost to those firms insofar as it can be recouped by increasing commission charges. However this is not without its adverse consequences and the degree to which the burden is shared between consumer and producer depends on the 'elasticity of demand' for the relevant financial services. If the client does indeed have to meet the cost of the compensation fund via higher charges then it becomes similar to any insurance policy: all contribute a small amount to meet the possibility of failures in the system which might have catastrophic consequences for some individuals.

(iii)   Regulatory Arbitrage

A third variant of cost arises where regulation causes firms to move to other financial centres. This possibility is particularly acute in cases where regulatory regimes in different countries are very different and the SIB has indeed been conscious of this as evidenced by its willingness to be flexible *vis-à-vis* the Eurobond market by granting Designated Investment Exchange status to the AIBD.

 If all economies were to implement similar sorts of regulation of course there is no incentive to move and with the growing internationalisation of capital markets there does appear to be pressure to move in the direction of similar rules with regard to capital adequacy and so on: this is certainly true in the banking world where the Bank for International Settlements is in the process of defining international capital adequacy standards which, if implemented, will result in a 'level playing field' in the sense of similar sorts of competitive environments. Perhaps ultimately a unified approach to supervision of banks will result (*The Economist*, June 23 1989). Similarly the Group of Thirty countries are trying to bring common standards throughout securities markets with respect to settlement and clearing procedures (*The Banker*, May 1990).

 In the present stage of increasing internationalisation and integration of capital markets most of the pressure has been in the direction of conformity via *deregulation*. As regulation is dictated by a number of influences only one of which is the idea of a 'level playing' field, it is likely to be some time before common regulatory principles can be universally applied. In the meantime discussions have accelerated about conditions required to achieve greater integration of capital markets within Europe. For example after a period of dormancy since the original directives about liberalisation of capital move-

ments in the early 1960s there have been over twelve different recommendations and directives proposed by the Commission and adopted by the
Council of Ministers since 1985. These cover both credit institutions and
securities markets.

Clearly there are powerful moves towards convergence but this process
will not necessarily be all one way, for example the recommendations on
prospectus requirements for securities offers has only been partly adopted. In
addition as was evident in the wake of the 1987 Crash, there is always the
possibility that political demands for tougher regulation may re-emerge
particularly in the derived markets – index options, financial futures and the
like.

(iv) Dynamic costs

These arise because regulation may prevent competition by establishing
'barriers to entry'. If this occurs then the regulatory system may have effects
contrary to what was intended. Thus, regulation is generally perceived as
serving the public interest but there is another argument which points to the
fact that regulation because it limits competition is often favoured by
producers in an industry as a way of protecting their position. While
proponents of regulation argue that it maintains standards, allows specialisation and so on, there is nevertheless the suspicion that vested interests are
being defended and that competition is the real fear.

Economists have developed the concept of 'regulatory capture' whereby
the agency charged with implementing regulation in the general interest
instead becomes a lobbyist in favour of the object of regulation. This
argument has particular force in cases of self-regulation: by definition this
involves individuals from a particular industry or sector regulating their own
industry so it is rather difficult to assume that they will be free of 'judicial
bias'.

If we take another facet of the regulator's duties, that between effective
regulation and disclosure of material information Kay has pointed out

> There is no point at which a regulatory authority is more tight lipped about the
> activities of bodies which it is regulating than when it actually has very serious
> doubts. (Seldon, 1988, p. 38)

This may not be too surprising when the staff appointed to regulatory
agencies are drawn from the industry itself. While the use of such personnel
can be supported by entirely reasonable arguments about the need to use
people with a detailed knowledge of practices in the industry nevertheless

they will be imbued with the ethos of the industry and therefore to a degree sympathetic to practitioners. This obvious conflict of interest between a body which is supposed to protect the interest of investors (customers) while simultaneously is staffed by producers has begun to look inappropriate in view of moves to 1992 and the different style of regulation which operates in Europe.

The suppression of competition which may be attendant on regulation means that innovation is held back and this damages the long term efficiency of the industry. It is relatively straightforward to estimate the costs associated with setting up and running the regulatory body itself. It is also possible to obtain rough estimates of the costs of compliance – in terms of in-house time and effort devoted to abiding by the regulator's position. However it is not so easy to obtain estimates of the effects of the suppression of competition and the slowing down in the implementation of technology. Yet over the longer period there is no doubt that the latter is the more serious issue.

3   THE REGULATORY FRAMEWORK IN THE USA

One of the most significant features of market regulation in the USA is the degree to which all parties accept that it is in essence a legal matter. In view of the discussion in the United Kingdom about the trade-off between regulation and market innovation and freedom it is ironic that the markets in the United States have been described as 'at the same time the freest, in the sense of innovation, and yet the most heavily regulated in the world' (Teweles and Bradley, 1987, p. 306)

The USA has regulation at federal, state and industry level. State regulation can produces some interesting variations in US corporate law and security dealing.[2] Although there is a gradual move toward uniformity it may still be feasible to find that an offer for sale of securities even by a well known national investment firm may not be legal in some States!

Federal Regulation

The 1930s ushered in a great flurry of legislation which altered the face of the financial services industry in the United States. Thus the Banking Act (more commonly referred to as the Glass-Steagall Act – after the Senators responsible) was placed on the statute book in 1933. One of its most important features was to separate banking and dealing in securities. To this end the Act forbade US banks from issuing or dealing in securities.[3] Just as significantly the Senate hearings leading up to the enactment of Glass-

Steagall were to be a prelude to fundamental changes in the regulation of securities markets.

Prior to 1933 there was virtually no regulation imposed on securities dealing by US federal authorities. In general a relaxed degree of self-regulation was applied and there was some criminal and civil law applicable at state level. In this respect the legislative framework of the State of New York was particularly influential because of the fact that the largest stock exchanges were to be found there.

(i)   The Securities Act 1933 and the Securities and Exchange Act 1934

These major Acts were passed by Congress in the wake of the market decline in 1929–33 and after the investigations of market manipulation by the Senate Banking Committee. The legislation had four main objectives:

o   To establish regulatory machinery;
o   To regulate practices of brokers and dealers in organised stock exchanges and over the counter markets;
o   To impose limits on speculative credit;
o   To ensure adequate disclosure of material information to members of the general public so that they would not be placed in a disadvantaged position *vis-à-vis* 'insiders'.

The last of these four objectives was viewed as particularly important and in order to give effect to the Act the Securities and Exchange Commission (SEC) was established with far reaching powers (Skousen, 1983).

The SEC is a federal agency with quasi-judicial status and carries out its mandate through the twin tools of registration and reporting requirements.

(a)   Registration
Exchanges which operate any inter-state or foreign commerce or through the US mails have to be registered with the SEC. This effectively means that their membership, constitution, rules, procedures and so on must be vetted by the Commission. Particularly important is the need to show adequate rules for disciplining the membership of the relevant exchange. In addition exchanges are allowed to impose other rules and procedures provided they do not come into conflict with the law. All the well known US exchanges are registered with the SEC including the Chicago Board Options Exchange. Futures exchanges are not registered with the SEC but instead come within the ambit of a separate body – the Commodity Futures Trading Commission (CFTC). The CFTC also employs the devices of registration and reporting as techniques of control. However there is a lobby in the United States to place the regulation of the futures exchanges under the SEC.

(b)   Reporting requirements
The SEC has, as part of its brief, the duty to ensure 'full and fair' disclosure of all material facts concerning securities offered for public investment. Hence the Commission has been an effective body imposing high accounting standards not only on the securities industry itself but on corporate America in general. There are however some who argue that the disclosure requirements have been more significant for the accounting profession than on securities markets themselves (Benston, 1969; Stigler, 1964).

In case of fraudulent behaviour the initiation of litigation became the responsibility of the Commission. In addition the SEC was charged with overseeing arrangements for the proper registration of securities.

(c)   Other mechanisms of control
The SEC is the most famous of the instruments used in the regulatory approach employed in the USA, it is not of course the only instrument. The Securities and Exchange Act also gives power to the Federal Reserve System to determine margin requirements which investors must meet when dealing in stock market activity. Thus if speculative activity is deemed to be 'getting out of hand' then they can raise these margins to cool it while they can lower them to encourage investment.

Similarly the Act identifies and prohibits a whole series of activities deemed to be manipulative and gives the SEC the right to make rules about other deceptive or manipulative devices.

A significant part of the legislation is also concerned with the activities of 'insiders' of one sort or another. This principally relates to shareholders owning more than 10% of the total and is used as a way of monitoring the actions of major shareholders who might be in a position to speculate in their own stock. Insider trading has in fact been at the root of some of the most spectacular and notorious cases prosecuted by the SEC in the USA in recent years.

(ii)   Securities Investors Protection Act 1970

This piece of legislation came on to the statute book in response to what came to be known as the 'back office crisis' in the late 1960s (Smith, 1973). The inability of brokerage houses to cope efficiently with the enormous increase in the volume of share dealings led to very great difficulties with the clearance and settlement procedures then in place. Indeed official estimates suggested that between $100m and $400m worth of securities were stolen because of the lack of control (Seligman, 1982, p. 457).

Prior to this episode investor protection seemed to be taken care of by the net capital requirements imposed on brokers under the 1934 legislation and the use of fidelity bonds to deal with dishonest behaviour. However there was little or no protection against sheer incompetence, and the bankruptcy of some brokerages combined with the last minute rescue of several others underlined how vulnerable the investor was to this incompetence.

The October Crash of 1987 has led to a new debate in the United States about the need for further regulation and there is considerable discussion about the need for more uniformity in the supervision of derivative markets and the underlying stock markets. This has been given further impetus by an investigation into trading practices on the Chicago futures and options markets which has led to series of indictments being served on a large number of traders. It would come as no surprise therefore to see the SEC spanning both sets of markets.

4 THE REGULATORY FRAMEWORK IN JAPAN

Financial institutions in Japan have historically been subject to considerable political control via the Ministry of Finance (MoF) which enjoys much more power than its Western counterparts. Since the Second World War, the Japanese have employed strategic state planning in many parts of the economy and this included the financial sector. The prime objective of banking institutions was to act as a conduit directing domestic savings (which have tended to be very high by UK or American standards) to Japanese industry (Ruehl, 1987). Indeed the detailed nature of these financial controls would have come as a profound shock to many who advocate the adoption of Japanese industrial practices in the UK and the USA. Not only were interest rates deliberately held down by government intervention but the banks were also given quotas for lending activity to particular sectors of the economy.

The American post-war occupation also left its mark via the notion that banking should be strictly seperated from dealing in securities – the position taken in the United States' Banking Act of 1934 (the Glass-Steagall Act). Hence Article 65 of Japan's Securities and Exchange Law (1948) maintains this separation although in Japan as elsewhere the pressure to modify the situation has become intense.

The Japanese therefore have followed a policy of specialisation or *segmentation* whereby different sorts of financial institution have their sphere of operations prescribed by the authorities. For example banking was compartmentalised into short and long term, city, regional and trust banks which were all given different roles.

The emphasis on bank lending had the impact of keeping the securities markets in Japan relatively underdeveloped. This was reinforced by other features of these markets for example the high costs of a quotation and the practice of issuing shares at their par value. Another consequence of the tight regulatory regime was that, with the relaxation of exchange control in the 1970s, Japanese financial institutions turned toward overseas capital markets to develop their business. In foreign markets the opportunity to deal in activities which were proscribed in the domestic sphere gave such institutions experience which they could bring to bear in the home market in due course. A further effect of segmentation was that the dominance of the 'big four' securities houses – Nomura, Daiwa, Nikko and Yaimichi – was sustained by these regulatory 'barriers to entry'.

The financial sector is controlled by the Ministry of Finance (MoF) via three divisions or 'Bureaux' – Banking, Securities and International Finance. In addition to this official layer of control, other institutions carry certain responsibilities for monitoring specific aspects of the financial system: the Central Bank oversees the banking system; securities markets are regulated by the Securities Bureau and the stock exchanges regulate themselves; finally there are various professional and institutional bodies which undertake degrees of supervision – for example the Japanese Securities Dealers Association offers an element of voluntary regulation of member firms involved in the marketing of securities.

The rate of change in financial markets is slower than in Western markets and this might reflect a number of factors. First there is a tendency for the three 'divisions' of the MoF to defend the interests of their constituents – an outcome consistent with the concept of 'regulatory capture'. But while there is an element of truth in the idea of regulatory capture the relatively slow pace of change also reflects a cultural preference to seek change via consensus.

As the MoF is responsible for the issue of licences it clearly has the power to accelerate the process of liberalisation when it is seen as politically advantageous and despite the underlying inertia, in the last decade and a half major changes have been under way. The oil crises in the 1970s forced the public sector into fiscal deficit and caused a substantial rise in government borrowing. This in turn led to the government relaxing its control over interest rates to facilitate extra borrowing by the state. At the same time as the public sector ran into deficit the corporate sector moved from being a net borrower into financial surplus. Companies which as borrowers had been happy to live with a regime of low interest rates started to look for higher rates of return from their financial assets!

The government also turned its attention to the Tokyo Stock Exchange and the MoF introduced a number of measures which were designed to ease the process of listing – eg reducing the listing fee and relaxing requirements about the breadth of public shareholdings. On the whole, change has been slow and cautious and considerable criticism has built up as to the transparency of the stock market: the very size of the big four securities houses allied to the fact that as many as half the companies on the First Section of the TSE have a share float of about 20%, have led to accusations of market manipulation and sharp practice. For example in the Tateho Chemicals case in 1987 (Matsumoto, 1989) the company faced bankruptcy as a result of ill-advised speculation in the financial futures market but the larger institutional investors sold out just before the company's position became public knowledge. Insider trading rules have been in place for some time in Japan but they largely went unenforced until 1988 when pressure from overseas investors led the Japanese government to take a more active approach. A number of major scandals involving businessmen and politicians have also contributed to an atmosphere where such legislation is deemed to be even more pressing particularly as more foreign securities houses with a different style of business penetrate Japanese markets.[4]

Since the oil price shocks of the 1970s the Japanese economy has returned to its more customary balance of payments surpluses and the combination of a strong Yen plus the continuing gigantic flows of domestic savings resulted in further pressures for change in the regulatory structure. In particular there is a desire by the banks to enter into what they see as the highly profitable oligopoly of securities broking, underwriting and trading enjoyed by the big four while the securities houses themselves want to deal in foreign exchange – traditionally the preserve of the banks (*Banking World*, April 1989).

It is clear that the Japanese approach to deregulation exhibits their usual caution so that there is unlikely to be the 'Big Bang' approach seen in London. Instead the same process may be played out in slow motion. Nevertheless those calling for greater financial liberalisation have become more insistent and in this respect the patterns set in other parts of the world are important. As Japanese institutions come to play a progressively larger role in Western capital markets so external pressures will be put on the Japanese to extend reciprocal access to their market. Already foreign securities houses have established subsidiaries in Japan and entry into the Tokyo Stock Exchange has become very much easier – indeed one-fifth of seats on the exchange are now allocated to foreign houses.

If however the Japanese authorities wish to bring to Tokyo much of the business which currently takes place in centres such as London (for example the issue of Yen denominated Eurobonds and the trading of Yen equity warrants) it is clear that there will have to be further liberalisation, greater efficiency and enhanced transparency in Japanese markets.

NOTES

1. The MMC is not however autonomous and cannot initiate enquiries of its own volition. The Commission must wait until matters are 'referred' to it by the Minister. In turn its recommendations have to be implemented by the Minister. A reference to the MMC might be as much feared for the time it was likely to take as for the ultimate report.
2. For example incorporation in certain states, e.g. Delaware allows a company the opportunity to develop highly innovative defence tactics against predators.

3. This remains the case in the late 1980s but there is considerable pressure for change in the United States as deregulation and securitisation have gathered pace.
4. A new law to deal with insider trading emerged in 1989.

8   Capital Markets: Some Critical Questions

Public capital markets are the subject of a number of major criticisms which exercise the minds of economists, politicians and regulatory agencies. There are five important areas which are the focus of concern:

o   Finance for Industry;
o   'Short Termism';
o   Institutional Dominance;
o   Insider Trading;
o   Volatility and New Trading Techniques.

1   FINANCE FOR INDUSTRY

In the past stock markets have been criticised for being inaccessible to small capital hungry companies and therefore for doing little to help new industries to develop. Undoubtedly listing requirements, the costs of flotation and questions of control have been forbidding disincentives. In recent years however most major markets have addressed this issue and there has been a substantial increase in listings via the use of special sections or categories. For example the USM and the Third Market in the UK, the 'Second Marché' in France and the Geregelter Markt (second segment) in Germany have all been developed to cater explicitly for the needs of smaller and riskier companies. Reflecting its OTC traditions NASDAQ in the United States has always been more accessible than the major floor exchanges and has reaped the benefits via a doubling of the number of issues traded and an increase in company listings of nearly 80% over the ten years 1978–88 (NASDAQ, 1989).

In aggregate terms however it is still fair to argue that markets are not very significant as providers of funds for long term investment projects. Even in the UK and the US, with financial systems widely perceived as market led, public capital markets play a minor role in the financing of a typical firm.

Indeed the 1980s could be characterised as a decade in which corporate America 'bought itself back' as leveraged buy outs financed by a mix of bank capital and junk bonds produced a net decline in the volume of public equity!

In other major economies such as Germany, Japan and France reliance on public markets has traditionally played an even smaller role with banks providing a major proportion of long term capital needs. However it should be pointed out that the role of equity markets in these economies has been growing rapidly as a result of privatisations, tax incentives, deregulation and international competition.

The relatively low profile of public markets in the financing of industry has led some commentators (especially from the left) to question whether there is any need for stock exchanges at all. After all the development of capitalism was not contingent upon the existence of such markets and they have only really become providers of capital to the private sector since the late nineteenth century. In addition many firms in the UK and the US have grown to a considerable size without the necessity of a public quotation. As has been pointed out in Chapter 1 there have been several notable examples of firms buying back their own equity and becoming private companies again. Some of course preferred to remain private all along (including ironically some major securities houses for example Goldman-Sachs in the US) while others decided to go public when they were already mature corporations (eg Pilkington Bros in the UK). Indeed this seems to suggest that the really significant use of a stock market is not to raise new capital but instead to allow entrepreneur-owners to realise their wealth.

The growth of private placements of company paper directly to institutional investors leaves yet another question mark as the technique raises capital and effectively bypasses public markets entirely. Thus the SEC in 1990 approved a new rule (Rule 144a) for international issuers to use the private placement market by selling to US institutional investors without first registering with the SEC. Similarly permission has been given to the National Association of Securities Dealers to introduce a system called PORTAL (Private Offering and Reciprocal Trading through Automated Linkages) which will deal with the issue and trading of such placements. Looking further afield, Germany has less than 500 companies quoted on its various exchanges and France has less than 650 so it is quite clear that a considerable volume of economic activity manages to be sustained without a stock exchange.

It is therefore feasible to argue that from the perspective of generating finance for industry stock markets are not an absolute necessity. Of course this leaves out of account the role of such markets for the financing of state activity. Many exchanges for example London, New York, Paris and Vienna owed far more to the growth of government borrowing than to providing finance for industry. It is ironic that the liberalising governments of Eastern Europe are considering the establishment of their own domestic stock exchanges not to provide newly privatised enterprises with finance but to bring *state* finances under control. In the first instance this reflects a desire to wean major industrial enterprises away from a complete dependence on state finance: a condition which has allowed many of these enterprises to persist with inefficient practices well beyond the point where bankruptcy would have intervened in a market economy. In addition the privatisation of state capital may provide an outlet for monetary savings which currently act as an inflationary overhang. So the answer to the question 'Do we need a stock exchange?' is 'Yes – but not necessarily to finance private industry!'

2 'SHORT TERMISM' AND THE INVESTMENT HORIZON

It has become a common charge in both the United Kingdom and the United States that stock markets are myopic and share prices give too much weight to short run events. There is some evidence to suggest that the market does tend to place greater emphasis on near term results (Nickell and Wadhani, 1986). Industrialists also frequently complain that in having to keep an eye on the level of the share price they may have to limit long term expenditure on research and development or major capital programmes because these are not adequately reflected in the company's share price which leaves the company vulnerable to takeover (*The Economist*, June 24 1988). This is a difficult argument as there is the contrary view that takeovers are beneficial partly because they reallocate resources to higher valued uses and partly because they may be a *potential* discipline or threat which makes management more efficient.

This issue has never been satisfactorily resolved as the evidence is mixed and it depends on how long a period after a takeover has occurred one uses to assess the effects (Scherer, 1980). Certainly there is some evidence put forward by Scherer (see Bruck, 1988, p.267) that taken over the longer run:

 (i) in general mergers/takeovers tend to be targeted at companies which are already competently managed but where assets appear to be undervalued;
 (ii) many takeovers result in short run cash maximisation strategies where the target is refused spending on new investment and product development while prices are hiked without regard for long run competitiveness;
 (iii) in a takeover where the acquirer has little management experience in the target's business the result is a deterioration not an improvement in efficiency;
 (iv) takeovers which are followed by divestment of subsidiaries can frequently enhance the efficiency of the core business.

Takeovers are not therefore unequivocally a 'good thing' and one can argue that the discipline which firms need is competition in the product market. This is the real spur to efficiency not the worry that a short term fall in the share price will precipitate a takeover bid.

3 INSTITUTIONAL DOMINANCE

If one grants that stock markets are indeed more influenced by short term factors to the detriment of longer term developments a further question arises as to whether this reflects changes in the nature of the typical investor – in particular does this 'short termism' reflect the growing significance of the investment institutions?

The increase in the financial power of the institutions in most stock markets is well documented and the institutions now account for the major flow of investment capital and asset ownership. If these institutions are more 'performance' conscious than individual clients this would go some way to explaining the emphasis on the short run. From common observation it seems to be the case that individual investors do develop a greater attachment to shares and defences against hostile takeovers have frequently been more successful where there is a widespread group of individual shareholders who can be mobilised.

Why should the institutions regard themselves as driven by their policy holders or prospective pensioners to obtain better than average performance? One possible explanation is that in the competitive struggle to increase business, fund managers can only differentiate their product from their rivals by exhibiting greater 'expertise': performance becomes the crucial selling point. By contrast individual investors rarely have exaggerated expectations about how well they are able to choose shares. However if they are paying a fund manager to do it and if the fund has attracted savings by emphasising that it can outperform the competition then the individual investor may well press for 'performance' inducing a short run focus in investment decisions. In any case individual shareholders have a disincentive to manage their portfolio actively because they face higher charges whereas fund managers have an incentive to 'churn' in an attempt to maximise commission income as well as to chase performance.

The hypothesis is that the market may be less short term oriented where thousands of individual shareholders dominate not because they are less greedy but because they have fewer illusions about their stock picking ability. It may become more myopic where investment becomes the province of an oligopolistic set of investing institutions. In a large population of shareholders views about the future performance of particular companies may well be distributed normally and hence for each pessimist there is an offsetting optimist. Where only a handful of funds dominate however consensual judgements can form more easily and cause excessive swings of market opinion.

On the other hand the emergence of a large number of indexed funds may in time produce greater stability of institutional holdings as the underlying philosophy is one of 'buy and hold'.

4 INSIDER TRADING

Stock markets are also criticised because of the problem of insider trading. This has been a criminal offence in the United States for many years but in the UK and Japan for example there has been a fairly tolerant acceptance of the fact that those who work in the markets are able to take advantage of emerging news and/or rumour. Legislation on insider trading is of very recent vintage in the UK (1985) and Japan (1988) but the issue has become much more sensitive as shareholding and interest in stock markets have become more widespread. Public perception of the integrity of markets may have altered as a result of a number of major scandals over the last few years. Nor have many markets emerged unscathed: London and New York have had major cases of insider trading and share price manipulation; Tokyo and the Paris Bourse have been tainted by political scandals and Chicago's futures markets have been shaken by FBI accusations of illegal practice. This sort of experience has already produced demands for regulation to be tightened once more but at the very least it demonstrates the need for greater vigilance within the regulatory regimes that currently exist. If there is cynicism in the public at large about the honesty and integrity of stock markets then it can only be fuelled by the increasing number of cases in which individuals who are well paid by every day standards appear able 'to resist everything except temptation'!

For a market to work efficiently and fairly then price sensitive information must be rapidly accessible to all potential investors. There has been growing disquiet in the United Kingdom about the practice of quoted companies offering confidential briefings to analysts prior to the publication of company news (*The Observer*, 8 Oct. 1989). It is argued that two sets of market users are thereby placed in a privileged position – institutional investors with their own in-house research teams and the analysts of brokers whose market makers may be briefed in advance of their clients. This could lead to the practice of 'front running' – buying or selling shares in advance of the client. The Securities Association has regulations to forbid firms from dealing in this way except in two sets of circumstances – when they have informed clients in advance and provided they change their book in such a manner as not to 'move the market price materially'. The existence of such regulations is testimony to potential conflicts of interest but does not in itself tackle the problem at source: it would be better to make all company announcements public immediately via the media.

There are two views on this practice of confidential briefings:

o First that it is unfair to private investors who are deprived of profitable opportunities: if the impression becomes widespread that there is no 'level playing field' (in terms of access to information) this will drive private investors away to the long term detriment of the market;

o Second the practice may be even more pernicious where it focusses attention on the *immediate* profit potential of a piece of market 'news'. This shifts analysis away from fundamental research and encourages the short term orientation of which markets already stand accused.

5   NEW TRADING TECHNIQUES AND VOLATILITY

A fifth issue which relates particularly to equity markets has come to the fore since the 1987 Crash: this is the accusation that they have become more volatile as a result of three factors: the existence of derivative markets, the emergence of new technology and the use of new trading techniques.

This accusation is not easy to sustain: the basic problem is to define exactly what is meant by 'volatility' and over what period of time is that 'volatility' being compared. Thus Fortune (1989) argues that volatility should be measured not simply in terms of price movements but in terms of the variability of *realised rates of return* – ie including annual dividends. Using this as a criterion he argues that in general US markets have not become more volatile, even allowing for the October Crash of 1987, when compared with the variability of returns in the 1930s. Schwert (1990) comes to similar conclusions using data on returns to market portfolios over the period 1885 to 1989.

This is not the concept of volatility which the majority of investors would understand or employ however. It usually relates simply to *price* movements. Even on this narrower definition of volatility however the evidence is not conclusive and studies done prior to the collapses of October 1987 and 1989 seemed to indicate that markets were *not* becoming increasingly volatile (*The Economist*, 26 Sept. 1986). Volatility was measured in this case by comparing the standard deviation of daily movements in equity prices over the period 1970-86. On this criterion there was no convincing evidence to show that markets had become more volatile in the mid-1980s.

However this analysis was done prior to the much larger price movements experienced late in the decade and the likelihood remains that given the inclusion of these admittedly extreme observations the standard deviations of the daily price movements would be larger.

As suggested above volatility can be measured in several ways and the data may be based on comparing prices when the market opens with those when the market closes or on a 'close to close' basis or even intra-day price movements may be evaluated.

Table 8.1 shows the behaviour of the major market indices in the UK, US and Japan over the period of the Crash of 1987.

TABLE 8.1   Volatility* of major stock exchange indices

	FTSE	Dow Jones	Nikkei Dow
Third Quarter 1987			
Close to close	0.91	0.93	1.10
5th Oct. to 12 Nov.			
Close to close	4.15	5.49	3.88
Open to close	2.08	3.66	na

*Standard deviation as a percentage of the index of daily price movements.
Bank of England Quarterly Bulletin, Feb. 1988.

Table 8.1 demonstrates the dramatic increase in volatility over the period in question when compared with the previous quarter: the standard deviation of changes in the main market indices in London and New York are four and nearly six times higher respectively. It could be argued of course that the Crash of 1987 was simply a one-off phenomenon (except that there was something of a mini-Crash in October 1989 when the Dow-Jones index fell by 190 points!) and reflected a very special set of events but the sheer speed of the price collapse was certainly unprecedented and no entirely satisfactory explanation has emerged since.[1]

In any case whether or not stock exchanges have *actually* become more volatile is less important than the public perception. If they are perceived as highly unstable then risk-averse investors, and that probably means a substantial group, will be repelled. There is also a tendency on the part of some smaller investors and some academics (Strange, 1986) to see what goes on in stock markets as merely a higher form of gambling and this is a view which will be given credibility by the periodic and substantial movements which have marked the last few years. Finally the sophistication and resources required to operate protective hedging strategies through futures and options markets places the smaller investor at a disadvantage compared with larger market operators. The net effect of these factors may be to limit even further the small investor's participation in the market to collective investment vehicles.

New Trading Techniques

A number of recent developments in stock trading techniques in major world markets have proved highly controversial over the last three to four years. These techniques are grouped together under the collective title of *programmed trading*. There is a great deal of confusion as to exactly what is meant by the term and for some people it has almost become part of the demonology of stock markets.

The notion of programmed trades is not in itself exceptional yet for one reason or another it has become part of the folk-lore associated with the Crash in October 1987. It is also unfortunate that the expression 'programme' has come to be used as it has overtones of automatic trading via computer. While computers frequently are used to implement programme trades they are not essential to the concept of a programmed trade.

A programmed trade is simply a buy or sell order which covers a number of different stocks simultaneously. It is more simply expressed as a 'basket' trade. Such basket trades might be undertaken for a variety of reasons: for example the decision to implement a completely new asset allocation strategy by a fund manager might prove an occasion for such a trade or perhaps the launch or close of a particular fund might occur. In principle it is not necessary to use computers to effect such trades – they can be carried out manually.

Clearly however the facility for buying and selling a group of stocks simultaneously has been enhanced by systems which can handle and execute the necessary procedures speedily and accurately. Thus for example the development of the Designated Order Turnaround system (DOTs) in the New York Stock Exchange in the late-1970s linked brokers' offices to the Exchange floor and gave extremely rapid and efficient automated execution of small orders – up to 2099 shares. The limit of 2099 shares was set because the NYSE was trying to reduce the costs of dealing with small scale transactions (average transaction size in 1988/9 was about 2000 stocks). In fact however *automatic* execution was restricted to only fifty designated shares (Kregel, 1988). In the case of other shares, orders of this size are guaranteed execution by the specialist at the market price within three minutes. Before the market opens DOT has an Opening Automated Reporting Service (OARS) which allows orders of up to 5099 shares to be executed automatically.

Somewhat later the up-graded SuperDOT system increased the size of order to be dealt with up to 30 099 shares without guaranteed execution during the trading day and has the capacity to handle limit orders of up to 99 099 shares. This is one point at which computers *can* and do come into the picture: instead of sending the order to the exchange floor and using floor brokers to 'hit' the specialists simultaneously, it is possible for the shares in question to be loaded into the broker's computer and via the super-DOT system to route orders to the various specialists for execution. Notice whether or not the particular shares belong to or mirror one of the main indices is irrelevant – a programmed trade simply involves the sale or purchase of groups of stocks at the same time.

The sale of stocks in a group in this fashion is accomplished by a broker acting in either an agency or a principal capacity. If it is the former then conventional execution at best price will be the duty of the broker. However when acting as principal a number of possibilities are available. Thus instead of the broker being made aware of the whole set of shares in the portfolio he may deal 'blind' ie he may only have a very limited description of the content of the portfolio in question. This sort of blind deal is done at higher commission charges but it acts as a safety device for the client: it prevents a broker from 'front running' – ie trading in advance of the client – because he knows the specific composition of the portfolio. This combination of automated trades plus changes in market practice in the US has accelerated considerably the ability of institutions to sell and buy large elements of a portfolio.

The ability to sell or buy shares 'en bloc' in this manner and very rapidly has led to a family of trading techniques which have tended to be put under the general label of programme trading. In particular the following strategies are associated with the notion of programme trading

o Equity Allocation
o Stock Index Arbitrage
o Portfolio Insurance

These differ in their effects on the market in terms of directional impact.

(i) Equity allocation

This is the simplest way in which programme trading may be undertaken. A fund manager may wish to restructure a large portfolio by shifting between particular equities or by moving out of equities entirely and going liquid or buying fixed interest securities. Clearly this can be more efficiently and rapidly executed if the whole package can be transacted simultaneously rather than selling tranches of the portfolio over a period of time. In this context one should not however exaggerate the speed of execution of a very large programmed trade. Rapid transactions may be feasible in the major world markets with their great depth of liquidity, efficient execution and settlement routines (as in the United States) but there can be many difficulties in terms of both costs, execution and settlement delays in minor markets. This is particularly true of a portfolio which may be a global in content and in the process of major reconstruction ('Anatomy of a Deal',

The Banker, Oct. 1989). Selling procedures and settlement in these cases may be labyrinthine, costly and uncertain.

Equity allocation strategies may result in the fund being a net seller or a net buyer of equities or alternatively the effect may be neutral where a switch across different equities is concerned. Thus the effect of this species of programme trading on the general level of the market depends upon which of the above outcomes occurs in the aggregate. Nevertheless it seems reasonable to argue that programme trading to facilitate equity allocation will have no *systematic* effect on the direction of the market.

There is always the possibility that several institutions might simultaneously restructure their portfolios in one direction or another in which case there would be a substantial impact on the market in a very condensed period of time. There are no secondary effects however other than what has come about as a result of a reappraisal of the market by fund managers. The best one can say for the effect of programme trading in these circumstances is that it can exaggerate any 'herd instinct' which may be at work. This in itself may not be particularly beneficial as a fall of 100 plus points in a given index in an hour will be distinctly more unsettling than the same fall over a period of days!

(ii)　Stock index arbitrage

The existence of futures markets offering contracts on particular stock market indices has given the idea of programme trading a new dimension. In 1984 the use of programme trading to facilitate arbitrage between index futures and the underlying stock market first occurred (*Financial Times*, 14 Nov. 1989, p. 36). In this case the technique was *not* deployed to restructure a portfolio but to close a position where the trader had already bought stock index futures and was short of the underlying stock. Hence a large programme trade offered a mechanism to facilitate this process.

In addition it was realised that the use of stock index futures to accomplish large portfolio readjustments was considerably cheaper than using the cash (securities) market itself. For example transaction costs are significantly cheaper:

> A single S&P500 futures contract has a value of $500 times the S&P500 index, or $175,000 at an index level of 350; a single S&P futures contract can be purchased at a transactions cost of about $95 which covers the round-trip commissions and fees. Assuming a $50 share price outright purchase of $175,000 of shares through a major retail broker requires one way commissions of approximately $1,500, while a major discount broker charges $315. In addition outright purchase requires payment of half the bid-asked spread on the common stocks; at a minimum bid-asked spread of 0.125 and a $50 share price, this comes to about $200. (Fortune, 1989)

There is also the impact of major transactions on the price of the securities being sold to consider:

As a measure of the cost involved with price change, it is estimated that a $20 million trade will move prices in the cash market by 0.27%. Thus in addition to commissions etc the cost of a block trade will include its negative impact on price. Adjusting a portfolio by a similar amount in the futures market moves the relevant stock futures price by only 0.04% and has no direct impact on the stock price. In dollar terms, a $120 million trade will have a transaction cost of $520,000 due to its impact on market price while the cost in the futures market would be only $20,000. (SEC, pp 3–5, n. 26, quoted in Kregel, 1988)

Partly as a result of these differential costs it has become commonplace to operate in futures markets rather than the cash market and frequently the value of the contracts traded in the futures markets is a multiple of the value of the underlying shares.

Programmed trades and the futures market are used in conjunction to carry out arbitrage operations: depending upon the relative value of the underlying shares in the cash market and the price of index futures it might be possible to arbitrage across the two markets and take advantage of price discrepancies. Thus for example should the futures index look cheap *vis-à-vis* its 'fair value' then the investor should buy the futures contract and sell the stocks thereby locking in a sure gain. On the other hand should the futures look expensive *vis-à-vis* their fair value then the contrary position should be executed – sell the futures contracts and buy the underlying stocks.

Notice the effect of these transactions is to move the market index and the futures price but *it will move them in the direction of closing any existing discrepancies*. This will tend to eliminate differences between markets and in essence should be inherently stabilising in its effect. In addition of course computers can monitor the price discrepancies referred to and execute the relevant trades if and when certain thresholds are reached. This should result in even greater stability as it would mean that large differences should not occur because they would be arbitraged away as the price gap begins to emerge.

The essence of the argument is that these arbitrage operations are not *momentum based*: they act simply to close discrepancies between futures and cash markets and therefore do not prolong or sustain a move in one direction or another (Hill and Jones, 1988). Nevertheless a considerable degree of opposition has built up against the use of index arbitrage.

The Brady Report, which emerged in the aftermath of the October 1987 Crash, offered one such negative appraisal (Brady, 1988). The main charge is that by moving large lines of stock simultaneously programme trading increases the volatility of the market undermining its credibility in the eyes of both investors and listed companies. In addition it is said that the trading specialists on the floor of the Exchange are particularly vulnerable as they are not sufficiently capitalised to be able to carry out their main function of keeping a continuous market.

There is evidence which suggests that the link between programme trading and market volatility is simply non-existent (Grossman, 1988; Schwert, 1990) but the perception of many investors is contrary to this view (*Financial Times*, Nov. 30 1989, p. 24).

The animus against programme trading has been sufficiently powerful that in November 1989 the NYSE asked member firms to suspend index arbitrage activity and suggested a series of trading halts when the Dow Jones dropped by more than thirty points. It has been argued that suppressing the link between futures and cash markets in this fashion will impair the efficiency of the market: if stock prices are determined according to the Efficient Markets Hypothesis then they will only exhibit volatility as a result of new information. If the futures market is better at ferreting out such information or is more sensitive to it then traders will adjust futures prices more rapidly and the result will then be transmitted to the main market via the arbitrage operation – this is the price discovery function of futures markets (Siegel and Siegel, 1990). According to this view the link between the markets fulfils a useful economic function of getting stock prices in the main market to reflect changes in economic fundamentals *more* rapidly than they would otherwise do so.

The logic of this economic argument may not be sufficient to allay the suspicions of ordinary investors however: if they feel that the market has indeed become more volatile as a result of the nature of block trading techniques and rules they may decide that the additional source of variation in share prices is simply not tolerable and be driven away entirely. This would hardly be regarded as a beneficial outcome for the longer term health of the market.

In the meantime the debate has been further complicated by rivalry between regulatory authorities in the US and also between respective markets – the NYSE and the Chicago Exchanges. The SEC and the NYSE have both complained that the treatment of the stock market and the futures market is so different with regard to margin requirements that block traders have every incentive to use arbitrage strategies (*The Banker*, Feb. 1990). The argument is that on the stock market the Federal Reserve requires a margin deposit of 50% of the value of the shares being bought. However in the futures market which is under the jurisdiction of the Commodity and Futures Trading Commission the margin is between 4% and 7%. Indeed the so-called locals in the Chicago market handling the S&P500 futures index do not have to deposit dealing margins at all: they merely have a requirement to match their positions at the end of the trading day. This obviously adds to the liquidity of the market but may also add to its volatility: the fact that margin deposits are small or non-existent keeps the cost of trading futures down and adds to the volume of arbitrage operations even for very small gains. There is therefore pressure to alter the minimum margin requirements for futures trades.

Index arbitrage is a relatively cheap strategy for the larger operator but before suspending the procedure or making it more expensive as the SEC/ NYSE appear to argue, the authorities must distinguish between trading strategies which are inherently stabilising (or neutral) and those which add to market instability. The academic evidence thus far on the whole suggests that arbitrage strategies are basically stabilising (Grossman, 1988). The same cannot be said of the third use of programmed trading – the strategy known as portfolio insurance.

(iii) Portfolio insurance

Portfolio insurance emerged in the wake of the market in stock index futures and stock index options. In principle the notion of portfolio insurance has an appeal to many investors as it suggests that it may be possible to lock in gains which have accrued during bull markets by selling as the market moves down. The strategy itself can be accomplished in a number of ways: by using traded options, futures and/or the underlying stocks themselves.

The procedure is easiest to understand where portfolio insurance is accomplished via the use of *share options*. However as traded options do not exist on every share which makes up a given index it is not possible to establish a perfect hedge.[2] It is easier and considerably cheaper to use option contracts based not on the value of the individual shares but on the value of the index itself. Such index options exist based on the FT-SE 100 in the UK as well as the S&P500 and S&P100 in the United States.

For example a fund manager who has enjoyed considerable gains on the underlying portfolio may protect those gains via a 'put' – the right to 'sell' at a fixed price – on the relevant stock index. A downward movement in share prices which would have undermined previous gains is now covered by the performance of the put option which will increase in value as the market falls. A simple example of the relationship between the value of the underlying shares and that of the put is shown in fig. 8.1 overleaf.

The remaining problem for the fund manager is to buy the requisite number of put contracts in order to get the optimum coverage of his portfolio.[3]

This hedging strategy would provide adequate protection against a downside market move and in so far as no underlying shares are traded it would have very little impact in the main market unless traders there took the increase in the volume of the put contracts as an indicator of bearish sentiment. This could then cause market makers to adjust their prices downward which would act as a disincentive for people to sell. The purchase of the 'puts' in other words sends a signal to the main market and action

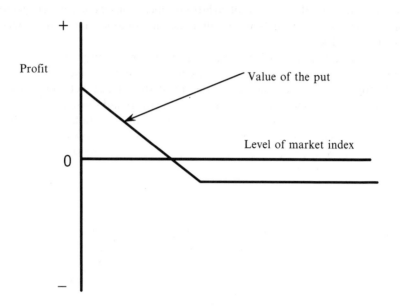

Figure 8.1   Profit and loss profile of a traded put

there takes into account the new information concerning the hedgers' perceptions.

Index options are not the only way in which portfolio insurance strategies may be undertaken however: the process may also be carried out by the use of index futures or *by using the underlying share portfolio itself.* If these techniques are employed they go under the name of 'dynamic hedging'. Using the futures index in this way simply means that a stated proportion of the underlying portfolio is covered or hedged by the purchase (or sale) of the relevant number of futures contracts on the index. Thus in a rising market stock index futures are bought while in a falling market they are sold. Again notice that the transactions in the futures contracts conveys information to market participants about the investor's expectations.

If 'dynamic hedging' is implemented using the underlying portfolio – ie the shares/stocks themselves – then this involves altering the balance of the portfolio as between shares and cash depending upon the direction of the market. Dynamic hedging sounds extraordinarily sophisticated but has been described by Joseph Grundfest (1989), a Commissioner of the SEC, as little more than a sophisticated stop loss order.

Whichever is the desired vehicle for implementing the strategy the result of using futures or the shares themselves to pursue portfolio insurance means that the decision of the fund manager reinforces a market change. An upward move in the market results in the balance shifting toward the purchase of shares or the futures index. A fall in the market would trigger the sale of stock or the futures. Hence portfolio insurance *adds* to an initial change and as a consequence this sort of approach has been termed a 'momentum' strategy (Hill and Jones, 1988).

However there is a major difference between a dynamic hedge using options and futures contracts and one which is based on the use of the share portfolio itself. In the latter case there is no information conveyed to the market about the hedgers' expectations

> when you buy a put you offer the world valuable information about your expectations that the market might decline, but when you rely on stop loss selling, you offer the market no information because your strategy is kept secret. (Grundfest, 1989, p 25)

Clearly then portfolio insurance based on dynamic hedging of the underlying portfolio itself blocks the price discovery function which is an important feature of futures and options markets. In doing so it may also result in a large overhang of potential sell orders which are unknown to the market makers.

Indeed the strategy of portfolio insurance is most effective in circumstances where the fall in the market is gradual and where only a small proportion of fund managers use the technique. This allows time for fund managers using a different philosophy to come in and buy the now cheaper shares and therefore to impart counter pressure on the direction of share prices. It must be emphasised that *for portfolio insurance to work there must be a set of buyers prepared to take the extra stocks as they come onto the market.*

For example it would be possible to envisage the situation where a fall in the price of the underlying stock leads portfolio insurers to sell shares. Buyers whose decisions are normally based on some concept of 'value' would come in to take advantage of lower prices. Also as the programmed sale of shares tends to open a gap between the underlying market and the value of the futures index, this might induce arbitrageurs to buy (the now cheaper) shares and sell futures. In this case the combined influence of the conventional investors and the arbitrageurs offsets the sellers and brings stability to the market.

The strength of these countervailing influences however depends on two sorts of 'structural' features:

1. The proportion of funds driven by portfolio insurance strategies compared to those following a more conventional 'fundamentals' approach and those indulging in arbitrage activity.
2. The relative speeds of implementation of the various types of strategy.

Thus where a substantial change in the level of the market occurs and a major proportion of funds are committed to a portfolio insurance strategy there will be a much greater increase in selling and significant downward pressure on prices. If funds following a fundamentals strategy have longer implementation lags then for a period at least there will be little buying just when the insurance strategies are being executed. The net result is that portfolio insurance adds to any incipient instability of the underlying market.

If on the other hand the market is well differentiated with only a small proportion of funds pursuing the insurance strategy while others follow strategies based on 'fundamentals', the extent of market falls will be more limited and depend upon how rapidly the other funds implement their own strategy.

The problem of differential speeds of strategy execution has resulted in calls for changes in trading rules in both Chicago and New York. As has already been mentioned above there are possible changes in NYSE rules on programme trading so as to build in longer execution lags and to introduce 'circuit breakers' – trading halts – after a specified fall in the index. In addition there may be stronger enforcement of the short-sales rule called the 'up-tick' rule. This applies to the sale of individual shares and is designed to prevent short selling cumulating into a continuous fall. Thus the short sale of individual shares (the seller does not currently own them) is forbidden unless there has previously been a deal at an *increase* in the share price immediately preceding it. Unfortunately this up-tick rule is not easily enforceable in the case of programmed trades – particularly when the broker may be dealing blind as described earlier.

This is just one example of a class of problems where markets break down: markets operate best where participants take different views about future behaviour – this imparts stability to the market – because there will be a mix of buyers and sellers. If however all market participants expect exactly the same outcome their behaviour will be modified: all either become buyers or all become sellers and the market collapses into illiquidity. This is a dangerous condition and it is made more likely where individuals and institutions delude themselves into believing that they have discovered techniques which lock in gains and assure liquidity.

The flaw at the heart of portfolio insurance is the assumption that because the market provides liquidity for an individual decision taker it does so for all. Liquidity however is only a characteristic of markets when participants take different views about the future. As was pointed out over half a century ago

> Of the maxims of orthodox finance none is more anti-social than the fetish of liquidity . . . . It forgets that there is no such thing as liquidity of investment for the community as a whole. (Keynes, 1936, p. 155)

Perhaps it would be salutary for stock markets to be reminded of this from time to time.

NOTES

1. An excellent survey of the behaviour of the different markets during and after the Crash is provided in Roll (1988) and an examination of the various trading techniques which are said to have contributed to it can be found in Hill and Jones (1988).
2. For example the Chicago Board Options Exchange only lists 206 stock options and the London Traded Options Market lists 64 UK and 4 non-UK.
3. At first sight this may appear to be a simple procedure:

    Buy the number of contracts n' such that

    $n \times$ Value of the index option $=$ Value of Portfolio

    $$n = \frac{\text{Value of Portfolio}}{\text{Value of the Index Option}}$$

    Difficulties arise because the movement in the underlying portfolio does not necessarily match the movement in the price of the index option on a 1:1 basis. Therefore the number of contracts has to be adjusted to allow for this differential relationship between the price of the portfolio and the behaviour of the index option.

Selected Bibliography

The bibliography is divided into three sections – books, articles and official sources – to make it more accessible to the reader.

BOOKS

Association of Investment Trust Companies (1985) *How to Make IT*, Woodhead Faulkner, Cambridge.

Association of Investment Trust Companies (1989) *Investment Fund Index - Investment Trusts*, Centaur Communications Ltd., London.

D. E. Ayling (1986) *The Internationalisation of Stock Markets*, Gower, Aldershot.

Bank for International Settlements (1989) *Annual Report*,

W. J. Baumol (1965) *The Stock Market and Economic Efficiency*, Fordham University Press, New York.

A. A. Berle and G. C. Means (1933) *The Modern Corporation and Private Profits*, Macmillan & Co., New York.

G. M. Bollenbacher (1988) *The Professional's Guide to the US Government Securities Markets*, New York Institute of Finance, New York.

R. Bosworth-Davies (1988) *Fraud in the City: Too Good To Be True*, Penguin Books, London.

M. Bowe (1988) *Eurobonds*, Dow Jones-Irwin, Homewood, Illinois.

N. F. Brady (1988) *Report of the Presidential Task Force on Market Mechanisms*, US Government Printing Office, Washington D.C..

R. Brealey (1983) *An Introduction to Risk and Return*, Basil Blackwell, Oxford.

—— and S. Myers (1981) *Principles of Corporate Finance*, McGraw-Hill, London.

C. Bruck (1988) *The Predators' Ball*, Simon and Schuster Ltd., New York.

J. Burnham (1941) *The Managerial Revolution*, John Day, New York.

N. M. Cavalla (1989) *GNI Handbook of Traded Options*, Macmillan, London.

J. Clements (1988) *Stock Answers: A Guide to the International Equities Markets*, Cassell, London.

P. H. Cootner (1964) *The Random Character of Stock Prices*, MIT Press, Cambridge, Mass.

J. G. Cragg and B. G. Malkiel (1982) *Expectations and the Structure of Share Prices*, NBER, University of Chicago Press, Chicago.

D. Courtney and E. C. Bettelheim (1986) *An Investor's Guide to the Commodity Futures Markets*, Butterworths, London.

S. Das (1989) *Swap Financing*, IFR Publishing Ltd., London

J. C. Dodds (1979) *The Investment Behaviour of British Life Insurance Companies*, Croom Helm, London.

J. A. Donaldson and T. H. Donaldson (1982) *The Medium Term Loan Market*, Macmillan, London.

H. E. Dougall and J. E. Gaumnitz (1980) *Capital Markets and Institutions*, Prentice-Hall International, Englewood Cliffs, New Jersey.

F. G. Fisher III (1987) *Eurobonds*, Euromoney Publications, London.

P. Gallant (1988) *The Eurodollar Bond Market*, Woodhead-Faulkner, London.

S. Goldenberg (1986) *Trading: Inside the World's Leading Stock Exchanges*, Sidgwick & Jackson, London.

A. Hamilton (1986) *The Financial Revolution*, Penguin Books, London.

L. Harris et al. (1988) *New Perspectives on the Financial System*, Croom Helm, London.

—— and J. Coakley (1983) *City of Capital*, Basil Blackwell, Oxford.

I. Hay Davison (1987) *A View of the Room, Lloyd's: Change and Disclosure*, Weidenfeld & Nicolson, London.

G. Ingham (1984) *Capitalism Divided? The City and Industry in British Social Development*, Macmillan, London.

International Stock Exchange (1989) *The Stock Exchange Survey of Share Holding*, ISE, London.

William Kay (1986) *The Big Bang*, Weidenfeld & Nicolson, London.

J. M. Keynes (1936) *The General Theory of Employment, Interest and Money*, Macmillan, London.

I. M. Kerr (1984) *A History of the Eurobond Market: The First 21 Years*, Euromoney Publications, London.

H. Levy and M. Sarnat (1984) *Portfolio and Investment Selection: Theory and Evidence*, Prentice-Hall International, Englewood Cliffs, New Jersey.

F. Macaulay (1938) *The Movement of Interest Rates, Bond Yields and Stock Prices in the United States since 1856*, National Bureau of Economic Research, New York.

B. G. Malkiel (1985) *A Random Walk Down Wall St.*, W. W. Norton and Co., New York.

H. M. Markowitz (1959) *Portfolio Selection: Efficient Diversification of Investments*, John Wiley, New York.

T. Matsumoto (1989) *Japanese Stocks: A Basic Guide for the Intelligent Investor*, Kondansha International, Tokyo.

J. Maycock (1986) *Financial Conglomerates: The New Phenomenon*, Gower Publishing Co., Aldershot.

R. Minns (1980) *Pension Funds and British Capitalism*, Heinemann, London.

J. Orlin Grabbe (1986) *International Financial Markets*, Elsevier Publishing Co., Amsterdam.

K. W. Peasnell and C. W. R. Ward (1985), *British Financial Markets and Institutions*, Prentice-Hall, Englewood Cliffs, New Jersey.

P. Phillips (1987) *Inside the New Gilt-Edged Market*, Woodhead-Faulkner, London.

J. L. Powell (1988) *Issues and Offers of Company Securities: The New Regime*, Sweet & Maxwell, London.

S. Prodano (1986) *Pension Funds: Investment and Performance*, Gower Publishing Co., Aldershot.

Report of the Committee on Finance and Industry (the Macmillan Committee) (1931) Cmnd 3897, HMSO, London.

Report of the Committee to Review the Functioning of Financial Institutions (the Wilson Committee) (1980) Cmnd 7937, HMSO, London.

J. Robinson (1964) *Economic Philosophy*, Pelican Books, London.

J. Rutterford (ed) (1988) *Handbook of UK Corporate Finance*, Butterworths, London.

—— (1983) *Introduction to Stock Exchange Investment*, Macmillan, London.

S. Sakakibara et al. (1988) *The Japanese Stock Market: Pricing Systems and Accounting Information*, Praeger, New York.
F. M. Scherer (1980) *Industrial Market Structure and Economic Performance*, Houghton Mifflin Co., Boston, Mass.
S.E.C. (1988) *The October 1987 Market Break*, A Report of the Division of Market Regulation, Securities and Exchange Commission, Washington D.C., US Government Printing Office.
—— (1971) *Institutional Investor Study Report of the Securities and Exchange Commission*, Washington D.C., US Government Printing Office.
A. Seldon (Ed.) (1988) *Financial Regulation - or Over-Regulation?*, Institute of Economic Affairs, London.
J. Seligman (1982) *The Transformation of Wall Street*, Houghton Mifflin Co., Boston.
D. R. Siegel and D. F. Siegel (1990) *The Futures Markets*, McGraw-Hill, London.
K. F. Skousen (1983) *Introduction to the SEC*, South Western Publishing Co., Cincinnati, Ohio.
A. Smith (1776) *The Wealth of Nations*, Pelican Edition, London.
A. Smith (1973), *Supermoney*, Michael Joseph, London.
R. Sobel (1975) *NYSE: A History of the New York Stock Exchange 1935-1975*, Weybright & Talley, New York.
R. Sobel (1972) *AMEX: A History of the American Stock Exchange 1921-1971*, Weybright & Talley, New York.
Spicer and Oppenheim (1987) *Guide to Stock Markets Across the World*, Spicer & Oppenheim, London.
N. F. Stapley (1984) *The Stock Market*, Woodhead Faulkner, London.
P. Stonham (1987) *Global Stock Market Reforms*, Gower Publishing Co., Aldershot.
—— (1982) *Major Stock Markets of Europe*, Gower Publishing Co., Aldershot.
S. Strange (1986) *Casino Capitalism*, Basil Blackwell, Oxford.
M. E. Streit (Ed.) (1983) *Futures Markets*, Basil Blackwell, Oxford.
R. J. Teweles and E. S. Bradley (1987) *The Stock Market*, John Wiley & Sons, New York.
W. A. Thomas (1986) *The Big Bang*, Philip Allan, London.
J. Wormell (1985) *The Gilt-Edged Market*, George Allen & Unwin, London.

ARTICLES

R. Banz (1981), 'The Relationship between Return and the Market Value of Common Stock', *Journal of Financial Economics*, Vol.12.
G. J. Benston (1969), 'The value of the SEC's Accounting Disclosure Requirements', *The Accounting Review*, July.
O. Blanchard (1979), 'Speculative bubbles, crashes and rational expectations', *Economic Letters*, Vol.3.
S. Brady (1990), 'Evolution not revolution', *Euromoney*, June
G. Bulkley and I. Tonks (1989), 'Are Stock Prices Excessively Volatile? Trading Rules and Variance Boundary Tests', *The Economic Journal*, Vol.99, Dec.
E. Dimson and P. Marsh (1989), 'The Smaller Companies Puzzle' *The Investment Analyst*, Vol. 91, Jan.
G. P. Dwyer Jr. and R. W. Hafer (1988), 'Are National Stock Markets Linked?', *Federal Reserve Bank of St. Louis Review*, Vol. 70, No. 6, Nov./Dec.
E. Fama (1970), 'Efficient Capital Markets - A Review of Theory and Empirical Work', *Journal of Finance*, Vol. 25, May.

B. J. Foley (1987), 'Pension Funds in the UK – Danger Ahead?', *Employee Relations*, Vol. 9, No. 1.

P. Fortune (1989), 'An Assessment of Financial Market Volatility: Bills, Bonds, and Stocks', *New England Economic Review*, Nov/Dec.

I. Friend and L. H. Lang (1988), 'The Size Effect on Stock Returns: Is it simply a risk effect not adequately reflected by the usual measures?', *Journal of Banking and Finance*, Vol. 12, No 1, Mar.

C. A. E. Goodhart (1987), 'The economics of "Big Bang"', *Midland Bank Review*, Summer.

K. Gordon (1987), '1992 Big Bang or Little Whimpers', *The Banker*, Oct.

P. De Grauwe and K. Matthews (1988), 'Black Monday and the Crash of Voodoo Economics', *Quarterly Economic Bulletin*, Liverpool Research Group in Macroeconomics, Vol. 9, No. 4

M. Grinblatt and S. Titman (1989), 'Mutual Fund Performance: An Analysis of Quarterly Portfolio Holdings', *The Journal of Business*, Vol. 62.

S. J. Grossman (1988), 'Program Trading and Market Volatility: A Report on Interday Relationships', *Financial Analysts Journal*, July/Aug.

—— (1986), 'An Analysis of the Role of "Insider Trading" on Futures Markets', *The Journal of Business*, Vol. 59 Part 2.

—— and R. J. Shiller (1981), 'The Determinants of the Variability in Stock Markets', *American Economic Review*, Papers and Proceedings, Vol. 71.

J. Grundfest (1989), 'Perestroika on Wall Street: the Future of Securities Trading', *Financial Executive*, May/June.

M. N. Guletkin and N. B. Guletkin (1983), 'Stock Market Seasonality: International Evidence', *Journal of Financial Economics*, Vol. 12.

G. M. S. Hammond (1987), 'Recent developments in the swap market', *Bank of England Quarterly Bulletin*, Feb. Vol. 27, No 1.

L. Herzel and L. Katz (1987), 'Insider Trading: Who Loses?', *Lloyds Bank Review*, No. 165, July.

J. M. Hill and F. Jones (1988), 'Equity Trading, Program Trading, Portfolio Insurance, Computer Trading and All That', *Financial Analysts Journal*, July/Aug.

M. C. Jensen (1968), 'The Performance of Mutual Funds in the Period 1945-64', *Journal of Finance*, May.

S. M. Keane (1989), 'Seasonal Anomalies and the Need for Perspective', *The Investment Analyst*, Vol. 91, Jan.

D. Keim (1983), 'Size Related Anomalies and Stock Return Seasonality: Further Empirical Evidence', *Journal of Financial Economics*, Vol. 12.

—— and R. Stambaugh (1984), 'A Further Investigation of the Weekend Effect in Stock Returns', *Journal of Finance*, June.

M. G. Kendall (1953), 'The Analysis of Economic Time Series, Part 1: Prices', *Journal of the Royal Statistical Society*, Vol. 96.

M. A. King and S. Wadhwani (1990), 'Transmission of Volatility between Stock Markets', *The Review of Financial Studies*, Vol. 3, No 1.

J. A. Kregel (1988), 'Financial Innovation and the Organisation of Stock Market Trading', *Banca Nazionale del Lavoro Quarterly Review*, Dec.

R. A. Levy (1967), 'Random Walks: Reality or Myth', *Financial Analysts Journal*, Nov./Dec.

C. Mayer (1987), 'The Assessment: Financial Systems and Corporate Investment', *Oxford Review of Economic Policy*, Vol. 3, No. 4, Winter.

S. Micossi (1988), 'The Single European Market: Finance', *Banca Nazionale del Lavoro Quarterly Review*, Dec.

H. D. Mills (1970), 'On the Measurement of Fund Performance', *Journal of Finance*, Dec.

F. Modigliani and G. A. Pogue (1974), 'An Introduction to Risk and Return', *Financial Analysts Journal*, Mar./April.
———————— (1974), 'An Introduction to Risk and Return: Part II', *Financial Analysts Journal*, May/June.
S. J. Nickell and S. Wadhwani (1986), 'Myopia the "Dividend Puzzle" and Share Prices', Centre for Labour Economics, mimeograph, LSE.
A. Prindl (1989), 'Change and continuity in Japanese finance', *Banking World*, Vol. 7, No. 3.
R. Roll (1988), 'The International Crash of October 1987', *Financial Analysts Journal*, Sept./Oct.
S. Ruehl (1987), 'Interest Rate Policy and Credit Rationing in Japan', in L. Harris et al. *New Perspectives on the Financial System*, Croom Helm, London.
G. William Schwert (1990), 'Stock Market Volatility', *Financial Analysts Journal*, May/June.
W. F. Sharpe (1963), 'A Simplified Model of Portfolio Analysis', *Management Science*, Jan.
—— (1966), 'Mutual Fund Performance', *Journal of Business*, Vol. 35.
H. Shawky (1982), 'An Update on Mutual Funds: Better Grades', *Journal of Portfolio Management*, Winter.
R. J. Shiller (1987), 'Investor Behaviour in the October 1987 Stock Market Crash', *National Bureau of Economic Research Working Paper*, No. 2464, Nov.
—— (1981), 'Do Stock Prices Move too Much to be Justified by Subsequent Changes in Dividends?', *American Economic Review*, Vol. 71, pp 421-36.
G. Stigler (1964), 'Public Regulation of the Securities Market', *Journal of Business*, Vol. 37.
G. Stigler (1971), 'The Theory of Economic Regulation', *Bell Journal of Economics and Management Science*, Vol. 2, No 1.
L. Summers (1986), 'Does the Stock Market rationally reflect fundamental values?', *The Journal of Finance*, July.
S. Tagaki (1989), 'The Japanese equity market: Past and present' in G. Tullio and G.P. Szego (eds) 'Equity Markets - An International Comparison Part A', *Journal of Banking & Finance* Vol. 13, Nos 4/5, Sept.
J. Tobin (1984) 'On the Efficiency of the Financial System', *Lloyds Bank Review*, Vol. 153, July.
R. S. Tondkar, A. Adhikari, and E. N. Coffman (1989), 'The Internationalisation of Equity Markets: Motivations for Foreign Listings and Filing and Listing Requirements of Five Major Stock Exchanges', *The International Journal of Accounting Education and Research*, Vol. 24, No 2.
S. L. Topping (1987), 'Commercial paper markets: an international survey, *Bank of England Quarterly Bulletin*, Feb. Vol 27, No 1.
D. Walker (1987), Speech to the National Association of Pension Funds reported in *Bank of England Quarterly Bulletin*, May, Vol. 27, No 2.

OFFICIAL PUBLICATIONS

Bank of England Quarterly Bulletin
Bank for International Settlements Annual Report
Federal Reserve Bulletin
Federation of German Stock Exchanges Annual Report
Financial Statistics, HMSO
ISE Quality of Markets Review Quarterly

NASDAQ Fact Book
OECD, *Financial Statistics*
SEC Statistical Bulletin
Société des Bourse Françaises Presentation Statistique de L'Année 1989.

Index

Index